"This fascinating collection of documents reveals American foreign policymaking at its most effective and compelling. What stands out is not only the professionalism of American diplomats but also their passionate devotion to liberal democratic ideals. This is a success story, much needed at a time when many have forgotten what that looks like."

—ROBERT KAGAN, Stephen and Barbara Friedman
Senior Fellow, The Brookings Institution; author of
The Jungle Grows Back: America and Our Imperiled World

"*Democracy's Defenders* is fascinating and instructive. It offers essential lessons about not only the past but the present and future of American foreign policy. They include how to promote human rights in authoritarian regimes and how to support new democracies."

—JOSEPH LIEBERMAN, former United States Senator

"*Democracy's Defenders* is a welcome and valuable addition to our ever-expanding volume of knowledge of the role of American diplomacy behind the Iron Curtain and particularly in Czechoslovakia at the end of the Cold War and in the first stages of the country's transition to democracy. The newly available cables establish a number of interesting new connections and fill in a number of gaps. The meticulous work of the editors and their insights make this a book worth reading by every serious student of recent Czech-American history."

—MICHAEL ŽANTOVSKÝ, former Czech ambassador
to the United States; author of *Havel: A Life*

"These cables bring to life the heady, bewildering, and sometimes frustrating days of summer and fall 1989, as depicted by the U.S. embassy staff who dealt with the Communist regime in Prague and the growing dissident movement that would topple it. Norman Eisen and his researchers have done a fine job in selecting and editing these important diplomatic records and framing them in the context of the Cold War and its aftermath. As an eyewitness to these events myself, I commend the clarity of the reporting and the analytical framework with which these able, patriotic, and highly professional men and women served their country—and the wider cause of freedom in Czechoslovakia."

—EDWARD LUCAS, senior vice president, Center for
European Policy Analysis; author of *The New Cold
War: Putin's Russia and the Threat to the West*

"In *Democracy's Defenders*, history comes alive through the vivid, lived experience of U.S. diplomats who were both helping to shape and respond to transformative events. At a time when authoritarianism has reemerged, this book offers powerful and timely lessons about how and why we should learn from a democratic triumph that was not at all inevitable."

—BEN RHODES, former deputy national security adviser; author
of *The World as It Is: A Memoir of the Obama White House*

DEMOCRACY'S DEFENDERS

DEMOCRACY'S DEFENDERS

U.S. EMBASSY PRAGUE,

THE FALL OF COMMUNISM
IN CZECHOSLOVAKIA,

AND ITS AFTERMATH

EDITED BY

NORMAN EISEN

BROOKINGS INSTITUTION PRESS
Washington, D.C.

Library of Congress Cataloging-in-Publication data
Names: United States. Embassy (Czechoslovakia), creator. | Eisen, Norman L., 1961– editor.
Title: Democracy's defenders : U.S. Embassy Prague, the fall of communism in Czechoslovakia, and its aftermath / edited by Norman L. Eisen.
Description: Washington, D.C. : Brookings Institution Press, [2020] | Includes bibliographical references and index.
Identifiers: LCCN 2019048150 (print) | LCCN 2019048151 (ebook) | ISBN 9780815738213 (cloth) | ISBN 9780815738220 (epub)
Subjects: LCSH: United States. Embassy (Czechoslovakia)—Records and correspondence. | International relations—History—20th century. | Czechoslovakia—History—Velvet Revolution, 1989—Sources. | United States—Foreign relations—Czechoslovakia—Sources. | Czechoslovakia—Foreign relations—United States—Sources. | Czechoslovakia—Politics and government—1968–1989—Sources.
Classification: LCC DB2233 .U55 2020 (print) | LCC DB2233 (ebook) | DDC 943.704/3—dc23
LC record available at https://lccn.loc.gov/2019048150
LC ebook record available at https://lccn.loc.gov/2019048151

9 8 7 6 5 4 3 2 1

Typeset in Minion Pro and Acumin Pro

Composition by Elliott Beard

CONTENTS

INTRODUCTION
U.S. Diplomacy in Czechoslovakia
at the End of the Cold War
NORMAN EISEN
WITH DAVID FISHMAN AND NARRELLE GILCHRIST

THE CABLES

AFTERWORD
The Aftermath of Revolution:
U.S. Support for Czech and Slovak Liberal Democracy, 1989–Present
KELSEY LANDAU, NORMAN EISEN, AND MIKULÁŠ PEŠTA

ACKNOWLEDGMENTS

First, I wish to acknowledge my friend Dan Berger, who provided constant encouragement during the long process of obtaining the cables from the State Department, and who otherwise supported this book in every way. I could not have produced this volume without the generosity of John Allen, president of the Brookings Institution, and Darrell West, vice president and director of the Governance Studies program at Brookings. I am grateful to them both.

My Brookings research assistant, Theodore Becker-Jacob, helped shepherd every part of this book to completion, and generously allowed others who led on individual portions to have the bylines. This volume also benefited in all aspects from the work of my co-contributors Kelsey Landau, Mikuláš Pešta, David Fishman, and Narrelle Gilchrist.

At the Brookings Institution Press, I wish to thank director Bill Finan, production manager Elliott Beard, and managing editor Cecilia González for their enthusiasm and care. The essays in this volume greatly benefited from the comments of Adrian Basora, Eric Edelman, Daniel Fried, Kenneth Juster, Igor Lukes, Andrew Kenealy, Vilém Prečan, Theodore Russell, Jiří Suk, and Jenonne Walker.

I am grateful to those who provided assistance in obtaining the materials and developing the ideas presented here while I was working on *The Last Palace*, including my former research assistant Andrew Kenealy and my first editor on that earlier volume, Domenica Alioto, as well as Richard Bassett, Charles Black Jr., Cliff Bond, Susan Black Falaschi, Curtis Grisham, Thomas Hull, Ed Kaska, Robert Kiene, John Macgregor, Robert McRae, Cameron Munter, Fernando Rondon, and Theodore Russell. Additionally, I would like to express my gratitude for relevant help to my former interns Agneska Bloch, Ladislav Charouz, Adrienne Epstein, Colby Galliher, Carolina Hernandez, Alexander Jin, Angela King, Madeline McCann, Kiersten Rhodes, Henry Robinson, and Meilin Scanish, and to Sarah Chilton and Laura Mooney of the Brookings Library. I would also like to thank Andy Schapiro and Tod Sedgwick, as well as my Brookings colleagues Alina Polyakova and Torrey Taussig, for their thoughts on essays I co-authored with Mr. Kenealy about the state of Czech and Slovak liberalism today that are here adapted and excerpted as part of the afterword.

Finally, I wish to thank Alden Fahy and Behar Godani of the United States Department of State for their assistance with obtaining the cables, including with the Mandatory Declassification Review request that resulted in their release.

As always, I relied most of all on the love and tolerance of my wife Lindsay Kaplan and my daughter Tamar Eisen.

TIMELINE OF EVENTS

AUGUST 21, 1989 Several thousand protestors march in Prague's Wenceslas Square to commemorate the twenty-first anniversary of the Soviet invasion of Czechoslovakia. The police disperse the demonstrators and arrest over three hundred people.

AUGUST 22, 1989 Shirley Temple Black presents her credentials as the new U.S. Ambassador to Czechoslovakia.

OCTOBER 1, 1989 U.S. Secretary of State James Baker meets with Czechoslovak Foreign Minister Jaromír Johanes in New York City, the first cabinet-level meeting between the two countries in eleven years.

OCTOBER 28, 1989 Nearly ten thousand people demonstrate in Wenceslas Square in Prague, marking the seventy-first anniversary of Czechoslovakia's founding. The police once again harass and arrest many of the protestors.

NOVEMBER 17, 1989 Students organize an on-campus demonstration in Prague to commemorate the fiftieth anniversary of a Nazi crackdown on universities. The students spontaneously march toward Wenceslas Square, their numbers growing to nearly fifty thousand along the way. The police prevent them from continuing and severely beat many among a core of about two thousand demonstrators.

NOVEMBER 18, 1989 Thousands continue to demonstrate in Prague, enraged over the police brutality and bolstered in part by false reports that a student died during the previous day's crackdown. Students and other activists call for a nationwide strike on November 27.

NOVEMBER 19, 1989 As demonstrations continue, Václav Havel and other dissidents announce the creation of Civic Forum, an organization that united all independent initiatives. In Bratislava, a similar organization called Public Against Violence is established.

NOVEMBER 20, 1989 Demonstrations in Prague reach one hundred thousand, with similar protests taking place in other cities.

NOVEMBER 21, 1989 Amid ongoing demonstrations, Czechoslovak Prime Minister Ladislav Adamec meets with members of the Civic Forum, though he does not allow Havel to participate.

NOVEMBER 22, 1989 Havel addresses a crowd of approximately two hundred thousand at a rally in Wenceslas Square.

NOVEMBER 23, 1989 As demonstrations continue in Prague, former First Secretary of the Presidium of the Central Committee of the Communist Party of Czechoslovakia Alexander Dubček speaks at an anti-Communist rally in Bratislava, calling for democracy and the resignation of the Communist Party of Czechoslovakia (CPCz) Central Committee leadership.

NOVEMBER 24, 1989 On the eighth day of protests, the CPCz Central Committee holds an extraordinary session. The leaders decide against using violence to stop the demonstrations. The entire Party leadership then resigns, leaving behind younger leaders and some hard-liners.

NOVEMBER 26, 1989 Prime Minister Adamec meets with Havel and other Civic Forum members to begin negotiations.

NOVEMBER 27, 1989 Much of the country takes part in a two-hour general strike to show the public's rejection of continued Communist rule.

NOVEMBER 29, 1989 The Federal Assembly of Czechoslovakia votes to eliminate language about the Communist Party from the constitution.

DECEMBER 3, 1989 The government proposes a new structure made up of mostly Communists, with some independent participants. Civic Forum, Public Against Violence, and the public reject the proposal.

DECEMBER 4, 1989 Hundreds of thousands continue to protest in Prague and other parts of the country. The Soviet Union and other Soviet Bloc states call the 1968 Warsaw Pact invasion of Czechoslovakia a mistake.

DECEMBER 7, 1989 Prime Minister Adamec resigns. Marián Čalfa, a Slovak Communist, succeeds him with the agreement of Civic Forum and Public Against Violence.

DECEMBER 9, 1989 Talks between the Communist Party, Socialist Party, Civic Forum, Public Against Violence, and other political actors end with an agreement to form the Government of National Understanding. Several dissidents, some of whom were formerly political prisoners, are chosen as government ministers.

DECEMBER 10, 1989 Czechoslovak President Gustáv Husák resigns, naming the new government in his last act as head of state. Civic Forum, meanwhile, announces the candidacy of Václav Havel for president.

DECEMBER 22, 1989 The major political actors agree that Václav Havel should serve as president while Prague Spring leader Alexander Dubček serves as the leader of the Federal Assembly.

DECEMBER 28, 1989 New members enter the Federal Assembly to replace those who have resigned. Dubček is among them and is quickly elected leader of the Federal Assembly.

DECEMBER 29, 1989 Havel is inaugurated as president after being unanimously elected by the Federal Assembly. Elections are scheduled for June 1990.

JANUARY 1, 1990 Havel, speaking from Prague Castle, delivers a New Year's address before the nation.

ACRONYMS AND ABBREVIATIONS

A/S	Assistant Secretary
AMCIT	American citizen
ATA	anti-terrorism assistance
BFWG	Business Facilitation Working Group
CA	Bureau of Consular Affairs, U.S. Department of State
CC	Central Committee
CCTV	closed-circuit television
CD	Concluding Document
CDO	Career Development Officer
CLO	Community Liaison Office
CPCz	Communist Party of Czechoslovakia; in the cables, sometimes referred to as Party
CPS	Communist Party of Slovakia
CPSU	Communist Party of the Soviet Union
CSCE	Conference on Security and Cooperation in Europe
CSSR	Czechoslovak Socialist Republic
COCOM	Coordinating Committee for Multilateral Export Controls
CODEL	congressional delegation, often followed by the name of the lead senator/representative (e.g., CODEL Cranston)

DAO	Defense Attaché Office
DCM	Deputy Chief of Mission
DOS	U.S. Department of State
DS	Bureau of Diplomatic Security, U.S. Department of State
EAP	Bureau of East Asian and Pacific Affairs, U.S. Department of State
EC	European Commission
EE	employee evaluation
EMBOFF	Embassy officer
EUR/EEY	Office of Eastern European and Yugoslav Affairs in the Bureau of European and Canadian Affairs, U.S. Department of State
EUR	Bureau of European and Canadian Affairs, U.S. Department of State
EXIM	Export-Import Bank
FBO	Foreign Buildings Office
FCA/JO	Junior Officer Division, Office of Foreign Service Career Development and Assignments, U.S. Department of State
FRG	Federal Republic of Germany, or West Germany
FS-04	rank for foreign service officers
FSN	Foreign Service National, a local citizen employed by the U.S. embassy
GDR	German Democratic Republic, or East Germany; sometimes referred to as DDR
GOC	Government of Czechoslovakia
GSA	General Services Administration, a U.S. government agency responsible for providing administrative and technical support for government offices
GSO	General Services Officer, a foreign service officer responsible for resources and logistics at U.S. embassies
HA	Bureau of Human Rights and Humanitarian Affairs, U.S. Department of State
HAWG	Humanitarian Affairs Working Group

HDM	Human Dimension Mechanism
IREX	International Research and Exchanges Board
KCS	Czechoslovak koruna, the currency in use at the time
LOU	limited official use
MFA	Ministry of Foreign Affairs
MFN	Most Favored Nation
MOU	memorandum of understanding
MSG	Marine Security Guard, a division of the U.S. Marines responsible for providing security at U.S. Embassies
MOTORPOOL	the embassy's fleet of motor vehicles for official use
NED	National Endowment for Democracy
OFM	Office of Foreign Missions, U.S. Department of State
OIG	Office of Inspector General, U.S. Department of State
PAO	public affairs officer
PER	Bureau of Personnel, U.S. Department of State
PLO	Palestinian Liberation Organization
PNG	persona non grata
POL	political
POL/EC OR POLEC	political-economic section of the embassy
PTPE	Participant Training Program for Europe
REFTEL	reference telegram
RFE	Radio Free Europe
RSO	Regional Security Officer, a special agent for diplomatic security employed by the U.S. Department of State
SEO	security engineering officer
SEPTEL	separate telegram
SPUSA	Society of Friends of the United States
TDY	temporary duty
UNGA	United Nations General Assembly
USG	United States government
USIA	United States Information Agency

USIS United States Information Service

VOA Voice of America

VRA voluntary restraint agreement, a trade agreement through which two countries agree to limit exports to one another in order to protect domestic industries

KEY TERMS, NAMES, AND EVENTS

LADISLAV ADAMEC: prime minister of the Czechoslovak Socialist Republic (1988–1989)

SHIRLEY TEMPLE BLACK: U.S. ambassador to Czechoslovakia (1989–1992)

CHARTER 77: initially a document signed by Czechoslovak dissidents in 1977 calling for the government to uphold human rights; evolved into an informal and influential dissident group

CLIFFORD BOND: foreign service officer at U.S. Embassy Prague

CZECH CHILDREN: group of dissident activists in their twenties

JÁN ČARNOGURSKÝ: Slovak lawyer and human rights campaigner jailed for dissident activities; later served as prime minister of the Slovak Republic within the Czech and Slovak Federal Republic (1991–1992)

PETR CIBULKA: dissident active in Charter 77, previously arrested for distributing banned materials

STANISLAV DEVÁTÝ: Czech dissident and political prisoner who engaged in well-publicized hunger strikes

JIŘÍ DIENSTBIER: dissident and Charter 77 signatory; supported reform movement in 1968

ALEXANDER DUBČEK: first secretary of the Communist Party of Czechoslovakia (1968–1969); a reformist who was forced to resign in the aftermath of the Prague Spring

LAWRENCE EAGLEBURGER: deputy U.S. secretary of state (1989–1992)

BRUCE GELB: director of the U.S. Information Agency; visited several Eastern Bloc countries in 1989, meeting with Communist leaders

VÁCLAV HAVEL: leading Czech dissident and playwright who later became president of Czechoslovakia (1989–1992) and of the Czech Republic (1993–2003)

HELSINKI ACCORDS: agreement signed in 1975 by the Soviet Bloc, Western European countries, and the United States at the conclusion of the first Conference on Security and Cooperation in Europe; in it, all signatories committed to the protection of human rights

HELSINKI WATCH: U.S. NGO set up to monitor compliance with the Helsinki Accords; later became Human Rights Watch

ERICH HONECKER: Communist leader of East Germany who was forced out of power in October 1989

MICHAEL HORNBLOW: U.S. diplomat responsible for Poland, Hungary, and Czechoslovakia (1988–1990)

MIROSLAV HOUŠTECKÝ: Czechoslovak ambassador to the United States (1986–1990)

HUMAN DIMENSION MECHANISM: a tool established by the Helsinki Accords that allows states in the Organization for Cooperation and Security in Europe (OSCE) to raise questions about the human rights situation in other OSCE states

GUSTÁV HUSÁK: president of Czechoslovakia (1975–1989)

INDEPENDENT PEACE ASSOCIATION: Czechoslovak dissident group formed in 1988

ALOIS INDRA: Czechoslovak government minister and Communist official

INTERNATIONAL HELSINKI FEDERATION: group of NGOs described as Helsinki Watch groups; dedicated to ensuring compliance with the human rights provisions in the Helsinki Accords

IZVESTIA: Soviet newspaper known for expressing the views of Soviet officials

JACKSON-VANIK AMENDMENT: congressional amendment to the 1974 Trade Act that prevents the United States from granting Most Favored Nation status to countries that deny citizens the human right of emigration

MILOŠ JAKEŠ: general secretary of the Communist Party of Czechoslovakia (1987–1989)

VLADIMÍR JANKŮ: director of religious affairs for the Czechoslovak Communist government; responsible for approving bishops

JANUARY 1989 DEMONSTRATIONS: widespread demonstrations commemorating the anniversary of Jan Palach's self-immolation that were met with police brutality and a government crackdown

JAROMÍR JOHANES: Czechoslovak minister of foreign affairs (1988–1989)

ED KASKA: U.S. foreign service officer responsible for human rights updates sent by U.S. Embassy Prague

ROBERT KIENE: junior foreign service officer at U.S. Embassy Prague

MIROSLAV KUSÝ: Slovak political scientist jailed for dissident activities

JOZEF LENÁRT: former prime minister of Czechoslovakia (1963–1968) and member of Czechoslovak Communist Party presidium (1970–1989)

TOMÁŠ GARRIGUE MASARYK: first president of Czechoslovakia (1918–1935)

TADEUSZ MAZOWIECKI: Polish leader who took office in September 1989 as the first non-Communist prime minister of Poland since 1946

ZDENĚK MLYNÁŘ: Czech politician active in the Prague Spring and later Charter 77

NATIONAL FRONT: coalition of Czechoslovak socialist political parties controlled by the Communist Party of Czechoslovakia

NĚKOLIK VĚT ("A FEW SENTENCES"): petition circulated in June 1989, ultimately with more than forty thousand signatories, urging the government to improve its human rights practices and open public discussion of the 1950s, the Prague Spring, and normalization

JULIAN NIEMCZYK: U.S. ambassador to Czechoslovakia (1986–1989)

OBRODA (*OBRODA - KLUB ZA SOCIALISTICKOU PŘESTAVBU*) (REVIVAL - CLUB FOR SOCIALIST RESTRUCTURING): Czechoslovak reform Communist dissident organization established in 1989

JAN PALACH: student who committed suicide by self-immolation in 1969 in protest of the invasion of Czechoslovakia that ended the Prague Spring

PLENUM: plenary session; in the cables, Plenum of the Central Committee of the Communist Party of Czechoslovakia

POLITBURO: executive committee of a Communist party

PRESIDIUM: council of policymakers within a legislative body in a Communist system; in the cables, Presidium of the Central Committee of the Communist Party of Czechoslovakia

RUDÉ PRÁVO: official newspaper of the Communist Party of Czechoslovakia

THEODORE (TED) RUSSELL: deputy chief of mission at the U.S. Embassy in Czechoslovakia

SAMIZDAT: term for a clandestine publication disseminating uncensored information; a form of dissident activity across the Eastern Bloc

ARTHUR SCHNIER: Austrian-American rabbi and activist for religious freedom and human rights; founded the Appeal of Conscience Foundation

RAYMOND SEITZ: career diplomat who served as assistant secretary of state for Europe and Canada (1989–1991)

FRANTIŠEK STÁREK: activist and journalist arrested for publishing *Vokno*, a dissident magazine

MIROSLAV ŠTĚPÁN: secretary of the Municipal Party Committee in Prague, member of the National Assembly of Czechoslovakia, and member of the Central Committee of the Communist Party of Czechoslovakia

JAN ŠTĚRBA: Czechoslovak minster of foreign trade

JIŘÍ TICHÝ: Czech football player

CARDINAL FRANTIŠEK TOMÁŠEK: archbishop of Prague (1977–1991)

ZDENĚK URBÁNEK: dissident at one point jailed for his activities

VIENNA CONCLUDING DOCUMENT: agreement signed by CSCE states at the end of the 1989 conference; re-affirmed Helsinki principles of human rights

IVA VOJTKOVÁ: dissident and Charter 77 signatory

ALEXANDR "SAŠA" VONDRA: dissident leader; post-revolution became a prominent cabinet member

VONS (*VÝBOR NA OBRANU NESPRAVEDLIVĚ STÍHANÝCH*) (COMMITTEE FOR THE DEFENSE OF THE UNJUSTLY PERSECUTED): an independent Czechoslovak dissident group founded by Charter 77 signatories that focused on human rights

INTRODUCTION

U.S. Diplomacy in Czechoslovakia at the End of the Cold War

NORMAN EISEN

with David Fishman and Narrelle Gilchrist

As the former United States ambassador to the Czech Republic,[1] a scholar of the history of the Czech lands,[2] and the child of a Czechoslovak expatriate, my experience of the country's turbulent history is punctuated by the miracle of the peaceful fall of Communism. In November 1989, countless Czechoslovak citizens took to the streets to call for an end to the repressive Communist regime, culminating in one of the most remarkable transfers of power in the twentieth century. In just over a month, Czechs and Slovaks had ousted the Communist government. After an initial night of police brutality, the days that followed were so peaceful that they became popularly known as the Velvet Revolution (*sametová revoluce*).

When looking in the rearview mirror at momentous historical events, there is sometimes the tendency to assume that events had to go as they did. But the Velvet Revolution easily could have been less smooth and soft. 1989 was not only the year of Tiananmen Square, but also of brutal repression elsewhere in the Soviet Bloc. In Romania, for example, one thousand civilians were killed by police during a cascade of anti-Communist riots.[3] Czechoslovakia also came close to seeing the use of lethal force, with the military poised to strike during a key moment that November.[4] Fortunately, circumstances instead aligned to create a peaceful transition of power.

The contents of this volume offer important new evidence about the Czechoslovak and American actors whose work throughout 1989 helped make that happy outcome possible. This book includes fifty-two recently declassified U.S. diplomatic cables originating from this period in Czechoslovak history. The cables—which were transmitted from the U.S. Embassy in Prague to the U.S. Department of State in Washington, D.C.—shed new light on why the revolution was velvet and in particular the American role in helping to establish some of the conditions that made it so. Together with the previously declassified set of cables printed in the excellent volume, *Prague–Washington–Prague: Reports from the United States Embassy in Czechoslovakia, November–December 1989* (Václav Havel Library, 2004), these documents offer a unique behind-the-scenes view of the events of 1989.

The present collection is intended to complement *Prague–Washington–Prague*, and to follow its exemplary model. I obtained these fifty-two additional cables while conducting research for my book *The Last Palace: Europe's Turbulent Century in Five Lives and One Legendary House* (Crown, 2018), a history of the twentieth century as seen from the U.S. ambassador's residence in Prague. Soon after I began studying the *annus mirabilis* of 1989 for my book, it became clear to me that, as valuable as *Prague–Washington–Prague* was, additional State Department materials remained under wraps. This was apparent from clues and the occasional gap in the cables in the earlier book, from conversations with former embassy officials, but also as a result of my wish to cover a broader period of time than the prior volume. I aimed to go back to the summer of 1989 and trace the societal and political tensions in the months leading up to the Velvet Revolution that November, whereas *Prague–Washington–Prague* includes cables almost solely from November and December.

More than two years of cordial negotiations ensued with my former employer in Foggy Bottom, first under the Obama administration and then continuing into that of President Trump. In retrospect, I probably should have done a Freedom of Information Act (FOIA) request of the kind that resulted in the release of the cables for *Prague–Washington–Prague*. But the State Department had an enormous FOIA backlog, and I feared that the process would be too slow. Finally, as the manuscript submission deadline for *The Last Palace* approached in 2017, the State Department kindly suggested I make a request under their Mandatory Declassification Review process.[5] In response to a list of twenty-four targeted questions I submitted on July 17, 2017,[6] the State Department produced the cables collected herein.

Written in the brisk style characteristic of internal State Department communications, the cables offer fresh insights into the historic events of the period—including the activities and deliberations of Ambassador Shirley Temple Black and her staff.[7] Taken together with *Prague–Washington–Prague*, these cables offer a more comprehensive look at the activities of the U.S. Embassy in Prague during this critical year, including how embassy staff processed and reacted to the first signs of upheaval and saw events through to the advent of a new democracy—both by observing and helping promote that happy outcome. This introduction briefly offers some context for reading the cables. It begins by discussing U.S. democracy promotion in Central and Eastern Europe at the end of the Cold War, a strategy carried out by American diplomats including those in Prague. Next it provides an overview of the events of 1989, showing the efforts of U.S. Embassy Prague at key moments of the Velvet Revolution and addressing some themes of the cables (although they speak for themselves magnificently).[8] The cables follow this introduction. Finally, an afterword carries the themes of the cables forward, describing efforts to promote U.S. democracy post-1989 and assessing the ultimate legacy of the Czechoslovaks and Americans who worked so hard for freedom: the current state of democracy in the Czech and Slovak lands.

HUMAN RIGHTS: THE FULCRUM OF U.S. DIPLOMACY IN CZECHOSLOVAKIA BEFORE THE VELVET REVOLUTION

The significance of Embassy Prague's engagement in 1989 is best understood within the context of a broader American strategy in the run-up to the end of the Cold War that stressed the advancement of human rights. While numerous factors contributed to the demise of Communism in 1989—including socioeconomic challenges, charismatic dissident leadership, and the reforms of Soviet leader Mikhail Gorbachev and his circle— U.S. advocacy for human rights played a part in fostering dissent and eventually revolution in the Soviet Bloc.[9] In Czechoslovakia, U.S. diplomacy long provided inspiration and protection for opposition movements.[10] Ambassador Black was the last in a line of Communist-era American diplomats and policymakers who supported the growth of dissent in Czechoslovakia, work that aided the peaceful downfall of one of the most oppressive regimes in the Soviet Bloc.

U.S. human rights advocacy behind the Iron Curtain marked an inflection point in 1975 with the signing of the Helsinki Accords. In this agreement, Czechoslovakia, along with the Soviet Union and other Communist states, reluctantly promised to protect human rights in exchange for diplomatic concessions from the United States and other Western powers, including the official recognition of post–World War II territorial boundaries.[11] When the Helsinki Accords were signed at the conclusion of the first Conference on Security and Cooperation in Europe (CSCE), neither the Soviet nor the Czechoslovak government expected the human rights provision to have a major impact on their affairs. Among other considerations, President Gerald Ford and his secretary of state, Henry Kissinger, showed no intention of making human rights predominate in their foreign policy because it would have jeopardized the détente with the Soviet Union that they sought. Within a few short years, however, a new consensus in U.S. foreign policy began to emerge—one that placed human rights advocacy at the core of Cold War strategy. Both the Carter and Reagan administrations were persistent in their pursuit of human rights—at times relentlessly so.[12] Ensuring compliance with the Helsinki Accords would become a focal point for American and international diplomacy, not to mention domestic opposition movements within Communist states. Indeed, as one historian puts it, "from Moscow's perspective, the path from Helsinki to the 'evil empire' speech was straight, and all downhill."[13]

By signing the Helsinki Accords, the Czechoslovak government had agreed to respect citizens' rights within its borders, a commitment that radically changed the dynamic for opposition movements in Czechoslovakia. The Helsinki Accords helped embolden a wave of dissent, as activists rallied around the idea of enforcing government compliance with the agreement.[14] Czechoslovak dissidents quickly signed and published Charter 77 in 1977, demanding that the government respect human rights and honor international norms. Prior to 1975, the Czechoslovak government might have responded by silencing the Charter 77 signatories with complete or at least substantial impunity. In the aftermath of Helsinki, however, the government risked losing legitimacy through accusations that it had flouted its obligations to the international community. For the first time in years, civil resistance groups were allowed a small sliver of space to operate above ground, a notable development in one of the more repressive states in Central and Eastern Europe.[15]

Over the next decade, sustained U.S. diplomacy and engagement on human rights issues supported opposition movements like Charter 77. Activists gained ground in part through their ability to link with transnational networks of human rights advocacy.[16] The U.S. Congress established a Helsinki Commission to monitor governments' compliance, and dissidents formed connections with U.S. politicians, NGO leaders, and journalists, as well as with ambassadors and foreign service officers like those serving in Embassy Prague. As one historian notes, "it became commonplace for an Eastern European dissident to write to an American diplomat asking that his plight be addressed in upcoming talks."[17] The Helsinki Accords created a standard under international law through which Western regimes could object to violations of human rights inside Soviet Bloc states.[18] The latter still fought human rights; the hard-line Communist regime in Czechoslovakia continued to periodically harass and arrest dissidents. Yet, bound by Helsinki, the Czechoslovak state could not stifle dissent entirely without incurring significant costs. The dissidents persisted, at one point declaring, "We must keep fighting, we must continually point to the Helsinki Accords and say 'You signed this, you must honour this.'"[19]

Despite the growth of domestic opposition after Helsinki, Czechoslovakia and other Communist governments continued to participate in the CSCE process throughout the 1980s, contending with the human rights provisions in hopes of gaining additional diplomatic and economic concessions from the West. Czechoslovakia was soon bound by its commitments not only to Helsinki, but also to follow-up agreements made at CSCE convenings in Belgrade, Madrid, Stockholm, and Vienna, amplifying the pressure on the government to abide by international standards of human rights.[20]

By 1989, the authority of the hard-line Czechoslovak Communists was beginning to fray. Gorbachev had made it clear that the Soviets would no longer interfere to stop political liberalization. As Czechoslovak Premier Ladislav Adamec would eventually admit, "the international support of the Socialist countries can no longer be counted on."[21] Throughout the international community, the protection of human rights had become an established norm—a prerequisite to being considered a legitimate, modern, European state. Robbed of the full backing of the Soviet Bloc, the Czechoslovak government's claim to legitimacy eroded.[22] Moreover, the regime aspired to strengthen its economic ties to the United States and Western Europe. Though the nation was more prosperous than most of its Communist neighbors, its standard of living paled in comparison with Austria or Switzerland, as leading Party officials admitted.[23] Communist hard-liners clung (at least publicly) to the notion that state Socialism would bring about modernization, but the reality that economic growth would benefit from trade with the West was not lost on the regime. Yet, since Helsinki, U.S. trade deals and other economic incentives had been firmly attached to human rights. Most notably, the United States long withheld most-favored nation (MFN) trading status from Czechoslovakia over human rights violations, a diplomatic "carrot" that was fervently sought by the Communist government.[24]

U.S. pressure on human rights issues continued throughout the pivotal events of 1989. After the dissident leader Václav Havel was arrested and ultimately sentenced to an eight-month jail term, the United States, along with other Western powers, invoked the Human Dimension Mechanism, the measure established by the Helsinki Accords that allowed countries to call out other states' human rights violations. Faced with international pressure, the government released Havel several months early under "protective supervision"; while not completely free, Havel was able to continue his activities as an opposition leader.[25] As Communist regimes toppled one by one in other parts of Europe, the Czechoslovak opposition continued to gain momentum. The hard-liners who still dominated the Czechoslovak government eventually faced a choice: attempt to violently end the protests or negotiate a peaceful transfer of power. Some in the government advocated for a crackdown, but ultimately the Czechoslovak Communists opted to peacefully cede power to the people, an effort that was led in the Czech lands by Havel's Civic Forum.[26] Though many factors influenced the Communists' fateful decision, the international ramifications of violating the protestors' human rights was one consideration.

U.S. diplomats made it clear that government brutality would have significant consequences. One U.S. official warned that if the regime chose to act with further brutality, it would "go down in history" as a government known for "senseless violence."[27] Their message undoubtedly left an impression on the Communist leaders as they debated whether to crack down on protestors. In a November 24 speech before the Party's Central Committee, Premier Adamec stated that, given Western support for human rights, the government could not "underestimate the international risks of a broad application of force. . . . Signed international treaties dealing with human rights cannot be taken lightly." Adamec also noted that Czechoslovakia could face a "political and economic boycott" from Western countries if protestors were met with violence.[28] At the most crucial moment, warnings from U.S. diplomats about the consequences of human rights violations resonated with key figures in the Communist leadership, contributing to the peaceful, "velvet" end of a hard-line regime.

FROM DISSENT TO DEMOCRACY: THE VELVET REVOLUTION AS SEEN FROM U.S. EMBASSY PRAGUE

The cables in this book provide new insight into the persistent advocacy for human rights by the U.S. Embassy in Prague.[29] They detail how Ambassador Black and other embassy officers engaged frequently with dissidents through meetings that encouraged and legitimized opposition groups.[30] Embassy officers used these meetings to gather information on government repression, which formed the basis of human rights updates sent to the State Department.[31] Embassy officers also attended demonstrations themselves, openly displaying support for dissidents' rights and rapidly communicating to Washington about any violence.[31]

In addition to supporting dissidents, the cables show Ambassador Black and other embassy officers persistently and effectively wielding the tool of economic leverage. They made clear in their meetings with Czechoslovak government officials that MFN status and other economic incentives would only be granted after significant improvements in human rights practices.[32] Ambassador Black also dangled diplomatic "carrots," bringing up the possibility of high-level visits from U.S. officials, even from President George

H. W. Bush.[33] The cables demonstrate how embassy personnel tied this human rights advocacy to the Helsinki Accords. Ambassador Black and other cable authors frequently invoked Helsinki and the follow-up CSCE meetings, most frequently the then-recent Vienna Concluding Document.[34] She and her staff hoped that, if put under enough pressure, Czechoslovakia would abide by the human rights norms of the international community.

The cables in this volume begin on August 2, 1989, four months before the Velvet Revolution, and detail the reactions and activities of the U.S. Embassy in Prague during that preliminary period. It was a brief stretch of time during which, as Havel would later put it, history in Czechoslovakia "accelerated."[35] In the decades that preceded the revolution, the mass of ordinary Czech and Slovak citizens had largely abstained from overt acts of dissent.[36] Pervasive threats and harassment by Czechoslovakia's notorious secret police, the StB (*Státní bezpečnost*), stimulated fears of retaliation and violence. The memory of the 1950s, when the newly installed Communist regime enacted Stalinist measures to crack down on political dissent, played a part as well. As a result of these and other factors, the general populace tended to mask its contempt for the Communist Party through jokes, evasion, and indifference.[37] Reflecting on Czechoslovakia at the time of her arrival, Black would later remark that the citizens seemed downtrodden: "It was an oppression you could see and feel. . . . It was spooky. It was strange. Even the children were silent."[38]

The cables describe how the tide turned. They begin roughly a month after leading dissidents, including Havel, launched the "A Few Sentences" (*Několik vět*) petition, which called for "free and democratic discussion" and demanded that the government release political prisoners.[39] The petition quickly garnered thousands of signatures from citizens across the country, raising government fears of a snowball effect.[40] Cables penned by U.S. officials in Prague provided updates on the petition's reception by the regime and among ordinary citizens. One sent on August 11, for example, notes that the petition had gained wide support among workers, but lacked buy-in from Slovaks.[41] Another details the embassy's "informal sampling" of support for the petition, which found "intense interest" among ordinary citizens coupled with a "fear of the dangers involved" in action.[42]

The first chance to test that intense interest came in late August at demonstrations marking the twenty-first anniversary of the Warsaw Pact invasion of Czechoslovakia that crushed the Prague Spring. Leading up to the demonstrations on August 21, 1989, embassy officers offered incisive commentary, including warnings of potential violence against unauthorized demonstrations. In one cable, the Deputy Chief of Mission Theodore Russell warns of a "bloody (August) 21ˢᵗ" and proposes a blueprint for Washington's response should violence break out.[43] Another cable sent just days before the demonstrations remarks on a "mood of tension" pervading the city along with palpable hope for change.[44] The embassy's warnings proved accurate. While the protestors remained mostly peaceful, police attacked demonstrators and arrested more than three hundred individuals for independent political activity.[45] In a cable signed by Ambassador Black, the embassy provided its assessment of the day: "The regime appears to have been the clear loser in the confrontation, demonstrating once again that its concept of the freedoms of assembly and speech are sharply at odds with the Western (and its own population's) understanding of such principles."[46] She knew whereof she wrote: she was present.[47] Following up a week later, the embassy conveyed three prescient takeaways from the demonstrations: "increased willingness by Czechoslovaks, especially the young, to challenge the regime, an 'internationalization' of the fight for human rights in Czechoslovakia, and the importance of pressure from both the governments in East and West in nudging the Czechoslovak regime towards a more tolerant view of political dissent."[48]

Around the same time as the August 21 demonstrations, the newly arrived Ambassador Black was preparing to present her credentials to President Gustáv Husák. In a cable sent several days before her credentialing, Black describes her "cordial" meeting with the East German ambassador, the dean of the Prague diplomatic community. While lighthearted in tone, the meeting provided Black an opportunity to pepper the man with questions about protests, independent activists, and Gorbachev. The East German in turn delivered some counsel of his own: "Do not ask Czech officials any tough questions."[49] Black did not follow his advice. In a meeting with Foreign Minister Jaromír Johanes on August 22, the new ambassador emphasized the United States' interest in the region and its desire to see progress in human rights.[50]

The cables from September show the Americans continuing their strategy of engagement with a hard edge. As summer ended, an important meeting loomed on the horizon. For the first time in eleven years, a Czechoslovak foreign minister was set to meet with his U.S. counterpart.[51] Recognizing the potential of the encounter, Ambassador Black and her staff cabled recommendations to Secretary of State James Baker. Human rights should be the focus of the conversation and be further stressed in any subsequent comments to the media.[52] Other agenda items should include access to officials, embassy housing, and war monuments. In a final word of emphasis to Baker, the embassy returned to the Helsinki Accords, pointing out that he could undercut the legitimacy Foreign Minister Johanes stood to gain from the meeting by "hit[ting] hard" on human rights.[53] The advice was well received. In his October 1 meeting with Johanes, Baker presented a list of political prisoners and tied economic reform to improved human rights.[54]

Notwithstanding that message, October saw harsh measures against independent journalists and activists, setting the stage for an end-of-month showdown.[55] October 28 marked the seventy-first anniversary of Czechoslovakia's birth and provided another occasion for independent political action.[56] Concerned about a "new crackdown" on activists in order to "minimize the size of October 28" demonstrations, the embassy recommended that Washington issue a forceful statement on the "deteriorating human rights situation."[57] It was a gray and cold autumn day when nearly ten thousand people spontaneously appeared on Wenceslas Square to express their dislike of the regime.[58] Carrying signs that bore slogans such as "Truth Prevails" and "We will not allow our republic to be subverted," demonstrators began to sing their national anthem.[59] Suddenly, riot police appeared just as they had during the August protest. After demanding that the protesters vacate the square, police waded into the crowd, randomly beating some demonstrators and detaining at least two hundred and fifty others.[60] In the aftermath of October's demonstration, U.S. officials assessed that "the wider population here is yet unwilling to risk direct confrontation with the regime," noting that the turnout at the demonstration was "relatively small" compared with protests in nearby countries like East Germany.[61] At the same time, however, the turnout far exceeded that in August and continued a trend of "increasing activism." Like in August, Ambassador Black again attended the demonstration to see for herself, this time at even greater personal risk.[62]

November 17 marked the fiftieth anniversary of a Nazi crackdown that targeted students protesting the Nazi occupation and shut down major Czech universities.[63] The planned protests on that chilly November day did not initially seem remarkable to embassy officers.[64] The anniversary was less high profile than those in August and October, and the initial gathering had been officially sanctioned by government officials and co-organized by the Socialist Union of Youth.[65] Nevertheless, the embassy tracked the coming event, remarking on the creation of two independent student groups a few days earlier and speculating about the new developments that November 17 could bring.[66]

Three U.S. foreign service officers traveled to observe the protests that day, just in case they proved consequential.[67] Upon arrival, the American onlookers found an unusually large crowd gathered on the university campus, which later marched to a nearby cemetery.[68] The formidable turnout and rousing speeches energized the students in attendance. Rather than disperse after the approved ceremonies concluded, the demonstrators turned toward Wenceslas Square chanting slogans like "Forty years of Communism is enough" and "Warsaw, Berlin, and now Prague."[69] The U.S. embassy representatives moved with the crowd, continuing to observe events. The protesters' path was blocked in a side street by riot police. After a tense standoff with a substantial fragment that lasted late into the evening, regime forces cut off all escape. Czechoslovak security waded into the crowd and severely beat hundreds of peaceful demonstrators.[70] The horrified U.S. diplomats watched the carnage, themselves ultimately having to flee from the advancing forces.[71]

News of the violence shot through Czechoslovakia, galvanizing civilian resistance and outrage among activists. Western journalists were present, and news of the events rapidly spread globally. From her perch at the embassy, Ambassador Black helped rally international attention. She told one reporter, "The government is scared and out of control. . . . We are very angered by it."[72] Black urged Washington to condemn the regime's "brutal" and "bloody-minded" response to the demonstrations and continued to file reports about growing unrest.[73] On November 20, three days after the regime attack on the student-led marchers, around one hundred thousand people gathered in Wenceslas Square.[74] The size of the demonstrations grew daily and by November 26 would balloon to more than half a million.[75] Initially diffuse, the dissidents soon gained an organizing structure. On

November 19, Havel and other dissident leaders announced the creation of a partnership of independent groups called the Civic Forum, which united most independent initiatives and representatives of churches, artists' unions, and other like-minded citizens' organizations.[76] Commenting on the week's developments, Black cabled the next day that "the official structures of power are beginning to creak" and "[General Secretary Miloš] Jakeš's chances of surviving this week are looking very unlikely."[77]

As pressure on the government mounted, the possibility loomed that officials would rely on violence to maintain power. Ominously, the army was put on alert, with preparations made for a possible intervention in the protests.[78] On November 24, Defense Minister Milán Václavík told the Communist leadership that they had the support of the army and made the case for military intervention to restore order.[79] The decision was in the hands of the Party leaders. Fortunately, more moderate voices carried the day. Most of the Communist leaders were unwilling to risk the domestic and international consequences of further November 17–style violence.[80] Bowing to pressure, the entire Party leadership resigned, leaving behind younger leaders to salvage the Party.[81] Speaking to a closed-door audience, Jakeš said the country sat at "fateful crossroads" and admitted that "our restructuring has been and is accompanied by many great words, without the necessary deeds."[82] Many of the hard-liners, including Jakeš, had been ousted, but the remaining Communists dug in their heels, attempting to present themselves as a legitimate reform government.[83] Frustrated by the unyielding officials, most of the country on November 27 took part in a two-hour general strike organized by the Civic Forum.[84] Independent leaders called it a referendum on support for the Communist Party and reiterated their calls to end one-party rule.

The embassy's primary role during those heady days in late November and into December was one of meticulous reporting—with a particular eye toward preparing Washington for a more active role in supporting the new regime that seemed likely to emerge. The embassy met with representatives of the Civic Forum and other dissidents, reporting on their assessments about unfolding events and analyzing their evolving tactics.[85] For their part, dissidents pressed the embassy to show political support for the opposition "in a way that would minimize the potential that force might be used to thwart the democratic forces and processes now present in Czechoslovakia."[86]

By the end of November, the Communists had begun a dialogue with opposition leaders, promising to compromise on a new government.[87] The initial proposals, however, were modest at best, leaving the Communist Party firmly in the majority in the government. Unsatisfied, masses of Czech and Slovak citizens continued to march and strike in protest.[88] The dissidents asked that the United States not prematurely extend MFN status to the weakened regime, a gesture that would overly legitimize the Communists' attempt at reform.[89] Keeping in mind the dissidents' requests, embassy officials met with the embattled Communists to discuss ongoing events and remind them that the world was watching.[90] In a meeting with Foreign Minister Johanes, Ambassador Black rebuffed his requests that the United States normalize relations with Czechoslovakia, telling him that it was "a little soon to raise some subjects," including MFN.[91] Devoid of both international and domestic support, the Communists reluctantly began to cede their grip on power—paving the way for a new, democratic government.[92]

The final cables from November and December reflect the embassy's growing role as a bridge from Prague to decisionmakers in the United States whose choices would help shape the future of a democratic Czechoslovakia. Members of the Senate and the House came to Prague for meetings facilitated by the embassy with emerging leaders.[93] These conversations between U.S. and Czechoslovak politicians foreshadowed the strong alliance between the two countries that would soon emerge. Czechoslovaks hoping to reestablish liberal democracy benefited significantly from the political and economic advice of American lawmakers highly experienced in the practice of that system.[94] In addition, meeting with U.S. officials lent the budding Czechoslovak democratic leadership encouragement and support as they struggled to replace the decaying Communist regime with a new political order.

Just six weeks after the revolution had begun, the Czechoslovak dissidents achieved that goal. Addressing a jubilant crowd outside Prague Castle on January 1, 1990, the newly-elected President Havel quoted the seventeenth-century Czech educator Jan Amos Komenský: "People, your government has returned to you."[95] With the election of the former political prisoner as the country's first non-Communist president since 1948,[96] the Communist regime had been formally replaced, and the hopes of the Czechoslovak people, and their interlocutors in U.S. Embassy Prague, had been achieved.

FROM THE AFTERMATH TO THE PRESENT

Jubilation soon gave way to the hard work of building a new democracy. The United States continued its active supporting role, now pivoting from human rights advocacy to a broader focus on the many modalities of liberalism. The afterword to this volume traces how the seeds of democracy that were planted in 1989 were cultivated in 1990 and the years that followed, including with support from the United States, as well as the evolution of aid from the United States and the assumptions that undergirded it. The aid included a focus on helping Czechoslovakia build free markets on the assumption that doing so would support (or even guarantee) concomitant political freedoms. The afterword argues that the successes and failures of American democracy assistance after the Velvet Revolution are reflected in the complex state of liberal democracy in the contemporary Czech Republic and Slovakia, which is subject to populist and other challenges that confront democracies across Europe, but is proving surprisingly hardy in both nations and is outperforming some of their neighbors in that regard. That would surely gratify the authors of the cables presented in this book, who witnessed and aided the efforts of the Czechs and Slovaks to secure that democracy in the first place.

––––––––

The cables follow this introduction, with annotations as needed to define unfamiliar names, terms, and events. The time that each cable was sent is derived from the originals and is listed before a "Z" for "Zulu Time," a military term for the time zone better known as Greenwich Mean Time. We have also corrected minor typographical errors made in the original cables; these changes do not affect the cables' meaning and enhance readability. For additional reference in reviewing the cables, please see the timeline of events; list of acronyms and abbreviations; and list of key terms, names, and events.

THE CABLES

----

02 August 1989 1130Z
PRAGUE 05232

FM AMEMBASSY PRAGUE | **TO** SECSTATE WASHDC PRIORITY 9658 | **INFO** EASTERN EUROPEAN POSTS, AMCONSUL MUNICH, USIA WASHDC 7311, MUNICH FOR RFE

SUBJECT: THE REGIME'S CAMPAIGN AGAINST NEKOLIK VET;
A STRONG WARNING ABOUT AUGUST 21

REF: PRAGUE 5146 (NOTAL)

1. Confidential—entire text.

2. Summary. Prague Party boss Miroslav Stepan[a] has publicly attacked the Nekolik vet petition and promised that order will be maintained in Prague even by force on August 21. An ongoing general investigation of Nekolik vet continues with interrogations and police surveillance of possible suspects. The official press claims Western radio broadcasts have incorrectly cited persons as Nekolik vet supporters. *Rudé Právo* has attempted to link the editor of the exile publication "Svedectvi" to a U.S. military attaché allegedly expelled from Czechoslovakia for espionage activities some 40 years ago. We believe the Stepan August 21 warning should be taken seriously since the GOC has followed through on such threats in the past. End summary.

3. In an August 1 speech before members of the People's Militia and police, Prague Party boss Miroslav Stepan sharply attacked the Nekolik vet petition. Stepan called the petition "an anti-people circular" and a counter revolutionary program for the destruction of socialism in Czechoslovakia.

4. Stepan also warned that calls for disorder or destabilization on August 21 need to get a cogent answer, even including "force in accord with valid Czechoslovak laws." He declared that "we cannot allow the streets of Prague to become a place of gathering for destabilizing forces," adding that the government will take such measures as necessary to ensure calm "in the coming August days."

---

a. Miroslav Štěpán, secretary of the Municipal Party Committee in Prague and member of the National Assembly of Czechoslovakia and Central Committee of the Communist Party of Czechoslovakia.

5. The investigation by police of the Nekolik vet petition continues. REFTEL reported the house searches of Nekolik vet petition supporters Stanislav Devaty, Sasa Vondra and Jan Urban. We have learned the apartment of Jiri Krizan, one of four organizers of the petition drive, was also searched July 27. Krizan's daughter told EmbOff that Krizan has been directed to report to police August 3 for questioning. Jan Urban told another EmbOff that he could not go home because the police were watching his house.

6. The press campaign against Nekolik vet has taken a new twist. *Rudé Právo* quoted several individuals who claim their names were read on Western radio as petition signatories even though they are not. *Rudé Právo* August 1, as an example, reported the case of television announcer Zdena Varechova as one whose name was purportedly misused by VOA. A dissident contact told us petition organizer Sasa Vondra did receive a letter of support signed by "Zdena Varechova," which he forwarded to VOA and RFE. Dissident circles are unsure whether the letter was a fraudulent document created by Czechoslovak security, or if it was genuine and Varechova was forced or freely chose to recant.

7. The regime also continues to attempt to link Nekolik vet and other independent activities to the West. Stepan and others have attacked RFE and VOA publicly concerning Nekolik vet. *Rudé Právo* went so far on August 1 to dredge up from obscurity a 40-year-old charge asserting that former U.S. military attaché in Czechoslovakia Charles Katko, reportedly expelled for espionage activities in 1948, then became the chief of the U.S. intelligence service in Frankfurt. During Katko's tenure in Prague, the paper asserts that he maintained a subversive relationship with a Czechoslovak dissident (Pavel Tigrid), who later published an anti-socialist newspaper in Paris.

8. Comment. The ongoing general police investigation of the Nekolik vet petition in-and-of itself does not mean that the arrest and indictment of the petition's organizers is inevitable. While arrests certainly are possible, dissident contacts indicate cases exist in which general investigations were used as "warnings" which did not lead to criminal prosecution. Stepan's speech is more ominous. Past warnings of a strong reaction by Czechoslovak authorities to illegal demonstrations have generally been kept. The fact that Stepan's speech was given before an audience of the People's Militia, a group which participated in last January's violence against demonstrators commemorating Jan Palach's[a] self-immolation, further underscores the threat. RUSSELL

---

a. Jan Palach was a student who committed suicide by self-immolation in 1969 in protest of the invasion of Czechoslovakia that ended the Prague Spring.

09 August 1989 1449Z
PRAGUE 05422

FM AMEMBASSY PRAGUE | **TO** SECSTATE WASHDC IMMEDIATE 9779 | **FOR** EUR/EEY ONLY | **FOR** SWIHART FROM RUSSELL

SUBJECT: OFFICIAL INFORMAL NO. 148

1. (C) For Mike from Ted[a] (State 135/4, Prague 5228). We are all frankly puzzled and disturbed by strong OFM reaction you report to our August 2 cable filling them in on state of play with GOC on leases. I assume their cable to us will clarify what fur we rubbed the wrong way. In any case, please assure them we greatly appreciate their support. We were simply trying to keep them informed and find out from them what GOC was up to in NYC and Washington on leasing and construction requests. We thought it was appropriate to do this open channel rather than via OI to EEY.

2. (C) CODEL Cranston[b]. For Jeanne[c] from Harvey. As we have mentioned in previous front channels, the CODEL will be staying at the Hotel Intercontinental and we have reserved a control room. We are still waiting for fiscal data, however, in order to pay for the room and to cover transportation costs beyond normal embassy resources. There should be no problem in setting up an appropriate appointment for Mrs. Sarbanes[d] in the education area. The senators' wives' desire to meet with "politically active women" may be more difficult, though we will do our best. Clearly this term has meanings here that would be different than in the U.S., and we may look at the cultural area for some possibilities. We had planned to get off a proposed wives' schedule today, but with these new requests it will have to wait for awhile.

3. (C) Anniversary press statement (State 135/6). For Jeanne. Although GOC will no doubt react badly to it, statement eloquently captures the meaning of the August 21 anniversary[e]

---

a. Michael Hornblow, U.S. diplomat responsible for Poland, Hungary, and Czechoslovakia. Theodore (Ted) Russell, deputy chief of mission at the U.S. Embassy in Czechoslovakia.

b. Senator Alan Cranston (D-CA).

c. Likely Jeanne Schulz, U.S. foreign service consular officer; in 1989, she served first as Hungarian desk officer, then as consul general in Berlin.

d. Christine Dunbar Sarbanes, wife of Senator Paul Sarbanes (D-MD), who was part of CODEL Cranston, so-called because it was led by Senator Alan Cranston (D-CA).

e. August 21, 1989 was the twenty-first anniversary of the 1968 Soviet invasion of Czechoslovakia.

and accurately reflects our policy towards Czechoslovakia and its poor human rights record. FYI. Many observers here remain gloomy about what August 20–21 will bring and fear bloodshed. Youth are apparently determined to demonstrate and regime shows every sign of being absolutely determined to prevent such demonstrations with whatever force they believe is necessary.

4. (LOU) Industrial management training. For Jeanne from Harvey. In wake of Ambassador Niemczyk's follow up call to Ted Tuesday on this subject, we plan to seek—or recommend to Ambassador Black that she seek—to obtain specific Czechoslovak proposal requesting short-term visits by management experts to Czechoslovakia. We want to make sure, however, that we do not raise hopes for USG or other financial support we cannot deliver. P&C tells us that funding from their sources for this type of activity is very limited: USIA Washington might have some "seed money" to start up a linkage between schools in the two countries, and this could get into the management area. There is also the new USIA funding which has been made available for Eastern Europe, some of which might be used for this purpose. We can raise this with Gelb[a] when he arrives. Otherwise, is the Department or Ambassador Niemczyk aware of other USG funding which might be available, or have some concrete indications of private sector willingness to pay for these visits? RUSSELL

11 August 1989 1246Z
PRAGUE 05480

FM AMEMBASSY PRAGUE | **TO** SECSTATE WASHDC 9815 | **INFO** EASTERN EUROPEAN POSTS
SUBJECT: HUMAN RIGHTS UPDATE

1. Confidential—entire text.

2. Summary. A Nekolik vet petition organizer is pleased with the response of workers to the petition, but admits Slovak support is not commensurate with Slovak representation in the population. The regime's campaign against independent initiatives is not limited to Nekolik vet supporters; Obroda, the Independent Peace Association, and Jiri Dienstbier[b]

---

a. Bruce Gelb, director of the U.S. Information Agency; visited several Soviet Bloc countries in 1989.

b. Jiří Dienstbier was a dissident and Charter 77 signatory who supported the reform movement in 1968.

have been recent targets of harassment. Independent initiatives appear divided over whether to endorse an August 21 Wenceslas Square demonstration, but a demonstration appears likely regardless of what the initiatives might decide. Cardinal Tomasek has proposed an open dialog between authorities and the people, and has offered the Church as a possible facilitator. No dates have been set for the trial of Petr Cibulka[a] or appeal of Frantisek Starek.[b] Authorities are still trying to link an arson ring named Wehrwolf to independent activists. End summary.

Nekolik vet petition

3. Petition organizer Jiri Krizan told EmbOff that the total number of signatories is approaching 15,000. He is pleased that approximately 80 percent of the signatories come from the ranks of workers. Krizan stated that only 10–15 percent of the signatories are from Slovakia. He attributed the relatively low Slovak figure to historical differences, but indicated the Slovak response to Nekolik vet has been better than to the petition supporting Havel earlier this year (Prague 784).

Other targets of regime harassment

4. The regime's current campaign against independent initiatives has been focused on the Nekolik vet petition (Prague 5389), but movements and individuals not directly associated with the petition have also been targets of regime harassment. The Obroda group of reform Communists seems a special target. In addition to suffering house searches and confiscation of materials (Prague 5146), Obroda members on two recent occasions have been detained by police and prevented from attending Obroda meetings. Thirty-eight-year-old Obroda activist Jan Urban also recently received a surprise letter ordering him to report for three weeks of reserve military duty in the Bohemian countryside. The duty ensures Urban will not be in Prague for the August 21 anniversary of the 1968 invasion.[c] One independent contact believes Obroda is especially frightening to the regime because of its overtly political program and because its membership includes persons with substantial (pre-1968) Party and government experience.

---

a. Petr Cibulka was a dissident active in Charter 77 who was arrested for distributing banned materials.

b. František Stárek was an activist and journalist arrested for publishing *Vokno*, a dissident magazine.

c. The Warsaw Pact invasion of Czechoslovakia in 1968, led by the Soviet Union to suppress reform movements within the Czechoslovak Communist government.

5. Another target of harassment has been the Independent Peace Association (IPA). Police detained IPA activist Jana Petrova, on her way to an IPA demonstration on July 31. About 50 persons were able to gather long enough at Prague's Peace Square to hear an IPA proclamation supporting draft resisters. Petrova told EmbOff she was searched and held at the police station until the IPA rally was over. Petrova also remarked that one of her police interrogators had small busts of both Gorbachev and Stalin in his office. He declined to answer when Petrova asked if he planned to follow the path of Gorbachev or Stalin.

6. Jiri Dienstbier, Charter signatory and long-time independent activist, has also drawn the regime's ire for his recent interviews with *Newsweek* and the *Washington Post*. Dienstbier has been told he will lose his telephone because "the number is needed for a public purpose." Dienstbier's interviews were also criticized by *Rudé Právo*. The *Rudé Právo* article seemed especially disturbing to Dienstbier, who requested that EmbOff provide him with a copy of the *Post* article (we did) so he might be in a better position to defend himself.

To demonstrate or not on August 21

7. Differences appear to exist among independents as to how best to commemorate the 1968 invasion anniversary. Generally, older activists believe initiatives such as Charter 77 should not officially call for or endorse an August 21 public demonstration on Wenceslas Square. They fear that such a demonstration will be turned back with force by the regime, that the use of force will strengthen the position of hardliners within the Party, and that the independent initiatives will be held responsible for any injuries.

8. Initiatives with younger followers, such as the Czech Children, apparently would support endorsing a Wenceslas Square demonstration. One exception is the Independent Peace Association, which apparently will not formally endorse a demonstration. Those who support a demonstration believe it presents a no-win situation for the regime. If the regime does not interfere with a demonstration, people will be encouraged to demonstrate in the future. If the regime disrupts the demonstration, the regime will at a minimum embarrass itself in front of Western and other observers and again reveal that its professed interest in human rights is disingenuous.

9. Representatives of various independent initiatives are attempting to achieve a consensus concerning August 21 activities. It seems likely that, at least, a joint declaration condemning the invasion will be issued. However, even if a consensus is reached that an August 21 demonstration should not RPT not be called, most activists feel a demonstration

will occur one way or another. One EmbOff has seen "cordial invitations" to an August 21 demonstration scrawled in a number of telephone booths, and activists feel persons, especially the young, will accept these and other encouragements. Those familiar with the January 1989 demonstrations[a] also say that many onlookers spontaneously joined those demonstrations, and believe an August 21 replay of such spontaneity is possible.

Cardinal Tomasek urges dialog

10. Cardinal Tomasek in an August 4 open letter to Czechoslovak authorities and citizens urged an open dialog between authorities and the populace and warned against violence. The cardinal indicated that he and the Catholic Church, independent of any political ideology, stand ready to contribute to the development of such dialog. The cardinal on August 7 met with First Deputy Prime Minister Lucan, and repeated his offer that the Church facilitate a dialog.

Starek and Cibulka cases

11. Court dates for the appeal of Frantisek Starek (Prague 5291) and the trial of Petr Cibulka (Prague 4018) have not yet been set. One independent contact said the Starek appeal had finally been assigned to a judge, but that appeal judges had been reluctant to hear the case and had argued amongst themselves as to who should do so. Cibulka remains in jail in Brno pending investigation of the case against him. Investigators have already interviewed several hundred witnesses in preparing the case against Cibulka. His trial is expected this autumn.

Authorities charge "Wehrwolf" connection to independent movements

12. Articles in the official press have attempted to demonstrate a connection between independent activists and a series of industrial arson cases and a murder. Authorities claim a criminal organization called Wehrwolf (Prague 4432) is responsible for the crimes which have occurred in Bohemia and Moravia since 1986. Four persons, all around 40 years of age, have been detained in connection with the crimes, and are under suspicion of inciting and directing acts of sabotage. Wehrwolf is supposed to have delegated actual execution of the crimes to persons between the ages of 16 and 20.

---

a. On January 19, 1989, thousands of Czechoslovak citizens demonstrated in commemoration of the 20th anniversary of Czechoslovak student Jan Palach's self-immolation. The gathering was dispersed violently by police, bringing international condemnation.

13. One of the four persons detained is Jakub Dubsky. Dubsky is the son of Charter 77 signatories Ivan Dubsky, who lives in Prague, and Irena Dubska, who since 1968 is the wife of Zdenek Mlynar and now lives in Austria with Mlynar. Petr Uhl, the VONS activist, has also been interrogated by police in the case. Uhl apparently was in the same prison as one of the four suspects. Followers of independent initiatives generally believe the Wehrwolf crimes are deliberately being linked to independent initiatives in an effort to discredit them before the general public. **RUSSELL**

15 August 1989 1509Z
PRAGUE 05536

FM AMEMBASSY PRAGUE | **TO** SECSTATE WASHDC IMMEDIATE 9845 | **FOR** EUR/EEY ONLY—FOR HORNBLOW FROM RUSSELL

SUBJECT: OFFICIAL INFORMAL NO. 151

1. (C) For Mike from Ted (State 137/4). Our thoughts on August 21 reaction. As our reporting has indicated, we share your concern that August 21 will witness a harsh confrontation between demonstrators and the regime. We have little doubt that the government's warnings that it will not tolerate demonstrations are no bluff and that it will crack heads as necessary. As requested, we provide below our thoughts on what the USG reaction should be to a harsh crackdown.

2. (C) August 21 reaction—cont'd. The USG, as we know, has little in the way of direct leverage on the GOC. What few substantive "carrots" we have, such as MFN, we are already withholding. Thus our strongest weapons are probably political and rhetorical. While the GOC will take whatever actions it ultimately feels it must, it does have a concern for its reputation in the West. This is one reason its human rights policies have not fallen to the level of Romania or Bulgaria. Its concern stems mainly from two factors. First, perhaps more than any other Eastern European state, the Czechoslovaks consider themselves part of the West. They are very sensitive to criticisms that their behavior is not up to the standards of Western civilization, especially if this criticism comes from more than just the U.S. Secondly, the GOC desperately wants increased Western trade and investment. Strong criticism of the regime by Western governments may deter this trade and investment.

3. (C) August 21 reaction—cont'd. In the event that August 21 produces a harsh crackdown, including arrests and police brutality, we recommend that the Department prepare a strong statement, preferably from the president, condemning the crackdown and emphasizing the degree to which the GOC's behavior deviates from its CSCE[a] obligations. We should also encourage other Western CSCE participants, both NATO members and key neutrals like the Austrians, to make similar condemnations.

4. (C) August 21 reaction—cont'd. In other steps:

—We should call in Houstecky[b] at a high level and express our condemnation of GOC repression. To the degree feasible, we can encourage like-minded Western governments to make similar protests here and in capitals. We do not think it useful to try to isolate Houstecky again, as this simply plays into GOC hands in terms of restricting our access here.

—We should restrict high level political visits for a period of at least several months except in cases where the advantages of moving forward (e.g., the Gelb visit) appear to be clearly on our side. Much as we have liked the idea of giving Sterba[c] decent treatment, we could make clear that he could not expect to be received at a high level if he chooses to go to Washington soon after a bloody "21st."

—We should also make clear to the GOC that the laundry list of potentially worthwhile initiatives Houstecky proposed to A/S Seitz[d] would have to be put on hold.

—As we have been doing, we should make vigorous use of the Vienna CD[e] and raise any specific cases stemming from August 21 in writing for a GOC reply.

—Increasing interest by the GOC in the IMF and World Bank suggest that, while in the longer-term Czechoslovak membership might be in our interest, in the short run we could oppose it.

—In addition, we should certainly try to get CODEL Cranston to express strong reaction of U.S. legislators to human rights abuses here. **BLACK**

---

a. Conference on Security and Cooperation in Europe was a forum for dialogue between Eastern and Western nations that began in 1973. Thirty-three European countries as well as the United States and Canada participated.

b. Miroslav Houštecký, Czechoslovak ambassador to the United States.

c. Jan Štěrba, Czechoslovak minister of foreign trade.

d. Raymond Seitz, U.S. assistant secretary of state for Europe and Canada.

e. CD (Concluding Document), here referring to the agreement signed at the end of the CSCE meeting in Vienna.

15 August 1989 1523Z
PRAGUE 05547

FM AMEMBASSY PRAGUE | **TO** SECSTATE WASHDC 9854 | **INFO** EASTERN EUROPEAN POSTS, AMEMBASSY LONDON, AMEMBASSY PARIS, AMEMBASSY BONN, AMEMBASSY VIENNA, USMISSION USNATO, USIA WASHDC 7352

SUBJECT: WHAT CZECHS ARE THINKING ABOUT POLITICAL ACTIVISM

1. Confidential—entire text.

2. Summary. An informal sampling by EmbOffs of ordinary Czechs revealed intense interest in the Nekolik vet petition, positive views of dissidents, a willingness even by the cynical to take more political risks, yet an abiding fear of the dangers involved. Another source reported tension in a factory over the petition. Several contacts commented that significant segments of the population were not likely to contest the regime's control for at least two years. End summary.

3. As the anniversary of the August 21, 1968, Warsaw Pact invasion of Czechoslovakia draws near, even ordinarily apolitical Czechs are busy debating politics. The powerful example of Polish and Hungarian liberalization and the government's savage attacks on the Nekolik vet petition have stirred up tensions in workplaces and aroused the interest of villagers. Because the government censors the mails through which Nekolik vet signatures are being sent, it presumably has a reasonably accurate count. The intensity of its vituperation against the organizers of Nekolik vet may indicate that the number of signatories is higher than anyone expected. Recognizing that the petition has made an impact outside of Prague, the regime has sent Central Committee members to large industrial enterprises to preside over anti-Nekolik vet meetings and Party aktivs.

4. What the broader, long-quiescent Czechoslovak population thinks about Nekolik vet and the more general issues of political activism is critical for the future political development of the country. But because the regime firmly controls the discernible political scene here, it is difficult to ascertain the public mood.

5. To get a feel for what Czechoslovaks think, EmbOffs spoke in passing with some 40 people in Bohemia and Moravia[a] (Slovak opinion was not assessed) and in detail with a half dozen. These reasonably well-informed, middle-class Czechs had no contact with dissidents and no previous contact with Western embassies.

---

a. Czech historic lands, along with Silesia.

6. To a person, our interlocutors had positive views of dissidents. An old lady called them "modern martyrs"; a middle-aged teacher, "the only decent people left in the country"; another said they were heroes. Even a senior economic manager and Party member stated, "everyone knows the system is cruddy. They are the only ones willing to do anything about it." Mr. M, a mid-level technical manager who was letting his secretary at her own initiative type copies of the Nekolik vet petition in the office and warning her of possible informers, had a more ambivalent view. He agreed with the petition ("it's what Helsinki[a] is all about") and admired the dissidents, but he thought they were tilting at windmills. If you can't change the system, then you shouldn't try was the gist of his argument. Many casual contacts agreed with him that dissent was justified but hopeless.

7. One contact reported that some people he talked with in a village accepted the media's characterization of the dissidents as immoral elements. A more sophisticated view came from a civil engineer, who said that without meaning to under-estimate Vaclav Havel's contribution, he thought Havel's writing at times suffered from not having a critical audience which could openly engage him in debate.

8. When the question of personal political activism is raised, these Czechs displayed nuanced and at times contradictory attitudes. Like moths drawn to a flame, they all wanted to read Nekolik vet. As one put it, how can the regime want us to condemn something we haven't even read? Yet getting one's hands on it is not easy. Few of our contacts had seen it. Some asked us for copies (requests turned down with regret). Even a parish priest who should be able to tap Church sources could not get ahold of it. Clearly, the dissidents have not yet developed an adequate distribution network.

9. Yet when our contacts managed to get a copy and read the petition, they were immediately confronted with the dilemma of signing and possibly suffering the (undefined) consequences, or being cowards and refusing to sign: a no-win situation.

10. Our contacts viewed political activism per se as potentially dangerous. As far as they were concerned, it was to be avoided. It was for other braver or perhaps more foolhardy souls.

11. Nonetheless, although they might not have been fully aware of it, their reports of their own activities showed that they are less afraid than in the past. Actions which a decade

---

a. Helsinki Accords, an agreement signed in 1975 by the Soviet Bloc, Western European countries, and the United States at the conclusion of the first Conference on Security and Cooperation in Europe. In it, all signatories committed to the protection of human rights.

ago they would have probably avoided as dangerous they now undertake as a matter of course.

12. Mr. M, the mid-level technical manager who considered activism quixotic, in fact engaged in a series of risky political acts:
—He read Nekolik vet and passed it on;
—He permitted his secretary to use company time and resources for illegal political activity;
—He did not report her illegal activity, as required by law;
—He warned her about a potential informer;
—He discussed the petition favorably with a fellow Czech; and
—He passed all the above information to a U.S. diplomat.

13. Mr. M does not realize it, but he is a political activist. Yet he considers himself inadequate and unmanly because he does not take an open political stance. His is a subterranean activism; others in our sampling were similarly involved.

14. Virtually all of our contacts engaged in activism by proxy:
—They flock to exhibits which include previously taboo political subjects;
—Some pass around books on the West—others follow American popular culture;
—They say they listen to RFE and VOA, and complain that VOA is too cautious; and
—They tell countless cutting political jokes about Czechoslovakia's Communist leaders.

15. Although our contacts were generally unwilling to translate their antagonism toward the regime into political activity, at least one—a 65-year-old woman—told us she would be demonstrating in Prague on August 21. As she walked out of an office building during the Palach demonstrations last January, the police beat and trampled her, breaking her hip. After this experience, she said it was her duty to demonstrate against the regime.

16. Although our sample is too small to generalize credibly to the entire country, a recent chat with a factory worker revealed that a very different slice of the population may hold parallel sentiments.

17. Our source, a 35-year-old Charter 77 signatory with an elementary education who works in a chemical factory in northern Bohemia, told of the tensions aroused in his workplace by the Nekolik vet petition. He said he collected 40 signatures and sent them to Havel. The Party, meanwhile, collected 24 signatures of Party members denouncing Nekolik vet and sent them to the Central Committee. (One of our 40 "ordinary" Czechs said that the Party unsuccessfully tried to collect signatures at his workplace for a letter denouncing Nekolik vet, but had to abandon the effort. Many denunciatory letters in the

media are signed only by Party members, indicating that workers may be refusing to sign them.) When the Chartist-worker petitioned the factory trade union chairman to allow the workers to read Nekolik vet, she refused. He was attacked by "Pruboj," the regional newspaper, threatened with loss of his job and relocation and told he would be detained on August 20. Even some Communists, he said, sympathized with him.

18. The "Pruboj" article, which he showed us, in a defensive tone argued that such activities should not be allowed to disrupt production and asserted that Prestavba was improving safety and the workers' lot in the factory.

19. Several of our sampling felt that Czechoslovaks were not yet ready for out-and-out political activism. It will take two years for ordinary people to get involved, we were told. Indeed, the penalties for opposition to the regime are palpable, although considerably smaller than several years ago. In preparation for August 21, for instance, a witness reported seeing Interior Ministry forces in a remote rural area practicing handling water cannons. Militia are said to be patrolling the streets in Plzen,[a] while police patrols have been stepped up on Vaclavske namesti[b] in Prague. One policeman there told EmbOff that he did not want to be there, and that the regime would bring in tougher units for August 21. BLACK

16 August 1989 1514Z
PRAGUE 05578

FM AMEMBASSY PRAGUE | **TO** SECSTATE WASHDC IMMEDIATE 9883 | **INFO** USIA WASHDC IMMEDIATE 7355, USIA FOR EU (JORIA)

SUBJECT: CZECHOSLOVAK GOVERNMENT WARNING TO
    EMBASSY ON AUGUST 21 ANNIVERSARY

1. Confidential—entire text.

2. Summary. The embassy has received a "warning" from MFA to stay away from any demonstrations on August 21. The warning included expressions of concern that diplomats might be caught in the "legitimate" efforts of security forces to maintain public order and also applied to accredited foreign journalists. We plan to reply to the warning stressing that observation of public events is a perfectly legitimate diplomatic function

---

a. Plzeň, a city in Czechoslovakia.

b. "*Václavské náměstí*" is the Czech name for Wenceslas Square.

which we intend to continue and our expectation that the GOC will fulfill its obligations to protect diplomats and foreign journalists. End summary.

3. The Deputy Director of MFA Consular Affairs Drahomir Kuban asked our consul to come in August 16 to collect copies of two diplomatic notes regarding visas for accredited journalists and new rules on obligatory exchange of hard currency by foreign visitors to Czechoslovakia (SEPTEL). After passing her the notes, Kuban read a prepared statement asserting that "certain illegal groups" planned to hold illegal demonstrations in Prague on August 21. He noted that, under the Fourth Article of the Vienna Concluding Document,[a] the Czechoslovak government had the right to enforce its laws and maintain public order.

4. Kuban then stressed that, while the GOC was committed to ensuring the free movement of diplomats in accordance with the Helsinki Accords, Western diplomats did not have a right to "participate" in illegal demonstrations. He urged that U.S. diplomats avoid the area of the demonstrations. He "expressed concern" that diplomats and accredited journalists might be caught up in the efforts of security forces to fulfill their "legitimate duty" of maintaining order.

5. We are seeking an appointment with appropriate MFA officials dealing with U.S.–Czechoslovak bilateral relations in order to reply to Kuban's statement. We plan to make following points:
—U.S. diplomats have never participated in any demonstrations in Czechoslovakia, illegal or otherwise.
—Observation of public events, including demonstrations, is a legitimate activity and responsibility of diplomats, and it is one that we will continue to fulfill.
—Such observation is also the legitimate activity of journalists, and we presume that U.S. journalists will be covering August 21 events in Prague.
—It is the obligation of the host government to ensure the protection of diplomats and accredited foreign journalists as long as they are engaging in legitimate activities.
—The U.S. government accepts and lives up to this responsibility for diplomats and foreign journalists and expects the government of Czechoslovakia to do likewise.

---

a. States that the participating nations "confirm that, by virtue of the principle of equal rights and self-determination of peoples and in conformity with the relevant provisions of the Final Act, all peoples always have the right, in full freedom, to determine, when and as they wish, their internal and external political status, without external interference, and to pursue as they wish their political, economic, social and cultural development."

6. Depending on the response we receive from MFA, we may ask the Department to follow up our demarche. **BLACK**

17 August 1989 1519Z
PRAGUE 05614

FM AMEMBASSY PRAGUE | **TO** SECSTATE WASHDC 9908 | **INFO** EASTERN EUROPEAN POSTS

SUBJECT: THE 1968 INVASION ANNIVERSARY APPROACHES - A MOOD OF TENSION
UNDERLINED BY HOPE

1. Confidential—entire text.

2. Summary. The approach of the twenty-first anniversary of the 1968 invasion finds a mood of tension here, although external changes in Hungary, Poland and the USSR, coupled with an increase in political activism internally, give hope that change is possible. No one is certain how protest actions called by various initiatives will play themselves out. Everyone takes regime threats to use force to keep order seriously, and riot police have been practicing their techniques in anticipation of protests.

3. Charter 77 and five other groups have limited their call to protest to two minutes of silence in town centers on August 21. The two-minute protest will provide little opportunity for violent confrontation, but an hour-long demonstration scheduled for August 21 and endorsed by three independent initiatives holds out a greater prospect for violent confrontation. Various other protest actions, scheduled for both August 20 and August 21, are planned, and a greater number of protest actions outside of Prague are anticipated than in previous years. End summary.

4. "The situation is so tense, anything is possible. August is crucial." Whether correct or not, this statement by an independent activist succinctly states what we believe to be the mood here as the twenty-first anniversary of the August 21, 1968, invasion approaches. The tension is felt not only by independent activists and the regime, but also by many politically aware citizens who must decide what, if anything, to do on August 21. No one knows for certain how many will answer the call of independent initiatives to protest actions, nor is there any certainty as to how strongly the regime and its security apparatus will react.

5. Beneath the tension and uncertainty, however, is a recognition that August 1989 is unlike the previous twenty Augusts. Both external and internal developments give

activists and common citizens some hope that genuine change is possible. Externally, changes in Poland, Hungary, and especially the USSR are the inspiration for optimism, while internally, the increased willingness of persons to speak out, whether it be in the form of demonstrations, signing of the Nekolik vet petition, or otherwise, gives hope that the long dormant populace is finally starting to stir.

6. The most immediate concern among activists is whether planned protest actions (described paras 10–13) may end in violence. The regime, frightened by the success of the Nekolik vet petition and fearful of losing its privileged position in Czechoslovak society, has promised it will use force to maintain order (Prague 5232), and every activist we talk to takes the threat seriously—as do we. The more excitable, less experienced activists even predict shootings and the use of tanks, and tell us temporary detention centers capable of holding 60,000 persons are being set up in the countryside. The calmer and more experienced activists count regime-provoked violence as a possibility, but believe any excessive crowd control measures are likely to follow the pattern seen during last January's clashes between police and demonstrators (baton charges, water cannon, tear gas).

7. We have heard that riot police have been training at Prague's military airport on a strip of land the size of Wenceslas Square, the traditional site of demonstrations in Prague. Reportedly Rudolf Hegenbart, director of the State Administration Department, Central Committee CPCz, has advocated a restrained response to any demonstrations, but is said to have been overruled by higher authorities. Some activists speculate that regime hardliners will seek excuses to use violence, hoping by doing so to gain the upper hand in Party circles and to teach a lesson to those who dare use "illegal means and structures" to voice their dissatisfaction.

8. Activists themselves generally do not fear for their own safety. Many of the more prominent dissident leaders have already left Prague in hopes of avoiding the arrests/ detentions which they think possible before August 21, and because they want to make it more difficult for the regime to blame them for any violence which might occur. Those activists (and other veterans of previous demonstrations) who will be in Prague seem to have reconciled themselves to the possibility of personal injury at the hands of security forces.

9. Rather, most activists fear violence for at least three other distinct reasons. First, there is on their part a regard for the wellbeing of their fellow citizens. Activist Jiri Dienstbier states it simply: "I don't want people to die. There are other ways." Second, some activists feel regime violence against demonstrators would strengthen the hand of Party hardliners. And third, activists fear a violent crackdown against demonstrators (coupled with

the arrests, convictions, and prison terms which would inevitably follow) would dissuade many verged on the step of political activism from becoming involved. As a consequence, the majority of activists have sought a means by which persons may express their dissatisfaction on August 21 while minimizing the potential for a violent regime reaction.

10. With these concerns in mind, Charter 77 and five other independent initiatives (the Independent Peace Association, Czech Children, the John Lennon Peace Club, SPUSA, and Polish-Czechoslovak Solidarity[a]) have issued a declaration asking that people on the afternoon of August 21 walk to the centers of towns and that at 5:00 p.m. each person is to stand in place for two minutes of silence. The two minutes of silence will, according to the proclamation, be a call for freedom, democracy and human rights. Otherwise the proclamation does not endorse other protest actions, but does caution those who engage in them to responsibly choose their steps and urges state powers to respect the rights of assembly and peaceful demonstration. The planned two minutes of silence tactically should minimize the risk of violent confrontations. In addition, the action is a low risk one for persons who would like to express dissatisfaction with the regime, but still fear regime retaliation for unapproved political expression.

11. However, at least three independent initiatives (the Movement for Civil Liberties, the Democratic Initiative, and Tomas Garrigue Masaryk Association) have published a declaration calling for protest activities to extend beyond two minutes of silence. The declaration urges that the two minutes of silence be followed by an hour-long peaceful citizens' protest in the pedestrian areas in Prague and other cities. Some activists think such a demonstration is likely to end with a violent confrontation, either because security forces will not allow people to assemble and demonstrate, or because the goal of some young people at the demonstration will be to confront any police present.

12. Not all protest activities are called for August 21. Warsaw Pact troops in 1968 actually entered Czechoslovakia late the evening of August 20, and several protest actions are planned for this date. A group of five Slovak activists has advised Slovak authorities of their plans to lay flowers in Bratislava and Kosice on Sunday evening August 20, while Charter 77 spokesperson Tomas Hradilek has indicated he will try to lay flowers in Prague on the same day. A religious service for the morning of August 20 at the cathedral in Prague is being discussed by activists, and the reform Communist group, Obroda, is planning an August 20 independent demonstration under the slogan "the policy of Gorbachev, the true reconstruc-

---

a. A federation of Polish and Czechoslovak activists, founded in 1981 partly to bring together members of the Polish Solidarity movement and Czechoslovak Charter 77 dissidents.

tion." Obroda has decided to not/not[a] participate or endorse any activities on August 21, saying that what August 21 symbolizes is not tied to that date.

13. Activists also expect that this year protest actions will take place in cities besides Prague. In addition to the protest actions in Bratislava and Kosice described above, activists anticipate protest actions in Brno, Olomouc, and Ostrava. Activists universally agree that protest actions, whatever their nature, will be more enthusiastically endorsed in the Czech lands than in Slovakia. **BLACK**

17 August 1989 1526Z
PRAGUE 05615

FM AMEMBASSY PRAGUE | **TO** SECSTATE WASHDC IMMEDIATE 9911 | **INFO** USIA WASHDC IMMEDIATE 7358, USIA FOR EU (JORIA)

SUBJECT: CZECHOSLOVAK GOVERNMENT WARNING TO EMBASSY ON AUGUST 21 ANNIVERSARY: EMBASSY RESPONSE

REF: PRAGUE 5578

1. Confidential—entire text.

2. MFA Third Department (bilateral political affairs) declined to accept our reply to the statement read to consular officer regarding August 21 as reported in REFTEL. Instead, it directed us back to the MFA Consular Department. Consequently, acting POLEC counselor August 17 called on Consular Affairs Deputy Director Kuban, who had read the MFA statement, and made points contained in REFTEL.

3. Kuban responded to EmbOff's comments by stressing that his statement had not been meant as a warning, but as consultation and advice. He was sure that no embassy officer would intentionally participate in a demonstration, but contended that there was always a danger of unintended participation. He added that the GOC was not opposed to normal journalistic activity, but expected journalists to work in accordance with the law. Responding to EmbOff's questions, Kuban also provided some additional information.

—His statement had not been given to all Western embassies, but to embassies of neighboring Western countries and other Western countries with whom Czechoslovakia has significant ties.

---

a. Note that certain negation words are repeated in the cables for emphasis.

—The statement applied not merely to diplomats and journalists, but to all "embassy protected nationals"—which Kuban defined as anyone carrying a U.S. passport.

—The statement applied not just to August 21, but to the period August 18–22, and it particularly covered Wenceslas Square, Old Town Square, National Street and Na prikope.

4. The West Germans have told us that the statement was not given to them, but that they were informally cautioned by the MFA German desk. The statement was read to the British, who protested at the time, along the lines of our response to Kuban. The British plan to follow up this protest at the chargé level and have called in the Czechoslovak ambassador in London. They also plan to issue a travel advisory to British tourists over BBC.

5. Comment. The head of the MFA Press Department has asked PAO to meet with him August 18. He did not give a subject, but it may well be related to journalistic activity on August 21. For the moment, however, we do not recommend that Washington call in Czechoslovak Embassy official on this matter. Nor do we recommend the issuance of a U.S. travel advisory given the limited duration of the "threat" and the very short time available. **BLACK**

17 August 1989 1601Z
PRAGUE 05619

FM AMEMBASSY PRAGUE | **TO** SECSTATE WASHDC 9913 | **INFO** EASTERN EUROPEAN POSTS
SUBJECT: AMBASSADOR'S MEETING WITH DEAN OF PRAGUE DIPLOMATIC CORPS

1. Confidential—entire text.

2. My one-hour meeting August 17 with the GDR dean of the Prague diplomatic corps, Helmut Ziebart, was relaxed, informal, and productive. Protocol points for my presentation of credentials were fully covered by the ambassador, who speaks excellent English, but who often used an interpreter, particularly when I asked political questions.

3. During the last half hour of the meeting I directed political questions to Ziebart.
—August 20–21. He said the CSSR government is very nervous about August 20 and 21st. They know there will be big demonstrations and will control the demonstrators. The CSSR government has been assured by the Charter 77 group that they will conduct their demonstration silently and peacefully. Other groups may be a problem. Ziebart hopes for Czechoslovakia's sake that there will be no big trouble.
—Polish and Hungarian attitudes. Today's vote by members of Poland's parliament asking for a reevaluation of 1968, and apologizing to Czechoslovakia for their participation

in the 1968 invasion, are only fueling and supporting the dissident groups in Czecho-slovakia. Hungary has made similar statements. This has made the CSSR government extremely nervous. Ziebart said: "the events of Prague Spring 1968 should be left to historians, not to current politicians."

4. I asked if Ziebart thought that the CSSR would liberalize their political as well as economic policies. He answered that they will eventually, on a "step-by-step" basis. "The GDR will do the same, but in their own time." He continued, "all countries are different, and we must not hurry."

5. Ziebart continued that "Czechoslovakia has already known democracy as they have already experienced it in the 1920's and early 30's." "The Soviets on the other hand have never had a democracy so perestroika[a] is something very new for them." Ziebart said he looks at the strikes and wonders if Gorbachev is right and if he may be "rushing too much for change."

6. Ziebart said that we must all work to improve relations with each other. He said that it should not be difficult for me as I am the only woman ambassador in the diplomatic corps here. However, he hopes I won't find it awkward to be placed between Afghanistan and Nicaragua in the diplomatic order of precedence. I told Ambassador Ziebart that I was very brave and that I would manage.

7. Ziebart said that I will have no trouble getting appointments with government officials here, particularly with Jozef Lenart[b] and Miroslav Stepan. The dean said I should not expect to see Prime Minister Ladislav Adamec until my final farewell calls, as he does not see ambassadors for courtesy or business calls. While Adamec is very friendly, his staff protects his time.

8. President Gustav Husak will probably ask me many substantive questions after I present my credentials. Ziebart said "the Czechs are not very formal about protocol and I should expect thirty minutes of conversation with Husak, unless another ambassador is presenting credentials the same day."

9. Ziebart clasped his hands together, looked around the room slowly, and then raised his eyes to the chandelier. He looked at me and said, "do not ask the Czech officials any tough

---

a. Russian for "restructuring"; a program of economic and political reforms under Mikhail Gorbachev.

b. Jozef Lenárt, former prime minister of Czechoslovakia (1963–1968) and member of the Presidium of the Communist Party of Czechoslovakia (1970–1989).

questions." Remember that "just because the food is well cooked does not mean that it cannot be too hot." I laughed and said that his excellent saying seemed the proper ending to a most enjoyable meeting. I am grateful that Ziebart and his wife have fond and misty memories of my childhood films. It was a most cordial meeting. **BLACK**

18 August 1989 1436Z
PRAGUE 05646

FM AMEMBASSY PRAGUE | **TO** SECSTATE WASHDC IMMEDIATE 9932 | **FOR** EUR/EEY ONLY—FOR HORNBLOW FROM RUSSELL

SUBJECT: OFFICIAL INFORMAL NO. 155

1. (C) For Mike from Ted. East Germans. FRG DCM told me today that he fears influx of GDR refugee seekers next week. His embassy is already housing 50 such persons. He warned that if his embassy "fills up," U.S. embassy may get the spillover and said he understands that our embassies in East Berlin and Budapest have already instituted access limitations to keep out potential East German refugees. Can you let us know whether this is true and if you have any good advice for us here? Many thanks.

2. (C) For Jeanne. We know that Jan Urban did receive orders to report for military duty (ref Prague 5480). VONS has advised us that Urban did not/not report for duty, but instead is now in the hospital "having been diagnosed as having possibly suffered a heart attack." FYI: a British diplomat told Ed Kaska[a] she saw Urban after he had received the notice of military duty. Urban is reported to have said he might attempt to avoid the military duty for medical reasons. This suggests that whatever medical condition sent Urban to the hospital may have existed prior to his receiving the notice. Info gained from the conversation with the Brit should not/not be shared with Helsinki Watch. End FYI.

Jiri Dienstbier told us last week that he had received notice his phone would be disconnected because "the number was needed for a public purpose." (Prague 5480) We cannot confirm whether the phone has already been disconnected, but several attempts to call Dienstbier's number yesterday and today always resulted in a busy signal.

We have seen Havel's statement concerning August 21 demonstrations and fear of shootings by the authorities. Havel expressed the fear that security forces might shoot at

---

a. Ed Kaska, U.S. foreign service officer responsible for human rights updates sent by Embassy Prague.

demonstrators—he used the Czech word "postrelit," which means to shoot with an intent to wound, not to kill. Havel believes that there is now genuine hope for change in CZ. He also states that actions, such as signing Nekolik vet, are as effective as demonstrations. Havel then points out that it would be a tragedy for people to be shot when other means are available to achieve change, and urges persons to carefully consider the potential consequences of any protest actions in which they might participate.

3. (U) Ed to Jeanne. Zdenek Urbanek told me his application for an exit visa for his U.S. travel has been denied. He plans to appeal the denial. Please pass this news along to USIA EU[a] for Cynthia Miller[b] to pass to Mary Gawronski and Jerry Joria. **BLACK**

22 August 1989 1717Z
PRAGUE 05726

FM AMEMBASSY PRAGUE | **TO** SECSTATE WASHDC IMMEDIATE 9987, AMEMBASSY BUDAPEST IMMEDIATE | **INFO** EASTERN EUROPEAN POSTS, USIA WASHDC IMMEDIATE 7376, BUDAPEST PASS TO CODEL CRANSTON, DEPARTMENT PASS TO ERIKA SCHLAGER, CSCE COMMISSION, USIA FOR EU (JORIA)
SUBJECT: AUGUST 21 DEMONSTRATIONS IN PRAGUE

REF: PRAGUE 5682

1. Confidential—entire text.

2. Summary: A call by independent groups for two minutes of silence on Prague's central square on August 21 to commemorate the Warsaw Pact invasion of Czechoslovakia was observed by perhaps fifty percent of the persons on the square. However, a group of approximately 2,000 demonstrators, including some Hungarians, Poles and Italians, began a more active demonstration shortly after the two minutes of silence, chanting "freedom" and other slogans. Czechoslovak security forces, showing relative restraint compared with earlier demonstrations, were able to move the protesters from the square. The demonstrators regrouped, however, and led security forces on a mostly peaceful but hectic three-hour march/chase through the city. The protest action was finally dispersed at approximately 9:00 p.m. when a force of one thousand riot police occupied Wenceslas

---

a. EU (Europe).

b. Cynthia Miller, officer at USIA.

Square. For the most part violent confrontations between police and demonstrators were avoided. *Rudé Právo* reports 320 Czechoslovaks and 50 foreigners were detained, but we have seen no reports of American detentions or injuries. The regime appears to have been the clear loser in the confrontation, demonstrating once again that its concept of the freedoms of assembly and speech are sharply at odds with the Western (and its own population's) understanding of such principles. End summary.

3. This report presents details concerning the protest action in Prague on August 21. The report is based primarily on the observations of three EmbOffs who viewed the protest actions at different times and places, but also includes details provided by other Western diplomats who viewed the events.

4. Prior to 5:00 p.m., the time designated for the start of protest actions (Prague 5614), the day passed pretty much as any Monday in Prague, but with a higher concentration of police on Wenceslas Square than usual. As 5:00 p.m. drew near, the police busied themselves checking the identity cards of individuals, especially those of young people with long hair or facial hair. An EmbOff was also politely asked to present his identity card just as 5:00 p.m. approached.

5. There were a number of camera crews on the square, both those of Czechoslovak security forces and domestic and foreign television. EmbOff at about 4:30 saw a uniformed police officer reach up and attempt to disconnect the camera of an ABC television crewman who was filming another police officer "card" a person on the square. A Czech language speaker accompanying the ABC crew identified himself to the policeman as being from Czechoslovak television and told the police that ABC had a right to film anything they wanted on Wenceslas Square. He also mentioned that "we have problems with the American embassy," implying that we would complain about undue restrictions and/or harassment of American TV crews by Czechoslovak authorities. The arguments of the Czechoslovak TV rep, which seemed passionate to EmbOffs, were successful and the ABC crew was allowed to continue filming. EmbOff later talked with an ABC crew member who said that the crew had been asked to present its papers authorizing filming several times during the day, but that this incident was the only one where they had been harassed in any way.

6. At 5:00 p.m. the two minutes of silence called for by Charter 77 and other independent organizations began. On the end of Wenceslas Square near the statue of St. Wenceslas, the traditional site of demonstrations, there was a diminution of sound at 5:00 p.m., but only about fifty percent of those present observed the moments of silence. Many of

those who continued about their business appeared to be foreign tourists who would not have been as likely to know about the event. After two minutes passed people resumed their normal activities and no further protest actions are known to have occurred there.

7. On the other end of the long square (a pedestrian area known as Na prikope), a diminution of sound also occurred at 5:00 p.m. However, within a minute a small group of young Hungarians briefly raised a paper banner, written in Hungarian, which said "the Bolsheviks came with tanks, we come with flowers." The Hungarians are believed to be members of a group known as the Union of Young Democrats (Fidesz). The banner quickly was pulled down and ripped (we believe by police), but in the meantime a crowd we estimate between two and three thousand people began chanting in unison "freedom," "we are at home here," "long live Poland," and "Havel." The crowd at this time included a core of several hundred young adults surrounded by a group of persons which included older persons as well as the young.

8. At about 5:15 p.m. a police truck with a loudspeaker arrived, advised the demonstrators that their assembly was illegal, and ordered them to disperse. Few, if any, did. A few minutes later a busload of regular uniformed police arrived and created a police line to separate the couple thousand demonstrators from the persons (also numbering several thousand) who were merely onlookers.

9. Once the police line had been established, another bus carrying uniformed police in riot gear also arrived. As the bus rolled up one by-stander stated: "Here come the twenty year olds," and indeed the riot-gear-equipped police (helmets and nightsticks, some with shields) appeared to virtually all be in their early twenties. At this point approximately fifteen demonstrators sat down and offered passive resistance as the riot-gear-equipped police approached. Four police officers picked up each of those sitting on the ground and carried them without incident to a waiting bus.

10. The remainder of the crowd retreated from the Na prikope area in the face of the approaching riot police, and headed in the general direction of Prague's Old Town Square. It appeared to EmbOffs at this point that the crowd had been dispersed with no violence, and it appeared that neither demonstrators nor police were eager for a fight. (Note: at this point a busload of People's Militia, dressed in fatigues, arrived and perhaps symbolically occupied the now liberated Na prikope area for the forces of socialism. End note.) The crowd was not pursued by the police at this point, but a large blue police van partially blocked off the entrance to Old Town Square and the demonstrators, now numbering

between one and two thousand, marched toward Prague's Mala Strana across the Manesuv Bridge.

11. By approximately 6:15 p.m., the crowd was made up almost entirely of young people between the ages of 16 and 30. The crowd continued to chant slogans and did not seem to seek confrontation. The demonstrators walked down the middle of the bridge, but cheerfully parted to allow trams using the bridge to pass.

12. After most of the demonstrators had crossed the bridge and stopped near the Mala Strana metro station, riot-equipped police appeared and the demonstrators scattered—some retreating back across the bridge, some heading through Prague's Mala Strana toward Charles Bridge (the pedestrian bridge across the Vltava), some hiding in bushes along the Vltava, and other acting nonchalant and trying to appear as if they had been there all along. Again, no serious confrontation between demonstrators and police was observed by EmbOff.

13. Many of those who were dispersed somehow managed to get back across the river and then joined with demonstrators who had been on the Charles Bridge. The time was approximately 6:45 p.m. and the crowd of approximately 2000 young people peacefully wound its way through the narrow streets of Prague's Old Town in the direction of and past the National Avenue Metro Station. The crowd at this point continued with its chant of "freedom," but added a new chant as well—"Dubcek."[a]

14. The demonstrators then walked past the National Avenue Metro Station one block and filled the entire block of the city. At this point the crowd, meeting a line of riot-equipped police, turned and retreated in the direction of the National Avenue metro stop. Several trams attempted to make their way through the crowd, and although the crowd parted to allow them to pass, several demonstrators roughly slapped the trams as they passed through the crowd.

15. At about 7:15 p.m. the line of riot-equipped police ran toward the demonstrators with nightsticks raised and the demonstrators once again scattered. One police officer plunged into a crowd of people in an attempt to detain a specific individual. The crowd closed around the police officer, five or six other riot police rushed in and people in the crowd ran. A diplomat from another Western embassy who saw the incident said the first police officer fell to the ground and was kicked by demonstrators.

------

a. Alexander Dubček, first secretary of the Presidium of the Communist Party of Czechoslovakia (1968–1969); a reformist who was forced to resign in the aftermath of the Prague Spring.

16. By about 7:45 the area around the National Avenue Metro Station had been cleared and it once again appeared that the day's protest actions had ended. Some seven or eight trams were now in line waiting to move down the street running past the National Avenue metro stop. However, their forward progress was blocked not by demonstrators, but by approximately fifteen police personnel carriers (each carrying about 20 police officers).

17. In fact, the day's events were not over. By approximately 8:15 p.m. several hundred demonstrators had returned to Wenceslas Square and were continuing with their chanting. Riot police once again arrived and those demonstrating ran. Some demonstrators ran into restaurants along the square, but many were pursued by police into the eating places and arrested. Police then filled the square with personnel carriers (we counted 53) and five or six buses with more than 1000 riot-equipped police. By 9:15 the square was quiet and at 10:20 p.m. most of the police vehicles and most of the police left the square.

18. *Rudé Právo* today stated that 320 Czechoslovaks and 50 foreigners had been arrested. We have received no/no report of any Americans having been arrested or injured. We have learned from Western embassies in Prague that two Dutch students were arrested and are in jail, two Austrian journalists were arrested, that two Italian journalists were beaten, and that a FRG journalist was very roughly handled and detained by GOC security forces. The FRG journalist reported he was detained on a bus with between 10 and 15 demonstrators who had been bloodied by police nightsticks (EmbOffs saw no police beatings of demonstrators). Austria, Italy and the FRG have already lodged protests with the GOC and the Dutch have indicated they will do so as well.

19. In addition to the Hungarians who participated in the demonstration, there are reports from various sources (including *Rudé Právo*) that Poles and Italians also participated in the protest action. We are told that Polish Solidarity[a] parliamentarian Adam Michnik[b] attempted to come to Czechoslovakia for the demonstration, but was turned away at the border. A commentary in *Rudé Právo* today claimed the foreign participation in the protest action was proof of a coordinated international program "to kick the CZ regime into surrendering power." The commentary contended that "CIA collaborator Tigrid"[c] sent instructions by means of VOA concerning this program (see Prague 5232).

---

a. A political party and trade union in Poland; had formed a non-Communist government in August 1989.

b. One of the leaders of Polish Solidarity.

c. Possibly Pavel Tigrid, a Czech writer and exile journalist.

20. Comment: The regime appears to have been the clear loser from the August 21 events. Its relative restraint compared with January and last August 21 and decision not to follow through on threats to use violent force win it some points. On the other hand, its disruption of the August 21 assembly once again demonstrates that its concept of the freedoms of assembly and speech have thus far been little influenced by glasnost[a] and still are incompatible with Western (and its own population's) understanding of these principles. Moreover, the regime is essentially in a no-win situation since restraint encourages demonstrations while harsh action draws greater international criticism and builds up pressures leading to even worse confrontations in the longer term. BLACK

23 August 1989 0900Z
PRAGUE 05736

FM AMEMBASSY PRAGUE | **TO** SECSTATE WASHDC 9994 | **INFO** EASTERN EUROPEAN POSTS | CONFIDENTIAL SECTION 01 OF 03

SUBJECT: AMBASSADOR'S CALL ON FOREIGN MINISTER JOHANES

1. Confidential—entire text.

2. Summary. I presented copies of my letter of credence and Ambassador Niemczyk's recall August 22 afternoon to Foreign Minister Jaromir Johanes. During the course of a cordial and substantive hour-long discussion I emphasized the president's[b] interest in Eastern Europe and the desire of the administration to work to improve U.S.-Czechoslovak bilateral relations. I emphasized that this would take time and involved problems with Czechoslovakia's performance in the human rights field. Johanes underscored the GOC's corresponding desire to improve our relations but raised the Czechoslovaks' usual concern regarding "economic discrimination" (MFN), outside interference in Czechoslovak internal affairs and our travel restrictions on Czechoslovak diplomats in New York. End summary.

3. During my initial call on Foreign Minister Johanes August 22, I mentioned the progress in U.S.-Czechoslovak bilateral relations under Ambassador Niemczyk but said that I thought we still had much to do. Johanes said that he hoped our bilateral relations could

---

a. A term meaning "openness," referring to increased freedom of information and other reforms within the Soviet Bloc initiated in the 1980s by Soviet Premier Mikhail Gorbachev.

b. U.S. President George H. W. Bush.

improve and thought that, indeed, progress had been made, particularly, in terms of his 1987 visit to Washington, the useful work of the U.S.-Czechoslovak working groups—business facilitation and humanitarian affairs, and parliamentary exchanges including Politburo member Stepan's trip to Washington last year. However, Johanes emphasized that a lot of work remains to be done.

4. I told him that I had met with the president for half an hour just prior to my departure for Prague and that the president had discussed his great interest in Eastern Europe and in bettering relations with the CSSR. I told Johanes I would be pleased if sometime during the president's first administration or even his second I could get him to visit Czechoslovakia.

5. Johanes expressed pleasure at this thought but said that we needed to move forward in our political dialogue, which should be raised in level, and that the United States still discriminated against Czechoslovakia on MFN.

6. I told Johanes that I hoped that if there could be improvement in the human rights area in Czechoslovakia that sometime during my tenure I could recommend to Washington that MFN be granted. I emphasized, however, that Congress still has to decide on MFN and the administration must make a recommendation. They would be discussing the issue not on the narrow basis of freedom of travel under Jackson-Vanik[a] but on the broader basis of such freedoms as freedom of assembly and religion.

7. I then told Johanes that I had had cordial talks with Czechoslovak Ambassador Houstecky in Washington prior to my departure and that I thought he was doing a good job there. I also mentioned Houstecky's meeting with Assistant Secretary Seitz. Johanes seized on this to lament Houstecky's lack of access in Washington compared to what he described as Ambassador Niemczyk's broad access to many high-level people here. When I told him I thought that Houstecky's access was being restored following the recent unpleasantness (Norman[b] PNG[c]), Johanes said that Houstecky has consistently had limited access in Washington. He said the GOC wished to give me every opportunity to hold discussions here but that they expected reciprocity.

---

a. Congressional amendment to the Trade Act of 1974 that prevents the United States from granting most favored nation status to countries that deny citizens the human right of emigration.

b. Robert Norman was a U.S. foreign service officer ousted from Czechoslovakia in July 1989 at the request of Communist government officials for his presence at demonstrations.

c. Declared persona non grata.

8. When I told Johanes I hoped that we could improve trade relations, he again raised the MFN issue and through it the lack of EXIM Bank credits as well as CoCom controls. He then went on to extol the progress in perestroika in Czechoslovakia which has included the new joint venture law.[a]

9. When I asked Johanes whether perestroika here is maly (small) or velky (big), he said it was big but "not easy." He then mentioned that many economic reforms were being introduced one year early, that self-financing was making progress and that the government was trying to "democratize" the situation to give people more access to discussing things.

10. We then spoke briefly about the environment and Johanes cited Premier Adamec's interest in this issue and the meetings he has sponsored with neighboring countries on environmental issues. I told Johanes that I had been deeply involved in environmental problems during my time at the UN and told him I hoped we could cooperate in that area.

11. Johanes then returned to the theme of the GOC's interest in improving relations with the United States and after reiterating the need for expansion of political dialogue and MFN, he said that while his government is willing to talk about humanitarian issues it does not like to be told what to do by other countries. He then brought up United States travel restrictions in New York City against Czechoslovak diplomats. He said the GOC wants to see these restrictions removed or they'll be forced "to reciprocity." When I said we were working on the status of the chiefs of mission covered by these restrictions at the UN, Johanes said the GOC wants the restrictions lifted "on everybody."

12. Johanes then raised the August 21 statement by the Department deputy press spokesman and said again that Czechoslovakia does not like having other people telling it what to do. The GOC does not like "interference" particularly when it involves people coming from abroad. He mentioned the Hungarians in this respect. That is why the GOC called in Western consuls to warn them to avoid incidents (Prague 5578).

13. I replied that there were of course, some things that I have not liked such as highly critical articles about the United States in *Rudé Právo* concerning radio broadcasts by American stations. We believe there should be freedom of the press and of expression. Johanes countered that the GOC does not like RFE and VOA telling it what to do and stirring up demonstrations by announcing where they will be held and what they will be about. The

---

a. Likely the 1989 Enterprise with Foreign Property Participation Act, a foreign investment law that presented a shift away from the statist economic system.

GOC, he said, raised some of these concerns at the London Information Conference. I told Johanes we would have to compare notes on respective media coverage and programs.

14. Johanes briefly brought up the "European house"[a] concept and said that, of course, there was a place in the house for us. He then reiterated that Czechoslovakia is in the midst of perestroika but that its perestroika aimed at socialist development and not at changing the present socialist system. However, he said that he did not wish to turn our first meeting into too much of a political dialogue and said he had only done so because "Americans are pragmatic" and like to talk about useful things. I reiterated the hope that he could cooperate with me in seeking better bilateral relations.

15. In closing Johanes mentioned that he would be going to New York on or about September 20 to the UNGA and might make a side trip to Washington. I told him how glad I was to be presenting credentials prior to the arrival of CODEL Cranston August 24 and the planned visit by USIA Director Gelb September 9. **BLACK**

25 August 1989 1523Z
PRAGUE 05828

FM AMEMBASSY PRAGUE | **TO** SECSTATE WASHDC IMMEDIATE 0068 | **FOR** EUR/EEY ONLY—FOR HORNBLOW FROM RUSSELL

SUBJECT: OFFICIAL INFORMAL 158

1. (C) It was Ed Kaska who was carded on August 21. The GOC has not/not commented on his presence, or any U.S. presence, during the demonstrations. Ted pointed out to Consular Department Chief Houzvicka[b] the discrepancy between vitriolic anti-U.S. campaign in *Rudé Právo* prior to August 21 and lack of any U.S. actual involvement in the event.

2. (U) Cloud consultations. Harvey Lampert[c] will be on a well-deserved leave the last week of September and the first week of October. We suggest John come the week of October 16 (unless he wants to arrive a few days earlier and join us on the fall wreath-laying in Slovakia). Please advise. **BLACK**

---

a. A term used by Soviet Premier Mikhail Gorbachev to advocate for a unified Europe, not divided by military blocs.

b. Josef Houžvička, head of the Consular Department, Czechoslovak Ministry of Foreign Affairs.

c. POL/EC officer at U.S. Embassy Prague.

25 August 1989 1532Z
PRAGUE 05830

FM AMEMBASSY PRAGUE | **TO** SECSTATE WASHDC IMMEDIATE 0070 | **INFO** EASTERN EUROPEAN POSTS | DEPT PLEASE PASS TO ERIKA SCHLAGER, CSCE COMMISSION

SUBJECT: HUMAN RIGHTS UPDATE

1. Confidential—entire text.

2. Summary. Stanislav Devaty[a] has been freed, but his trial has been scheduled for August 29. Frantisek Starek's appeal will be heard August 28. Police detained or placed under house arrest at least eight prominent dissidents prior to the August 21 demonstration. Four Bratislava activists have had criminal charges filed against them. Only two of fifty foreigners arrested for participating in the August 21 demonstration will face criminal trials. The GOC has not provided information concerning the names of Czechoslovaks arrested August 21, but few, if any, prominent dissidents are believed among those arrested. Neither has the GOC indicated what kind of punishment those arrested face, but a dissident contact believes most will ultimately pay a 5000 crown (about US dols 500) fine and be released. Jan Urban is out of the hospital, but is "lying low." New bishops for Litomerice will be consecrated over the August 26–27 weekend. The phone service of Jiri Dienstbier, Petr Uhl, Jiri Krizan and Jan Urban has been cut off. End summary.

Devaty freed, but trial date set

3. SPUSA founder Stanislav Devaty has been freed from jail by Czechoslovak authorities after staging his third hunger strike of the year (Prague 5616). However, a trial of the charges pending against him has been set for August 29 in Gottwaldov. Activists generally characterize Devaty's hunger strikes as courageous, but do not expect other jailed dissidents to follow Devaty's example.

Starek appeal hearing date also set

4. The appeal hearing in the Frantisek Starek case (Prague 5291) has been scheduled for August 28 in Hradec Kralove.

---

a. Stanislav Devátý, Czechoslovak dissident and political prisoner who engaged in well-publicized hunger strikes.

Activists detained before August 21

5. Police detained and jailed, but did not charge, the following activists prior to the August 21 demonstrations: Petr Uhl, Ladislav Lis, Sasa Vondra, Jana Sabata, Martina Vondrova, and Jiri Ruml. Most were detained the weekend before the demonstration, except for the Vondras, who were jailed August 21. We have no/no report that any of those detained have been released. Czechoslovak authorities have in the recent past held dissidents without charging them for as many as six consecutive days.

6. Charter spokesperson Dana Nemcova and her son and activist David Nemec were placed under house arrest prior to August 21 as well. Police apparently intended to jail Nemcova and Nemec, but agreed to house arrest so that Nemcova and Nemec could remain with Nemec's infant son, who was ill. As of the afternoon of August 23, police stationed outside the Nemcova/Nemec apartment were preventing visitors to the apartment.

Bratislava activists face criminal charges

7. Bratislava authorities last week charged four Slovak activists for the offense of "incitement." Those arrested are Jan Carnogursky, Miroslav Kusy, Hana Ponicka and Anton Selecky. Carnogursky and Kusy, who were both also charged with "subverting the republic," are in jail. Ponicka and Selecky are free pending trial. The "subverting the republic" charge carries a maximum sentence of ten years' imprisonment, as opposed to the maximum five-year penalty for incitement. The criminal charges against the activists apparently stem from their work with the Nekolik vet petition and from a letter Carnogursky and Kusy wrote to Bratislava officials announcing their plans to lay flowers in Bratislava and Kosice on August 21 to commemorate the death of Slovaks killed during the 1968 Warsaw Pact invasion.

Note by OC/T: Not passed to CSCE commission

8. Activists find these arrests especially disturbing. They mark an escalation in Slovakia of the regime's campaign against independent initiatives—a campaign which in the recent past has been concentrated in the Czech lands. Activists also fear that resurrection of the harsher "subversion of the republic" charge as a prosecutorial weapon against dissidents (it had not/not been used as such now for over two years) marks the start of a general campaign to get tough with dissidents throughout the country.

Most foreigners arrested August 21 to be expelled

9. Only two of the fifty foreigners arrested during the August 21 demonstration will be held for trial. We believe them to be Hungarian citizens Tamas Deutsch and Gyorgy Kerenyi. The remaining foreigners (1 Arab, 3 Poles, 9 Hungarians, 7 Dutch, 8 Italians, 20 German speakers) have been or will be expelled.

GOC mum about Czechoslovaks arrested August 21

10. Although details concerning foreigners arrested have become known, the GOC has thus far remained silent about the fate of Czechoslovaks who were arrested. One embassy contact in the dissident community believes those arrested will be charged with "disrupting public order," fined five thousand crowns (about US dols 500), and released. We do not know the names of any Czechoslovaks arrested during the demonstration itself, nor do those we have talked to in the independent and diplomatic communities. However, few, if any, prominent dissident leaders would have been arrested because they either were outside of Prague voluntarily on August 21 or were detained by police before the demonstration.

Jan Urban update

11. Jan Urban, who apparently checked into a Prague hospital to avoid reserve military training, is out of the hospital (Prague 5480, Prague 0-I 155/2). However, Urban is lying low and has thus far avoided returning to his Prague apartment.

Bishops for Litomerice and Olomouc to be consecrated

12. Cardinal Tomasek will preside this weekend (August 26 and 27) at the consecration ceremonies for the new bishops of Litomerice and Olomouc. Consecration ceremonies for the new archbishop of Trnava and the bishop of Spis are expected to be held in September.

13. Vatican envoy Francesco Colasuonno will also be present for the consecrations. Church sources believe that Colasuonno will meet with GOC officials during his visit to discuss filling of the remaining seven empty bishoprics.

14. Church activists are taking a "wait and see" attitude toward the new bishops. They hope that at least one will display the leadership qualities Cardinal Tomasek has demonstrated. Archbishop Sokol of Trnava is known to be sympathetic to the "illegal Church structures" the GOC criticizes, and Sokol perhaps is the most likely of the new bishops to assume a prominent leadership role.

Phones zapped

15. We have confirmed that Jiri Dienstbier's phone has been removed. Other dissidents experiencing recent phone service problems include Petr Uhl, Jiri Krizan, and Jan Urban.

16. The dissident community has learned to use the phones to good advantage. During our visits with dissidents we have seen them frequently use the phones to brief Western journalists on developments in Czechoslovakia. In addition, we have seen them exchange information concerning criminal proceedings and even the Nekolik vet campaign by phone. Apparently the Czechoslovak security apparatus decided the advantage it gains from bugging the telephone is outweighed by the benefits the dissidents gain. **BLACK**

28 August 1989 1433Z
PRAGUE 05861

FM AMEMBASSY PRAGUE | **TO** SECSTATE WASHDC PRIORITY 0093 | **INFO** EASTERN EUROPEAN POSTS, USIA WASHDC 7396, USIA FOR EU(JORIA)

SUBJECT: CODEL CRANSTON: MEETING WITH CZECHOSLOVAK FOREIGN MINISTER

1. Confidential—entire text.

2. Summary and comment: Czechoslovak Foreign Minister Johanes' meeting August 24 with CODEL Cranston was cordial but broke no new ground. In an hour-long monologue covering the world situation, bilateral relations and internal developments, Johanes reiterated standard GOC views: economic and political reform must be done within the context of maintaining the socialist system; Czechoslovakia did not like being told what to do by others, and improved relations must be on the basis of equality and non-interference; the U.S. should look to its own human rights problems before criticizing others; Czechoslovak authorities have a right to maintain public order; and petitions and demonstrations were not an acceptable way to deal with Czechoslovakia's problems. In responding to the senators' questions, Johanes also took a swipe at RFE for "almost organizing" demonstrations. End summary and comments.

3. CODEL Cranston met with Foreign Minister Johanes for almost two hours on August 24. Among the other Czechoslovak participants were Acting Third Department (Western countries) Director Rychlik[a] and U.S. Desk Officer Kubista. On the U.S. side were the

---

a. Ivan Rychlík, deputy director of the Third Department of the Czechoslovak Ministry of Foreign Affairs.

ambassador, Senators Cranston, Sarbanes,[a] Graham[b] and Robb,[c] senate staffers Ritch[d] and Winik[e] and POL/EC officer Lampert (notetaker). Johanes, a former ambassador to the U.S., spoke partly in English and partly in Czech. Much of his remarks echoed his comments to the ambassador August 22 (Prague 5736). The atmosphere during the meeting was cordial.

4. The first hour of the meeting was a monologue by Johanes.[f] He spoke first about the general world situation, noting both positive and "unfortunate" developments. Among the former were the signs of progress on disarmament issues, and he asserted that Czechoslovakia for its own part had made more than a symbolic force reduction—850 tanks, 50 aircraft and 12,000 troops (as well as shifting another 20,000 troops into construction units). He said that these conversions were "not very easy" and Czechoslovakia would like more international cooperation in the effort.

5. Among the negative developments were "relapses into power politics"—particularly in some countries telling other countries how to behave. He stressed that what was needed was "new thinking," i.e., that this was one planet, that all people must learn to live together and that all things were interrelated. He insisted that this was not merely a philosophy to the Czechoslovak government, but a practical policy.

6. Turning to bilateral relations, Johanes appreciated some of the progress which had been made, but focused primarily on "certain obstacles." On the economic side, he particularly cited lack of MFN, the "too large" CoCom list, and refusal to provide EXIM loans. He contended that these violated the Helsinki process documents on free trade, limiting the free flow of technology. He described U.S.-Czechoslovak trade as "peanuts."

7. On the political side, he noted that there had been several high-level visits between the two countries in recent months, but complained that there had not been a foreign minister level meeting since 1975. This was not normal, since such meetings had been held with every other country with which Czechoslovakia has significant relations. He then reiterated his earlier point that Czechoslovakia "did not like anyone to tell it what to do," and that relations should be improved on the basis of equality and not interference.

---

a. Senator Paul Sarbanes (D-MD).

b. Senator Bob Graham (D-FL).

c. Senator Chuck Robb (D-VA).

d. John Ritch, congressional staffer.

e. Jay Winik, historian and staffer for Senator Chuck Robb.

f. Jaromír Johanes, Czechoslovak minister of foreign affairs.

8. Moving to Czechoslovakia's political and economic reform efforts, Johanes said that the July Warsaw Pact meeting had recognized that the pace of change in each country was different. For Czechoslovakia political reforms would include more democratization and more public participation, but together with more public responsibilities. He rejected Western charges that there was no perestroika in Czechoslovakia, stating that perestroika here meant reinvigorating and developing the potential of the socialist system, not eliminating it.

9. Johanes then attempted to preempt questions about the August 21 demonstrations (Prague 5726). He said that no one was happy about suppressing them, but that every country had to maintain order—including the U.S. He noted that even the Western press had admitted that the police had handled the demonstrators in "a calm fashion." He also could not understand why a tourist in a foreign country would participate in a demonstration, contending that the common people here had felt great indignation at the misbehavior of foreigners. The government had made clear to the embassies of arrested foreigners that it cannot tolerate such behavior. He said that all the arrested foreigners had been sent home. (Note: this assertion is incorrect. Two Hungarians are still in detention and the public prosecutor has indicated he plans to bring them to trial. End note.)

10. At this point Johanes turned the floor over to the CODEL for questions. Senator Sarbanes asked why the demonstration had been broken up if it was, as he understood, a peaceful one. Johanes responded that some of the demonstrators had been peaceful, others not. Moreover, the government had not granted a permit for the demonstration and the crowd had refused to disperse when ordered to do so by the police. When Sarbanes pursued the question, Johanes shifted tactics by arguing that "nobody was perfect," that there were other human rights besides political ones and that the U.S. had its own human rights problems: unemployment, the homeless, debt, child abuse, etc. Thus, the U.S. should look at itself first before criticizing others.

11. Senator Cranston acknowledged that these problems existed in the U.S., but saw the distinction between the two situations in that the U.S. problems were despite government efforts to correct them; the Czechoslovak government was the cause of the problem here. Sarbanes added that in the U.S. it was possible to criticize the government, but that was not the case in Czechoslovakia. Johanes sharply disagreed, saying that many Czechoslovaks criticized their government, but the situation was not improved if people disturbed order.

12. Sarbanes then asked why the government has a problem with the Nekolik vet petition (Prague 5232), since it did not seem to him to contain anything subversive. Johanes answered that a petition was not the proper way of dealing with these matters, that they should be brought up and discussed through such legal organizations as the National Front. In a non sequitur, he then said that the situation in Czechoslovakia is good compared to its neighbors Poland and Hungary. There was no inflation or foreign debt, and the people would not like to see Hungarian or Polish problems here. He reiterated that the country needed a calm and stable situation to deal with its problems, and that this would not be helped by demonstrations.

13. Senator Graham asked Johanes whether he agreed that the Brezhnev Doctrine[a] had been repealed. Johanes denied that such a doctrine had ever existed, emphasizing that the Warsaw Pact meeting had agreed that each country was responsible for its own development.

14. Senator Robb returned to the question of Nekolik vet, asking why the government—even if it disagrees with the petition—was unwilling to publish it to allow the population to discuss it. Johanes said that while the government was for a dialogue, that dialogue had to be about changes within the socialist system. He reminded the CODEL that this system had been adopted in the elections of 1948, which even Western observers admitted was a free choice. He argued that those few who rejected the socialist system were being openly supported from abroad by dissatisfied émigrés. In his one reference to RFE, he accused the station of "almost organizing" demonstrations and meetings, and asked rhetorically if that was right. He derided the idea of a free press in the U.S. by declaring that newspapers could only be owned by the rich and thus represented only their views.

15. Finally, Sarbanes noted that in the past Czechoslovakia had been considered one of the closest imitators of the Soviet Union, but this seemed no longer the case with the Gorbachev reforms. Johanes laughingly observed that in the past we had urged Czechoslovakia to move away from the policies of the Soviet Union, but that now we wanted it to move closer. He added, seriously, the claim that Czechoslovakia and the USSR were just as close today as in the past. **BLACK**

---

a. A Soviet foreign policy developed in 1968 that held that "socialist" countries had both "the right and duty" to militarily interfere with those countries where Socialism was under threat. Soviet leaders used this policy to justify the Warsaw Pact invasion of Czechoslovakia in 1968.

PRAGUE 05910

FM AMEMBASSY PRAGUE | **TO** SECSTATE WASHDC PRIORITY 0141 | **INFO** EASTERN EUROPEAN POSTS

SUBJECT: CZECHOSLOVAK-HUNGARIAN RELATIONS: DETAINEES
AND THE NAGYMAROS-GABCIKOVO DAM

1. Confidential—entire text.

2. EmbOff took advantage of request by Hungarian embassy official Georgy Tatar for briefing on CODEL Cranston to ask him for status report on Hungarian-Czechoslovakian relations. Specifically he requested information on Hungarian detainees from August 21 demonstrations (Prague 5726) and on where things stood regarding the Nagymaros-Gabcikovo dam.[a]

3. Tatar confirmed that only two Hungarian citizens were still being detained. These two, who were members of a "radical" Hungarian youth group, had read the statement which allegedly had set off the demonstration. Tatar said that their trial was going on today (August 29), and they were using the lawyer who had defended Vaclav Havel. For the purposes of the trial, the defendants were contending that they had been caught up in the demonstration by accident. Tatar acknowledged that this was not true and said that the organization which had sent them to Prague was unable to comprehend why the defendants were taking this line.

4. Turning to the question of the dam, Tatar said that the recent trip by Czechoslovak Prime Minister Adamec to Budapest had accomplished nothing in solving the dispute. The prime ministers of the two countries are supposed to meet again in October, probably with Hungarian Prime Minister Nemeth coming to Prague. Tatar reiterated earlier comments (Prague 3482) that the Hungarian decision to suspend construction on the dam was based on economic rather than environmental factors, noting that the Hungarian ecological arguments were weak. The Hungarian debt situation and the fact that it would need large sums of money to pay for a planned Budapest/Vienna world fair in 1995 required the government to cancel some large project. The dam was a convenient victim, especially as the Hungarian population did not support the project nor have much trust that

---

a. In a 1977 agreement, Hungary and Czechoslovakia agreed to jointly build and operate a complex of dams on the Danube River. Following protests in Hungary in 1988 and 1989, the Hungarian government paused construction on the project. Negotiations over the dam complex would continue for another decade.

their government could ensure that the Czechoslovaks would live up to their ecological commitments. On the other hand, the cost to the Hungarian government in compensation to Czechoslovakia and Austria would also be very large, and so Tatar thought that some kind of compromise would eventually be reached. BLACK

29 August 1989 1442Z
PRAGUE 05911

FM AMEMBASSY PRAGUE | **TO** SECSTATE WASHDC IMMEDIATE 0142 | **FOR** EUR/EEY ONLY—FOR HORNBLOW FROM RUSSELL

SUBJECT: OFFICIAL INFORMAL NO. 160

1. (LOU) Bernthal visit. We believe that a visit by Assistant Secretary Bernthal[a] is an excellent idea, but it is essential that he be aware and be prepared to discuss the difficulties we are having with the Czechoslovaks on that part of S&T exchanges not covered by MOUs. Background on this subject can be found in Prague 1092; Prague 3251 contains a letter we solicited from the State Commission listing possible areas for S&T cooperation, and to which we have never received a response from Washington. In addition, would Bernthal be prepared to discuss the president's Eastern European environmental initiative? Would Marty Prochnik come with him? It would be better if visit was not during first week in October since Harvey, who covers S&T matters, will be on leave. If this is only time possible, however, then we should go ahead anyway. Ted will also be away that week.

2. (U) Hungarian detainees. Hungarian embassy has informed us that two remaining Hungarian detainees from August 21 demonstration are having their trial today (August 29). The embassy hopes that they will simply be ejected from the country. We are reporting a few more details by front channel cable.

3. (U) Munter[b] travel. (Aug. 29 Munter/Russell Telcon). Oct 16–20 approximate dates for Cameron's travel look good. We look forward to his visit and John's.[c]

------

a. U.S. Assistant Secretary of State for Oceans and International Environmental and Scientific Affairs Frederick M. Bernthal.

b. Cameron Munter, desk officer at the U.S. Department of State; later U.S. ambassador to Serbia and then to Pakistan.

c. Presumably another U.S. Department of State officer visiting Embassy Prague.

4. (C) The dynamic Dillons. Ken and Zuzana[a] have done a superb job here this summer, as they did last year. They provided a number of excellent trip reports and helped out in myriad ways, including invaluable work with CODEL Cranston. Embassy will be considering possibility of trying to get Zuzana out here in an analyst position.

5. (U) CivAir. For John from Harvey. Prague 4503 of July 6 (slugged for Michael Goldman of EB/TRA) transmitted text of proposed Czechoslovak diplomatic note formally extending commercial annex of CivAir agreement negotiated in June. We have not received a response yet to the Czechoslovak draft. Can you check with Goldman to see where things stand?

6. (U) Fax. Please provide us a fax number for transmitting unclassified documents to EUR/EEY. **BLACK**

30 August 1989 1516Z
PRAGUE 05959

FM AMEMBASSY PRAGUE | **TO** SECSTATE WASHDC 0169 | **INFO** EASTERN EUROPEAN POSTS
SUBJECT: THE AUGUST 21 DEMONSTRATION: A RETROSPECTIVE LOOK ONE WEEK LATER

REF: PRAGUE 5726

1. Confidential—entire text.

2. Summary: The August 21 demonstration in Prague provided evidence of several factors/trends which characterize the current state of the struggle between the regime and independent groups. These include: (1) an increased willingness by Czechoslovaks, especially the young, to challenge the regime, (2) an "internationalization" of the fight for human rights in Czechoslovakia, and (3) the importance of pressure from both the governments in East and West in nudging the Czechoslovak regime towards a more tolerant view of political dissent. The "success" of the demonstration will encourage further demonstrations, with the most likely date for the next one being October 28, the anniversary of the founding of the Czechoslovak Republic in 1918. End summary.

3. Some activists tell us they were surprised by the size of the August 21 demonstrations in Prague. They believe that the fact some two to three thousand persons were neither

---

a. Kenneth Dillon, U.S. foreign service officer on temporary duty in Czechoslovakia. Zuzana Dillon appears to have worked primarily for USIA.

intimidated by the regime's threatened use of force nor dissuaded by the words of caution of the respected Vaclav Havel is evidence that Czechoslovaks continue every day to be more willing to challenge the regime. However, the size of the turnout is consistent with other recent evidence—such as the success of the Nekolik vet petition campaign and the recent proliferation of independent groups—that political activism is growing.

4. The predominance of those ages 16 to 30 among the demonstrators also illustrates the increasing activism of youth. No one reason exists why some of the young are turning to political activism. However, one married couple who participated in the demonstration noted to EmbOff they had decided to become involved politically, despite the risks, because they realized their future was at stake and that they had no other choice.

5. We see several telling points in this more active youth. First, it simply reflects a generational change: the coming of age of those who were too young to have direct memories of the crushing of Prague Spring in 1968 and do not feel bound by the unofficial agreement after the invasion to give up political involvement in return for relative material well-being. Second, it also means that this group is beginning to think that change is possible, that the regime can no longer count on Moscow to save it. Third, and perhaps most important, while this generation respects the older dissident leadership, it may not share their relative restraint and moderation, and certainly appears more willing to engage in confrontation. This does not bode well for the regime. As one dissident reportedly said, his generation is at least willing to have a dialogue with the government, but the next generation may not be.

6. The August 21 demonstration also provided further evidence of the internationalization of the conflict between independent initiatives and the regime. As regards the rally itself, most observers believe it was the unfurling of a banner by a core group of Hungarians and their chanting of "freedom" which sparked the demonstration and set its tone. However, in a larger sense, the internationalization involves the now open rhetorical conflict between the Czechoslovak regime and the people and governments of Hungary and Poland. Our activist contacts believe this open conflict raises the consciousness of persons in Czechoslovakia, making them more likely to question why things are not changing, and they believe such questioning is the first step of the process which leads persons to political involvement.

7. We think it also important to consider why police on August 21 acted with such relative restraint after the threats of use of force made before August 21 and after the precedent set by the indiscriminate use of force against demonstrators last January. Certainly security forces were prepared to take stronger measures. One usually reliable contact

from the dissident community told EmbOff that he had learned "from good sources" that Gorbachev had told General Secretary Jakes and Prime Minister Adamec during their vacations in the USSR "to avoid brutality" on August 21. This seems a credible explanation to us, though it may also be that the regime wanted to avoid provoking the Western outrage that had greeted the harsh suppression of the January demonstrations.

8. A re-reading of *Rudé Právo* in the weeks before August 21 does give some support to the Soviet theory. Before the return of Jakes and Adamec to Prague, *Rudé Právo* was filled both with promises of use of force against demonstrators as well as vitriolic attacks on the Nekolik vet petition campaign (Prague 5232). However, the August 16 *Rudé Právo* carried on page one both an article announcing the return of Jakes and Adamec from the USSR and a statement of the official Czechoslovak Human Rights Committee. The committee's statement, in a conciliatory tone, asked persons to express their views through legal means and structures. Missing from *Rudé Právo* on August 16 and the remaining days leading to the August 21 demonstration were articles threatening the use of force. Even the campaign against Nekolik vet has lessened since August 16, with fewer and milder attacks against the petition than before.

9. We also think the incident on Wenceslas Square in which a Czechoslovak state television (CST) representative defended the right of ABC television to film (REFTEL) is a reminder that Western pressure on the Czechoslovak regime, at least sometimes, can have an effect. The CST rep's lament that "we have trouble with the American embassy" underscores that judicious use of diplomatic pressure by the U.S. and other Western nations can make a difference.

10. A week after the event it is still clear that the regime was the loser on August 21. Its failure to prevent any demonstration despite massive, nationwide security measures and harsh warnings means such threats in the future will be taken less seriously. Activists are already looking forward to the next demonstration—most likely October 28, the anniversary of the founding of the Czechoslovak Republic in 1918—and expect a bigger turnout than was witnessed on August 21. **BLACK**

30 August 1989 1534Z
PRAGUE 05960

FM AMEMBASSY PRAGUE | **TO** SECSTATE WASHDC PRIORITY 0171 | **INFO** EASTERN EUROPEAN POSTS, DEPT PASS TO ERIKA SCHLAGER CSCE COMMISSION

SUBJECT: HUMAN RIGHTS UPDATE

REF: PRAGUE 5830

1. Confidential—entire text.

2. Summary. A trial court in Gottwaldov convicted Stanislav Devaty of "incitement" and sentenced him to twenty months' imprisonment, but Devaty remains free pending appeal. The appeals of the convictions of Frantisek Starek and Iva Vojtkova have been rejected by a court in Hradec Kralove. Two Hungarians tried for their participation in the August 21 demonstration have been convicted and expelled from Czechoslovakia. Prominent dissidents detained before August 21 have been freed without charges being filed against them. All Czechoslovak demonstrators arrested on August 21 apparently have been freed, and we have no/no report any have been charged with violations of the criminal code. The Movement for Civil Liberties has called for support for five Bratislava dissidents facing criminal charges. Over 20,000 persons have now signed Nekolik vet. The GOC has criticized the decision of a juvenile court in the FRG to sentence the Czechoslovak hijackers of a Hungarian Airlines plane to only two years in a youth home. End summary.

Stanislav Devaty convicted of incitement—free pending appeal

3. A three judge panel of the district court in Gottwaldov found Stanislav Devaty guilty of "incitement" on Thursday, August 29 (ref). Devaty was sentenced to twenty months imprisonment, but is free pending appeal. The appeal is expected to be heard in Brno in September. A separate charge of "attack against a public official" which Devaty also faces was not tried on Tuesday and remains pending against him.

4. Approximately 100 Devaty supporters (as well as reps from the International Helsinki Federation and the American and Canadian embassies) were present at the courthouse. The supporters applauded as Devaty entered and left the courthouse. Upon conclusion of the trial the supporters handed him red carnations to form a bouquet of several dozens.

5. Only 32 seats for spectators were available in the courtroom. At least a third of the seats were filled by men in their sixties who smiled when the verdict against Devaty was announced. One Devaty supporter called the men "retired policemen." As Devaty exited the courthouse upon the trial's conclusion, one elderly spectator shouted to him "it should

have been twenty years instead of twenty months" (but many of those passing by on the street stopped and applauded Devaty).

6. Devaty appeared pale and tired from his prior hunger strikes, but in his closing statement his voice was strong. Devaty told EmbOff who attended the trial that he was not/not surprised by the trial's outcome, and that he was not/not sure if he would undertake another hunger strike if he is actually imprisoned. Devaty also thanked the American embassy for its support.

7. We note for the record that EmbOff attended the trial with a Canadian diplomat, and that both were able to gain access to the courtroom. However, both diplomats, who rode together in the Canadian's car, were stopped by police on four occasions for identity card checks. The checks occurred between Gottwaldov and Brno (a distance of about 55 miles) as the diplomats were returning from the trial. All the checks were obviously planned beforehand, but individual police officers were "correct" in their dealings with the diplomats.

Starek and Vojtkova convictions upheld on appeal

8. A regional appeals court in Hradec Kralove on August 28 upheld the convictions of Frantisek Starek for "incitement" and Iva Vojtkova "for accessory to incitement" (Prague 5290). Starek, who already was serving the two-and-a-half-year sentence which had been imposed earlier by the trial court, will be eligible to apply for release after having served one half of his sentence. Starek has told friends he will not apply for early release as a protest against what he believes to be the illegitimacy of the charges against him. However, under Czechoslovak law friends or family members may and are expected to petition for Starek's early release.

9. Vojtkova, whose sentence was suspended by the trial court, of course remains free. Starek, in a closing statement, said that the Czechoslovak security apparatus decision to bring charges against a family member (Vojtkova) because of Starek's activities was "Stalinism."

10. About fifty Starek supporters were present for the trial, as were reps of the International Helsinki Federation, British embassy, and American embassy. Unlike the Devaty trial, there appeared to be no "packing" of the fifty-seat courtroom with pro-prosecution spectators.

Dissidents detained before August 21 released

12. According to dissident contacts, all prominent activists (Petr Uhl, Ladislav Lis, Sasa Vondra, Jana Sabata, Martina Vondrova, Jiri Ruml) detained before the August 21 demonstration have been released. None of those detained were charged with new violations of the criminal code.

Charges against Sasa Vondra revived

13. Sasa Vondra, a current Charter spokesman and Nekolik vet petition organizer, is now facing a possible two-month jail term. Convicted earlier of a "trespass against public order," Vondra's two-month prison sentence was suspended. However, the prosecutor claims that Vondra has violated the terms of his probation, and is now asking that Vondra actually serve the two-month sentence. A hearing on the prosecutor's request is scheduled for September 4.

August 21 demonstrators released

14. Dissident contacts tell us that they believe all Czechoslovak citizens arrested during the August 21 demonstration have been released from custody. The official Czechoslovak media remains silent on the situation of those detained. We are not/not aware of any Czechoslovak citizen facing criminal charges stemming from an arrest at the August 21 demonstration.

Movement for Civil Liberties (HOS) proclaims support for Bratislava activists

15. The Movement for Civil Liberties has issued a proclamation calling on Czechs and Slovaks to support five Bratislava activists (Jan Carnogursky, Miroslav Kusy, Hana Ponicka, Anton Selecky, and Vaclav Manak) facing criminal charges (ref). Activists believe Carnogursky and Kusy are facing the more severe "subversion of the republic" charge because the regime sees them as influential leaders in the Slovak dissident community and because both have been active in supporting the Nekolik vet petition. The petition, however, does not form a part of the charges against them. Rather, Carnogursky is charged because of his articles in a samizdat publication called "Brx Petition."

GOC criticizes sentence given to hijackers

17. Both *Rudé Právo* and Czechoslovak television have criticized the decision of a juvenile court in Frankfurt am Main to sentence the Czechoslovaks who hijacked a Hungarian airliner in Prague in March to two years' stay in a youth home in Karlshof (Prague 3529). *Rudé Právo* said the verdict has no deterrent effect, while Czechoslovak TV called the sentence "very lenient." **BLACK**

07 September 1989 0756Z
PRAGUE 06121[a]

FM AMEMBASSY PRAGUE | **TO** SECSTATE WASHDC 0277, OIG CHANNEL

SUBJECT: OIG INSPECTION OF PRAGUE: POST MEMORANDUM

REF: STATE 155407

1. Confidential—entire text.

2. This cable is keyed to REFTEL para 5 request for a concise review of mission operations, highlighting areas needing particular attention.

3. State of relations with Czechoslovak government:

(A) Political relations are cool and occasionally rocky because of the generally poor GOC performance on human rights. Although travel restrictions have been lightened and substantial progress has been made on resolving bilateral consular problems, including divided families, the regime's hard line on political dissent has prevented normalization and warming of U.S.-Czechoslovak bilateral relations.

Although willing to discuss individual human rights cases under the CSCE mechanism, the GOC accuses Western countries of using CSCE to destabilize Czechoslovakia. The USG is pictured as a prime offender in this respect and the GOC recently PNG'ed our political officer charged with following human rights here on the specious grounds of participation in illegal demonstrations. The GOC consistently criticizes the activities of VOA and RFE and charges that they are actively fostering anti-regime, illegal activities and demonstrations.

Another political bone of contention is the GOC's intense displeasure over USG travel restrictions on Communist diplomats in New York, which require advance notice for all travel outside a 25 mile radius. The MFA has repeatedly warned that the GOC will retaliate against us here unless our travel rules in New York vis-à-vis their U.N. and commercial office diplomats are removed or substantially eased. We have made clear that we do

---

a. The text of this cable was duplicated in another cable sent by the U.S. Embassy in Prague specifically to the attention of Mike Hornblow at the State Department in Washington, D.C. The duplicated cable, Prague 06136, begins with the following note to Hornblow: "For Mike for Ted. Herewith for your info is our post memorandum sent September 7 to OIG. Entire text is confidential. All sections plus RSO have cleared. Please let us know your views, particularly if you believe we have left out anything noteworthy or if you have a different slant on any issue discussed. Begin post memorandum." It is otherwise identical.

not see a reciprocity issue here, while at the same time working with OFM to ease the controls on the Czechoslovak ambassador to the U.N. and make certain other minor travel facilitations. Progress on this has been very slow because all East European diplomats in New York are affected. A near term confrontation with the GOC on the issue appears probable. Retaliatory limits on travel out of Prague by U.S. mission personnel could severely affect our operations.

On the positive side, the U.S.-Czechoslovak Humanitarian Affairs Working Group has had success in dealing with bilateral consular problems and in promoting a rather free exchange of information on individual human rights cases. Our increasing resort to invocation of the CSCE mechanism in soliciting information on individual human rights cases here, while appropriate and necessary, may lead to more formalistic exchanges on such cases in the working group.

(B) U.S.-Czechoslovak commercial and economic relations are better than our political relations, although they fall short of "normality." The regime here is more interested in economic reform than in political liberalization, although it makes clear that economic changes must strengthen the socialist economic system. The regime thus wishes to expand economic and commercial contacts with the West and it is possible to have meaningful discussions with a growing range of government officials and semi-independent economists. Cooperation with the Ministry of Foreign Trade and other trading organizations is good and we have completed highly successful negotiations on new textile and steel VRAs. In addition, discussions with foreign trade and banking officials in the U.S.-Czechoslovak business facilitation working groups have been cordial, frank and useful.

Despite the relative warmth in our economic relations, the GOC constantly expresses its annoyance at being deprived of MFN status. Although MFN would probably no more than double the present low level of bilateral trade, the GOC seeks MFN for reasons of political recognition as much as for trade facilitation. The regime also criticizes the USG for its support of CoCom controls on technology transfer and for failure to grant EXIM credits. We reply that MFN status and other trade concessions can only come from a better Czechoslovak performance on human rights. Such an improvement is unlikely under the present regime, installed in the wake of the 1968 Soviet invasion and highly resistant to change.

(C) Cultural and technical relations are productive and cordial. The 1986 Exchanges Agreement, amended in 1988, is highly satisfactory and provides for the exchange of 23 lecturers and researchers traveling yearly from each country on the Fulbright program, 25 Czech and Slovak leader grantees visiting the U.S. and 12 AMPART specialists visiting Czechoslovakia. In addition, USIS Prague also supports private sector exchanges, youth and sports exchanges and offers facilitative support to English teaching seminars sponsored by the GOC.

The one less than satisfactory area in our exchange program is in science and technology exchange. Those programs handled by the Czechoslovak Academy of Science and U.S. governmental institutions like the National Science Foundation run smoothly. However, the GOC has been slow to specify its precise interests and thus provide enough information to interest non-governmental U.S. sponsors. For its part, the GOC complains about lack of adequate U.S. assistance.

Bilateral civil air relations are excellent and we are in the process of formalizing a revised commercial annex to our bilateral civil air agreement. We have good, but limited, relations on narcotics control and are working to develop ways to increase cooperation on environmental information exchange and management training. Cooperation on counter-terrorism issues has not gotten off the ground, although our RSO has established a first-time link with the MFA on security matters.

4. Goals and objectives, workplan and accomplishments. (ref A. 88 Prague 6452; ref B. 88 State 394652; ref C. Prague 2841).

(A) Mission goals and objectives and workplan are accurately described in REFTEL A and were approved by Washington in REFTEL B above. The extent to which each goal is being accomplished is described in the FY-1989 mid-year report, REFTEL C. The following comments elaborate on the above information and bring up to date mission accomplishments in implementing our workplan. Our FY-1990 goals and objectives statement, due in October, will be available for the OIG inspectors upon arrival.

(B) Recent workplan accomplishments.

—Goal A: Increase effectiveness as a listening post. By bringing in inexpensive TDY assistance in the POLEC section this summer while the section chief was on home leave, we were able to provide Washington end users with a number of well received reports on conditions in Bohemia and Moravia. Regular POLEC and consular officers also were able to send in trip reports from Bratislava and Eastern Slovakia, which increased mission coverage of local conditions outside Prague. Ease of access to factories increased in recent months and the arrival of Ambassador Black will produce a unique opportunity for access to high level officials in her initial, and we hope, follow-up round of calls.

—Goal B: Ensure GOC awareness of U.S. policies. Progress has been made on this objective through the arrival of a new ambassador and by the very direct message on human rights conveyed by a recent CODEL.

—Goal C: Expand dialogue to gain more favorable response to issues of U.S. concern. See goal B.

Although our human rights concerns are getting through loud and clear, the GOC is unlikely to give us much satisfaction as long as the current, hard line leadership remains in charge. The arrival of a new ambassador will give us the chance to raise other concerns, such as the replacement of war memorials to U.S. forces removed by the regime, better access for all embassy reporting officers to government and Party officials and better GOC support on embassy housing needs.

—Goal D: Continue implementation of Exchanges Agreement. This goal continues to be met in exemplary fashion. Recent U.S. sponsored events, including a highly successful U.S. film exhibit in Prague and Bratislava, illustrate the success of our cultural exchange program.

—Goal E: Extend public diplomacy and keep alive historic and cultural ties. The former ambassador's spring wreath-laying program in western Bohemia was the most successful ever in terms of crowds and lack of any police harassment. Ambassador Black's participation in the Bratislava U.S. film exhibit drew large crowds and her high public diplomacy profile and interests open unique opportunities in furthering this mission goal.

—Management goal A: Improve quality of life for embassy personnel. The mission has made considerable progress in recent months in restoring the core areas of the embassy to functionality and attractiveness. Much remains to be done and chancery suffers from a serious imbalance of too much core space and too little space outside the core. Progress has been made on increasing the stock of embassy housing, but shortages still exist and the GOC has not been very helpful. Progress has been made under a new CLO in offering cultural opportunities for embassy staffers to understand and enjoy their host country despite security, travel and language constraints. The work order management system has improved, but needs further attention. Only one out of six cleared American technicians required has arrived at post. The arrival of an embassy nurse has improved health care and provided a greater sense of health security to the embassy community.

—Management goal B: Increase effort to conserve scarce resources. The complete reorganization of the GSO maintenance section has resulted in greatly improved responsiveness and efficiency, although problems remain. The use of GSA contract supply sources has considerably increased, with less dependence on West German outlets. The local, Czechoslovak market is of virtually no use to our administrative operations. The motorpool has improved considerably with the conversion to U.S. subsidiary/German-make trucks. The program needs to be expanded to cover embassy sedans, which are deteriorating and hard to repair U.S. models.

—Security goal: Enhance embassy security and safety. Additional recent progress has been made on enhancing embassy counter-intelligence capabilities thanks to the aggressive work of a TDY security officer sent to fill in after the early departure of the previous RSO. Embassy access and contact reporting procedures have been strengthened and non-fraternization policy is under review. However, Washington has been unable to recruit Czech speaking, cleared American personnel to serve as telephone operator/receptionists. Long requested, adequate alarm systems for the attic, which DS was unable to fund, have finally been procured from another agency and will be installed ASAP. FBO has indicated that they intend to proceed next year on the long overdue chancery roof replacement. The revised emergency action plan is overdue, but is being worked on. Drills are now being conducted with greater regularity. Morale of the MSG detachment is high. Much work will be necessary to rectify shoddy construction work, particularly on access doors, stemming from the core project.

5. Policy, operational and administrative problems and steps taken to rectify them.

(A) Policy problems: The embassy gets excellent support from the European bureau and most Washington offices/agencies in resolving policy problems. The following issues are often discussed formally and informally with EUR/EEY and other offices. Their resolution typically depends on allocation of scarce resources or reconciliation of understandably differentiated Washington and mission perspectives.

—Bratislava: The mission believes and has recommended that Bratislava be opened as a cultural center and eventually as a consulate. The former would require USIS staffing for which funds do not appear to be available, together with additional administrative backstopping in Prague. The Department has opposed Senator Pell's[a] efforts to earmark funds to open a consulate in Bratislava. Both resource scarcity and security concerns,

---

a. Claiborne Pell (D-RI).

involving predictable Czechoslovak demands for reciprocity, appear to be involved. The issue has been discussed by Ambassador Black with USIA Director Gelb in Washington.

—Level of visits: The mission has, on occasion, found itself on a different track from Washington in advocating higher-level visits to Czechoslovakia and higher-level access for Czechoslovak visitors or the Czechoslovak ambassador in Washington. With the arrival of a new U.S. ambassador, this discrepancy has been toned down. However, it may well arise on occasion in future. While no specific case is now under discussion, the difference in perspective has usually been due to Washington taking a tougher line regarding GOC human rights violations with respect to avoiding or turning off contacts above the deputy secretary level. While the mission has itself advocated this approach, it has also pressed in the past for higher level reception of Czechoslovak visitors, e.g., the foreign minister at the yearly UNGA opening, than the Department has favored.

—FSNs vs. cleared AMCITs: This hot issue seems to have cooled off a bit over the last year and the embassy has been informally advised by visitors in the security field that we are not expected to fire all or most of our FSNs on security grounds. While it is reasonable from a security perspective to replace FSNs with cleared, Czech speaking AMCITs, in practice Washington has found it virtually impossible to recruit any clearable, adequately Czech qualified personnel and exceedingly slow and difficult to recruit clearable, non-language qualified Americans as technicians/handymen (see operational problems para (B) below). This, plus the enormous extra costs and administrative overhead involved in use of AMCITs vice FSNs, suggests that our FSNs will be with us for some time, unless the GOC chooses to pull them out as a crippling form of harassment. We have also been informed by Washington that none of the unappealing, distant alternative sites for a new chancery offered by the GOC are satisfactory. We have been told informally that money would not, in any case, likely be available for a new chancery. Thus, we are likely to have to live for the foreseeable future with our present insecure and hard-to-maintain, but ideally located facility.

(B) Operational and administrative problems.

—Staffing: The POLEC and Admin/GSO sections are currently inadequately staffed for embassy reporting and operating needs. POLEC needs another reporting officer, probably a political officer, in order to do more out-of-Prague reporting and to respond to increased Washington end-user interest in Czechoslovak political and economic developments. The feeling in some quarters in Washington that "Czechoslovakia is next" after Poland and Hungary supports the need for beefed up reporting resources.

The inspectors' views on the matter will be welcomed. When the issue has been raised informally in Washington, the reaction has been that additional POLEC staffing would be desirable, but that resources are unlikely to be made available.

The administrative section is not adequately staffed to support the mission properly and simultaneously ensure appropriate internal controls. Specifically, there is a requirement for an additional position to supervise budget and fiscal and personnel operations, both now handled by the overworked Admin officer. This position has been requested. In addition, the post needs an additional GSO position. The scope of GSO responsibilities has grown tremendously with increased staffing, dispersed housing and the extra administrative work generated by ongoing security and other construction projects and requirements. The GSO man-hours required are simply not available with present staffing. The inspectors' views on Admin/GSO staffing would be appreciated, as it is our understanding that no additional GSO position is likely to be made available.

—Core maintenance: The European bureau has made an enormous effort to identify, recruit and process cleared American contractors to support the core areas of the chancery. However, it has been an extremely slow process and, after a year and a half, the post has just received a cleared electrician with the promise of a handyman/custodian to follow in October. This leaves us without a second handyman, a plumber and two Czech language qualified receptionist/telephone operators. In the meantime, our efforts to maintain the core are incomplete and we are unable to meet our ongoing program of replacing those FSNs in the more sensitive positions.

—Space shortages: We are long on core space and short on space outside the core. Administrative and consular operations are greatly cramped as a result. GSO employees, in particular, have little room in which to operate and store supplies and equipment. The newly constructed consular waiting room, already too small when it was built, is now cramped by visa applicants resulting from liberalized GSO travel regulations. In the short term, every effort is being made to make the best use of available space. The long-term solution is to find a nearby facility for the GSO unit. The problem is that a GSO annex could not function properly without an additional GSO position to assure proper oversight.

—Lack of classified word processing equipment: The lack of classified word processing equipment slows embassy operations considerably, particularly in the POLEC section. Security constraints make it unlikely that we will receive early relief in this area. The PTPE program, while promising newer equipment (typewriters and copiers) and better alarms, has so far resulted in the replacement of large, relatively fast copiers with small, slow desktop copiers, thus compounding secretarial problems. We have reported the situation to Washington and asked for at least two, larger and faster copiers for core use.

—Core construction follow-up: Some of the core construction was carried out in a shoddy fashion, despite the supervision by an FBO resident manager. This has become clearer in a recent security survey of chancery secure doors (18), most of which were found to be defective to some extent and possibly in need of replacement. The inspectors should plan to discuss this issue with Admin/GSO personnel and the RSO (if TDY RSO is present).

—Security of the ambassador: Particularly during wreath-laying trips, our new, high visibility ambassador will require additional security. This issue has been discussed with the RSO, who is working to improve both residential security and the security of the ambassador when involved in public diplomacy efforts involving mixing with crowds. Resources for additional residential security have been requested. Additional security needs while the ambassador is traveling will be assessed on an ad hoc basis by the RSO, who will accompany the ambassador when appropriate.

—Security and operational requirements: Increasing security requirements risk cutting across mission operational effectiveness. Thus, growing emphasis on contact reporting and non-fraternization consume reporting officers' scarce time and reduce staff cultural outlets. Physical and technical security constraints impede office machine operations and overload our already hard-pressed secretaries. Physical security projects have created increased Admin and GSO headaches, particularly when the construction work involved turns out to be defective, ill-considered and/or shoddy. While many of the enhanced security measures are clearly necessary in this critical hostile intelligence threat post, the inspectors will wish to look at the overall security vs. operations balance, which may have relevance for other high threat posts.

The embassy has sought to overcome these problems by a greater focus on the dangers of technical and personnel penetration and an effort to rectify some of the problems generated by past efforts to turn the embassy into a fortress. At the same time, we are seeking to strike a balance between legitimate security concerns and excessive drag on operational effectiveness. The recent assignment (ETA March 1990) of a qualified, permanent RSO will be helpful in this respect.

6. Performance of operating sections and other agency contributions.

(A) POLEC: The POLEC section is very successful in covering the complex and potentially dramatic Czechoslovak political and economic scene. It is strongly and effectively led and individual staff members do an excellent job covering their respective areas. As discussed above, however, POLEC is understaffed and not able to do as much trip reporting as Washington would like. This has been partially rectified by use of summer TDY assistance this year and last. POLEC faces the usual problems of circumscribed access to Czechoslovak officials, although this situation has somewhat improved over the last year. Aside from overwork and inadequate and poorly ventilated office space, the section operates without particular problems. Its reporting officers and staff are, however, sensitive to security restrictions which they feel excessively impede operational effectiveness.

(B) CONS: The consular section is ably led and appropriately staffed. It does a consistently excellent job in handling a wide range of potentially sensitive visa and U.S. citizen problems, while coping properly with a substantial number of walk-in visitors. Cooperation with other sections and with the front office is excellent. The section faces a serious space shortage, built into the recent core construction project. The consular waiting room, in particular, is too small and the situation is compounded by a sharp increase in visa business. FSN morale has been impaired by the move of the CONS section out of light and spacious offices in the core into more cramped surroundings. "Commuting" to the core consumes much time of the American officers. Security restrictions, including ambiguous Washington non-fraternization and contact reporting rules, adversely affect U.S. staff morale.

(C) Admin: The administrative section has more work than it can handle. That said, it is ably led by a first class officer backed by two excellent GSOs, an aggressive and experienced TDY RSO assisted by a qualified SEO, a superb MSG detachment, a newly arrived, highly qualified nurse, a first tour American secretary shared with the RSO unit, a PIT B&F assistant and a PIT American secretary. The section provides excellent administrative support to all embassy sections/agencies and does a fine job coping with the management of a local staff which largely lacks a positive work ethic and generally makes liberal use of sick leave.

Significant difficulties faced by the Admin section have been identified in para 5 above. The principal problem is the need for a B&F/personnel officer and an additional GSO to cope with increased workload generated in part by the core construction project and additional security measures and personnel (cleared American contractors). Maintenance of a secure core is a major problem for which we are not yet staffed. Restrictions on availability and use of modern word processing equipment (and on conversations outside

ACRs) severely hamper staff effectiveness, although such restrictions are generally justifiable. The inability of FBO to fund necessary chancery and residence maintenance projects and flaws in restricted area renovation design have also caused difficulties.

(D) Other agencies: Relations with all agencies represented at post are excellent. There is a fine sense of team spirit and interest in serving in Czechoslovakia at such a dramatic time in East-West relations.

—USIS: Relations between POLEC and the press and culture section are friendly and productive. Although two out of three USIS staffers are new to Prague, the section is already making a good contribution to realizing embassy goals and objectives. As discussed in para 3 above, the cultural exchange program with Czechoslovakia is one of the few success stories in our troubled bilateral relationship. The USIS counselor provides effective assistance to the ambassador in organizing her participation in embassy cultural outreach programs.

—DAO: Although DAO activities in general are compartmentalized, cooperation with POLEC and Admin is good. DAO plays a key role in organizing the semi-annual wreath-laying programs in western Bohemia (spring) and Moravia/Slovakia (fall). Important reports are shared with EXEC and POLEC as appropriate. DAO intelligence reporting often directly relates to "key areas of continuing interest" in the post's goals and objectives.

—End of post memorandum. **BLACK**

08 September 1989 1553Z
PRAGUE 06223

FM AMEMBASSY PRAGUE | **TO** SECSTATE WASHDC 0367 | **INFO** EASTERN EUROPEAN POSTS, DEPT PASS TO ERIKA SCHLAGER CSCE COMMISSION

SUBJECT: HUMAN RIGHTS UPDATE: CZECHOSLOVAKIA

REF: LAST UPDATE PRAGUE 5960

1. Confidential—entire text.

2. Summary. Alexander Dubcek is among those Czechoslovaks who have asked that charges against Jan Carnogursky and Miroslav Kusy be dropped. Independent activists have asked the USG and seventeen other signatories of the Vienna Concluding Document to use the Human Dimension Mechanism on behalf of Stanislav Devaty. A young Brno

man is on a hunger strike in protest of his arrest on August 21. A two-month suspended sentence against Charter spokesperson Sasa Vondra has been reinstated because Vondra has not been living "an orderly socialist lifestyle." The press campaign against the "Nekolik vet" petition has all but disappeared, but those circulating the petition are facing criminal charges and harassment. Two Prague dissidents have been beaten by police. Petr Cibulka's mother was allowed to visit her son in prison. Czechoslovak Helsinki Committee members were detained and questioned after a September 6 meeting. Bishops for two dioceses in Slovakia will be consecrated over the September 9–10 weekend. Jiri Tichy has been released from prison. End summary.

Dubcek among those asking for release of Carnogursky/Kusy

3. Prague Spring Party boss Alexander Dubcek was one of some thirty (mostly Slovak) signatories of a public letter to President Husak asking that criminal proceedings against Jan Carnogursky and Miroslav Kusy (Prague 5960 and earlier) be stopped. This marks the first time that Dubcek has joined with a group of persons publicly protesting the criminal prosecution of human rights activists.

4. A committee for the "freeing of the Slovak democrats" has also been formed to support Carnogursky, Kusy and the three other Bratislava activists facing criminal charges. A Swiss diplomat has also told us a Slovak emigre group in Switzerland has asked his country to become involved in Carnogursky's (but not Kusy's) case, but that no decision has been made whether or how the Swiss will protest. The trial of the five activists is expected to be held during the second half of September.

Support for Stanislav Devaty

5. Czechoslovak independent activists on September 1 delivered a letter in support of Stanislav Devaty (Prague 5960) to the embassies of the United States and some 17 other nations (including Hungary, Poland, and the USSR) which are signatories of the Vienna Concluding Document. The petition, signed by 32 prominent activists, asks that the U.S. and other nations use the means provided by the Concluding Document to secure a re-examination of Devaty's case by the GOC. We, of course, have already invoked step one of the Human Dimension Mechanism (HDM[a]) in the case (Prague 6040). EC diplomats have told us that the European Community (the French, in Prague) will also approach the GOC next week within the HDM framework. The EC demarche concerning Devaty will be part

---

a. Human Dimension Mechanism, the measure established by the Helsinki Accords that allowed countries to call attention to other states' human rights violations.

of a larger demarche including expression of surprise at GOC handling of the August 21 demonstration and the Starek case. The GOC will be asked to provide information on these matters.

Another hunger striker

6. At least one Czechoslovak has decided to follow the example of Stanislav Devaty and is using a hunger strike to protest what he considers illegitimate criminal proceedings. Vladimir Veselsky, a 23-year-old waiter from Brno, is charged with an "attack against a public official" in connection with an incident which occurred during an August 21 demonstration in Brno. Veselsky is said to have commenced the hunger strike when arrested.

7. On August 29 Veselsky was transferred to a prison hospital in Prague, where he has been artificially fed on at least four occasions. It is reported that Veselsky will be returned to Brno and placed on trial in middle to late September. A group of Brno citizens has asked Amnesty International to intervene in the case.

Sasa Vondra facing two-month jail term

8. Sasa Vondra, Charter 77 spokesperson and "Nekolik vet" petition campaign organizer, is facing two months in jail. Vondra earlier this year received a two-month suspended sentence for attempting to lay flowers on Wenceslas Square to commemorate the 1969 self-immolation of Jan Palach. The court on September 4 ruled Vondra has not been living "an orderly socialist lifestyle" since his original trial, and Vondra was ordered to serve the sentence. He is free pending appeal.

Nekolik vet update

9. As of September, over 23,000 persons have signed the Nekolik vet petition.

10. The official press now rarely carries articles criticizing the Nekolik vet petition (Prague 5232), but those collecting signatures for the petition are facing harassment and criminal prosecution. Miroslav Crha, from Volary in southern Bohemia, is believed to be among the first to receive a prison sentence (three months suspended) for circulating the petition. Activists tell us that they believe persons in Olomouc have also received suspended sentences for their work with the petition.

11. Police have also conducted recent searches of the residences of those collecting petitions. We have reports of searches and seizures of petition materials in Brno, Gottwaldov, and several smaller towns in southern Moravia. The individuals whose homes

were searched are suspected of "breaches of public order," but thus far we have no report these individuals have been formally charged with violations of the criminal code.

Two attacks by police against dissidents

12. Two Prague activists, Josef Kuhn and Stanislav Penc, have been the victims of recent physical attacks. On both occasions dissident sources say that Czechoslovak security officers carried out the attacks.

13. Kuhn was attacked on the evening of August 29 by three men in plain clothes. The three men jumped from a Skoda and one is reported to have shouted "that's him" when they saw Kuhn. Kuhn's watch and money were taken, and he was then beaten until he fell stunned to the ground. Kuhn had been detained by police several times in August prior to the attack.

14. Penc was attacked by five police officers on August 30 a few minutes after police had broken up a discussion group meeting on Prague's Charles Bridge. Two of the five persons who attacked Penc had broken up the discussion group. Passers-by came to Penc's defense and chased away the police.

Mother of Petr Cibulka allowed visit

15. The activist Petr Cibulka imprisoned while awaiting trial for "illegal enterprising" and "economic speculation" (Prague 5480) was allowed a 30-minute visit with his mother, Vera Cibulkova, on August 21. It was the first time Cibulka was allowed to see his mother since he was imprisoned last October. The British embassy in Prague, which had raised Cibulka's case with the Czechoslovak MFA during August, told us they had stressed Cibulka's inability to see his mother and other visitors during their demarche.

Czechoslovak Helsinki Committee members detained

16. Seven members of the Czechoslovak Helsinki Committee were detained and questioned for two hours after a meeting the evening of August 6. Among those detained was Dubcek-era foreign minister Jiri Hajek. All were released after questioning. One dissident says the detentions are a tactic by Czechoslovak security to obtain any documents those detained might have.

Slovak bishops to be consecrated

17. The consecration of the bishop of Spis (Tondra) and elevation to archbishop of the diocesan administrator of Trnava (Sokol) are scheduled for the September 9–10 weekend

(Prague 5096). Ninety-year-old Cardinal Tomasek will not attend the rites because of the distance to Slovakia, but Vatican envoys Colosuonno and Tomko (a cardinal of Slovak origin) will be present. Colosuonno is expected to use his visit to Czechoslovakia as an opportunity to discuss filling of the remaining seven empty Czechoslovak bishoprics.

Jiri Tichy released

18. Jiri Tichy, sentenced in March to six months imprisonment for circulating a petition in 1988 that criticized the GOC, has been released from prison. Friends of Tichy had petitioned for his early release from prison (early release for good behavior is permitted as early as the mid-point of a sentence), but foot-dragging by judicial authorities resulted in Tichy being released only 35 days early. Ivan Jirous, sentenced to 16 months for circulating the same petition, remains in prison. **BLACK**

11 September 1989 1452Z
PRAGUE 06252

FM AMEMBASSY PRAGUE | **TO** SECSTATE WASHDC 0390 | **INFO** EASTERN EUROPEAN POSTS

SUBJECT: SOVIET DIPLOMAT ON 1968 AND OPPOSITION WITHIN THE CPCZ

1. Confidential—entire text.

2. Summary. Soviet POL counselor Filippov (strictly protect) has told EmbOff that a Moscow re-evaluation of 1968 invasion is on its way. Recent "Izvestia" reporting on the August anniversary was one step in that direction. When re-evaluation comes, though, it will be narrowly restricted to the military action, not internal Czechoslovak developments of the time. (Comment. This may give the Jakes[a] regime an out to continue to justify post-invasion purges as necessary to correct a counter-revolutionary situation. End comment.) While Filippov sees no reform wing forming in the CPCz "so far," he believes internal Party pressure for change is building and will become more pronounced as the May 1990 CPCz congress nears. Very soon, decisions must be taken on draft Party rules and a Party program to be considered by the congress. He views the Slovak Party as cautious about reform and its economic benefits for Slovakia and unlikely to play the catalyst role for change it did in Dubcek's day. End summary.

---

a. Miloš Jakeš, general secretary of the Communist Party of Czechoslovakia.

3. Embassy POLEC chief had a long conversation on September 8 with Soviet Political Counselor Vasiliy Filippov (strictly protect). Both had spent periods out of Prague during the summer vacation and the exchange was very much in the vein of catching up on what had occurred and could be expected in the months ahead on the local scene. Some of the subjects touched on are summarized below.

A Soviet re-evaluation of 1968

4. According to Filippov "Izvestia" reporting on this August 21's invasion anniversary, including the interview with former CPSU Politburo member Kirill Mazurov, was a step in the direction of an official Moscow re-evaluation of the action. This should be clear to the local Prague leadership, he said, even if CPCz Presidium members Husak, Jakes and Indra continue to voice opposition to the idea (Note: Filippov did not speak to Mazurov's later and more critical remarks on Hungarian television and may not yet have heard or read the text of that interview. End note.) When the re-evaluation comes, said Filippov, it will be limited to the military decision to invade which, in any case, had not been taken by the full CPSU Presidium. Internal Czechoslovak developments, he said, would not be a subject of the re-evaluation. Asked if he thought the CPSU Central Committee would reply to Dubcek's letter requesting a re-evaluation of 1968, Filippov said he ("###). (##=#)

Note by OC/T: (##=#) omission at end of paragraph 4. Correction to follow

Weight with the public, said our contact, would not prevent the leadership from using it to try and preserve as much of the official version of the events as possible. End comment.

Opposition within the CPCz

6. Filippov said there was much sympathy for a re-evaluation of 1968 and a more decisive reform program among the 70 percent of Party cadres who entered the CPCz since the post-invasion purges. However, he saw no visible evidence of a reform wing taking shape within the Party "so far." Recently announced plans for an extraordinary meeting of leading district, city and regional Party secretaries called for September 15–16 would, he thought, be an attempt to put a cap on internal criticism building in the Party. Jakes would make a tough, orthodox speech at this meeting. While individual secretaries might raise critical voices, no serious challenge to the leadership would be mounted at this session or in an October CPCz plenum, now scheduled for October 16–17.

7. Comment. The leading secretaries meeting may in fact be intended to head off any criticism spilling over into this plenum. In a cosmetic display of glasnost the media here

has recently been giving more coverage to plenum discussions. Jakes may want to stifle criticism before it shows up embarrassingly on the television screen. End comment.

8. Filippov saw pressure for change building from below, but slowly. The driving force as he saw it, would be preparation for the May 1990 Party congress and the documents to be considered there: a new draft Party program, Party principles and a draft federal constitution. Decision on these documents would force the leadership to take opposition within the Party into account. Filippov continues to hold to the view that the congress will be a real watershed in terms of policy and personnel changes.

Slovak Party views on reform

9. Filippov characterized the Slovak Party grassroots as more cautious on reform than its Czech counterpart. He had been to Banska Bystrica with CPSU Politburo member Vorotnikov to hear Jakes deliver a speech last month on the anniversary of the Slovak National Uprising. Jakes' hardline speech, he said, would never have received the long and sustained applause in Prague, or the Czech lands, that it did in central Slovakia. The Slovak Party would focus, in his view, on bread and butter issues in its dealings with Prague: guarantees of a Czech/Slovak balance in Party and government positions, and preferences for Slovakia in investment and budget policy.

10. In Filippov's view reformers within the CPCz could not count on Slovak (###) secretariat and Central Committee, essentially putting it on a par with the CPSU.

August 21 and future demonstrations

Note by OC/T: (###) omission in paragraph 10. Correction to follow.

11. Filippov, who was in Prague for the August 21 demonstrations, did not believe they had produced any "winners or losers." Police reaction had been restrained because the opposition had opted for a moderate way (i.e., a few moments of silence) of marking the anniversary. August 21 was no guide, he felt, to possible public demonstrations on the October 28 anniversary of the founding of the republic. Filippov suspected these would be both broader-based and include demonstrations outside the capital. Support for independent demonstrations by official and semi-official persons would be easier to justify since, he said, this was a nationalist action and did not carry the taint of dissent associated with August 21. Filippov did not preclude support for independent actions coming from basic Party organizations.

Comment

12. Filippov's manner in discussing these issues depicted the Soviet embassy as a very interested observer, though not a player in these internal developments. That, of course, is consistent with the official Soviet line that Czechoslovakia's reforms are its own affair. CPSU Presidium member Vorotnikov in fact restated that position in his own speech at Banska Bystrica last month. (Even using a Czechoslovak turn of phrase, Vorotnikov said that socialist countries must choose the pace and content of reform based on their own conditions.) Though Filippov displayed considerable sympathy for potential change and reform coming to Czechoslovakia, he clearly believes the present leadership will tough it out as long as it can—certainly through the next Party congress, even in the face of a Moscow re-interpretation of 1968. **BLACK**

20 September 1989 1503Z
PRAGUE 06521

FM AMEMBASSY PRAGUE | **TO** SECSTATE WASHDC 0580 | **INFO** EASTERN EUROPEAN POSTS
SUBJECT: PRAGUE REACTS TO IZVESTIA LETTER ON 1968

1. Confidential—entire text.

2. Prague's reaction to *Izvestia*'s publication of a letter by Dubcek-era foreign minister Jiri Hajek last week has been muted, at least publicly. In fact, it has appeared only as a reference in a speech by Presidium member Miroslav Stepan. A Soviet embassy officer, however, has told us that his embassy has received stiff criticism from government and Party officials on *Izvestia*'s action and he implied that his embassy may have been called into the MFA to receive a protest.

3. The single reference appeared in Stepan's speech to the chairmen of Prague's basic Party organizations on September 18 and was front page news the following day. Stepan warned that efforts to reassess history (he later mentioned the Hajek letter as an example) made a gross mistake by failing to see the whole period of 1968 in its objective historical context. Stepan did not challenge, however, Hajek's contention in the *Izvestia* letter that the basis for the invasion (i.e., a fear that Czechoslovakia might withdraw from the Warsaw Pact) was groundless since it had never been considered by the Dubcek regime.

4. The selection of Stepan to voice this objection to *Izvestia* is interesting in itself. By using the 44-year old Presidium member the Prague leadership may wish to make the point that opposition to a re-evaluation of 1968 cuts across generational lines in the CPCz.

5. This is not the first time the older generation in the Presidium has chosen to use Stepan to carry water for it. It was a Stepan speech earlier this year that opened the campaign against the "Few Sentences" petition[a] and also Stepan who warned Party members off signing the petition to release Vaclav Havel. His name, as Prague Party boss, was also linked to police actions to put down demonstrations in August, 1988 and in January this year, though he reportedly denied making those decisions.

6. Some observers see a pattern in this. The older generation in the Presidium in their view is having Stepan sign on to orthodox and unpopular measures. These will compromise him in the long run and make it that much more difficult to present himself as a pragmatic reformer in the Gorbachev mold should he ever choose to challenge the Jakes leadership, as many think he is waiting to do. **BLACK**

21 September 1989 1559Z
PRAGUE 06551

FM AMEMBASSY PRAGUE | **TO** SECSTATE WASHDC IMMEDIATE 0606 | **FOR** EUR/EEY ONLY—FOR SWIHART FROM RUSSELL

SUBJECT: OFFICIAL INFORMAL NO. 174

1. (C) UNGA bilateral. We are sure you are working hectically to put together briefing materials for the secretary's meeting with Johanes. We include some thoughts below on what the secretary might raise and the subjects we think that Johanes in turn will bring up. If there is any other way we can be helpful in the process, let us know.

—Human rights. This should dominate the Johanes/Baker[b] exchange and be stressed in any comments the secretary or Department spokesperson make to the press about the meeting. We still have received no response to our latest demarche on the Carnogorsky, Kusy and Devaty cases (Prague 6040). When we have received replies, as on the Starek case (Prague 5291), they have been perfunctory. We have no evidence of the GOC attempting to resolve our human rights differences as it has committed itself to do in

---

a. The Několik vět petition.
b. U.S. Secretary of State James Baker.

the Vienna Concluding Document. The human rights situation continues to deteriorate. Vondra returned to prison earlier this week and actions against the "Few Sentences" petition organizers multiply (Prague 6525). USIA director Gelb took a good tack in his meeting with Johanes and others in Prague on human rights, which may be worth repeating. He argued that they were trying to hold back the democratic tide in Eastern Europe. It would not work and political reform would come, whether it took two or three years. He told them not to waste time fighting it. We wanted, he said, to cooperate economically and extend MFN to Czechoslovakia but we had to see progress on the human rights front to do so.

—Access. Access to Party and government officials for the ambassador has been improving. We would like that to continue and see it extended to the whole embassy, particularly in terms of better access to the Central Committee and Party organizations outside of Prague.

—Embassy housing. We need better GOC cooperation on making housing available for the embassy staff. The local diplomatic housing authority (Sprava Sluzeb) has turned down three out of eight of our last lease requests.

—War monuments. The embassy has had an on-going debate with the GOC about the replacement of memorials put up in western Bohemia to commemorate its liberation at the end of the war by U.S. forces. We have argued this is the sort of action the GOC should take to display its good faith in improving relations. Our interest is in restoring the original plaques and markers, not erecting new ones, which might distort the role of U.S. forces or carry a propaganda message. (In our view the action would be more than symbolic. It would help correct the official GOC line which plays down the role of the U.S. forces in the war and legitimize our wreath-laying activities.)

2. (C) UNGA continued. We would expect the Czechoslovak side to raise the following:

—MFN. Johanes will complain about how we have dangled MFN in front of Czechoslovakia for years to get it to change its behavior; first to negotiate a gold claims settlement,[a] then to develop an independent foreign policy from the Soviet Union and now to change its human rights practices. Johanes is well aware of the necessary human rights

---

a. The U.S. and Czechoslovak governments engaged in decades of negotiations regarding Czechoslovak claims to gold stolen by the Nazis and recovered by the Allies in World War II. The governments eventually reached an agreement regarding the return of the gold in 1981.

changes required before Congress will approve MFN, but that will not prevent him from trotting out this old line.

—Travel controls. It would be very good if the secretary could reply to Johanes's complaints on this by stating that we were waiving the controls on their UN permanent representative. Perm rep Zapotocky may actually sit in on the meeting.

—High level consultations. The GOC has pushed for regular political consultations at the deputy foreign minister level and for better access in general. We can point out that they are getting it with this bilateral. If they want to continue the dialogue, however, they will have to show some recognition of our human rights concerns. We will be watching developments inside Czechoslovakia very closely on this point.

3. (C) UNGA. A final point. The GOC here is feeling increasingly isolated. It is responding to developments in Poland, Hungary and the Soviet Union by building up links with other conservative socialist states. Internally, it is cracking down on the dissidents. We expect it will try to make the most of the Baker/Johanes meeting to show that it is taken seriously by us and play that message to its people. As the ambassador noted in her cable recommending the bilateral, we think the best way to counter this is by using VOA and other media to demonstrate that Johanes got hit hard on human rights. That is the best way to turn this sort of dialogue to our own longer-term advantage.

4. (C) For Mike from Ted. HAWG[a]/BFWG[b]. As stated in our last OI and previously, we think it would be a very bad signal to suggest to the GOC that we drop to only one HAWG and BFWG per year. The GOC now touts these working groups as a model for their relations with other CSCE countries and has been more forthright than normal in providing information, including on human rights cases, during WG sessions. Please try to turn Commerce around on this.

5. (U) For Mike from Ted. Your visit. I have yielded gracefully. You are cordially invited to stay at the residence.

---

a. Humanitarian Affairs Working Group, a U.S.-Czechoslovak bilateral governmental committee set up to discuss human rights issues.

b. Business Facilitation Working Group, a U.S.-Czechoslovak bilateral governmental committee to discuss issues related to business relations and commerce.

6. (LOU) OIG inspection. We now have the official word on the October 21–November 4 inspection. Please give us any feedback from your discussions that indicate areas of particular interest to the inspectors or particular desires during their visit. Can we assume that myriad security inspections over last year, including full OIG SY inspection in July, mean that upcoming inspection will not have heavy security focus?

7. (C) Appeal of Conscience Foundation delegation visit. Rabbi Schnier and the other delegation members provided Ed Kaska with a readout on their visit. Ed and Cliff had briefed them before their meetings with Fojtik,[a] Lenart, Johanes and Janku, the government's secretary for Church affairs. Fojtik and Lenart made the usual pitch for MFN and high-tech sales, Johanes pressed for more high level exchanges, and Janku outlined "progress" made on religious affairs. The delegation specifically raised the issues of filling remaining empty bishoprics and the possibility of allowing someone to undertake rabbinical studies abroad (so Slovakia can have a rabbi). Rabbi Schnier also expressed his interest during the meeting in having the Appeal of Conscience Foundation sponsor exchanges of American and Czechoslovak clergy, an idea which he will be pursuing with GOC officials. Rabbi Schnier also attempted to heal divisions in the Jewish community by arranging a meeting between the community's current leadership and representatives of the young members of the community who have complained about the current leadership.

8. (LOU) Security clearance. For John Cloud. Under the new access regulations you will need to provide us by front channel cable confirmation of your top secret security clearance in order to move around the chancery unescorted. **BLACK**

06 October 1989 1630Z
PRAGUE 07042

FM AMEMBASSY PRAGUE | **TO** SECSTATE WASHDC 0969 | **INFO** EASTERN EUROPEAN POSTS, DEPT PASS TO ERIKA SCHLAGER CSCE COMMISSION

SUBJECT: HUMAN RIGHTS UPDATE -CZECHOSLOVAKIA

REF: PRAGUE 6525

1. Confidential—entire text.

2. Summary. The charges pending against Jan Carnogursky and Miroslav Kusy have been reduced, and activists now hope that any prison sentence which might be imposed against

---

a. Jan Fojtík, chief of ideology of the Communist Party of Czechoslovakia.

them will be suspended. The appeal hearing of Stanislav Devaty is scheduled for October 11 in Brno. An activist says that members of Pacem in Terris[a] have decided to cease activity by the organization. A crowd of several thousand gathered on Wenceslas Square on St. Wenceslas Day. Independent activists have asked for a permit to hold a rally on the October 28 anniversary of the 1918 founding of Czechoslovakia. Some thirty thousand people have signed the Nekolik vet petition. Petition supporters continue to be harassed by the regime. Petition organizers have written Prime Minister Adamec and asked for a dialogue between the government and Nekolik vet supporters. Two Czech Brethren ministers have lost their licenses because of their connections with independent groups. End summary.

Charges reduced against Carnogursky and Kusy

3. Both domestic and international protests against the criminal prosecution of Jan Carnogursky and Miroslav Kusy continue. Over 10,000 Czechs and Slovaks have signed a petition demanding their release. Polish Prime Minister Mazowiecki has sent a message to Vaclav Havel saying Mazowiecki will take action to support Carnogursky and Kusy. And Alexander Dubcek, in an interview with Austrian television, called the indictment against Carnogursky and Kusy unacceptable and weakly founded.

4. Czechoslovak authorities, in the face of these and other protests, have reduced the charges against Carnogursky and Kusy. Although both still face Criminal Code Section 98 "subversion of the republic" charges, they will now be prosecuted under the first rather than second paragraph of the article. The change means that the maximum sentence which now can be imposed against them is five years imprisonment rather than ten.

5. Perhaps more importantly, the first paragraph of Article 98 allows a judge to suspend any sentence imposed. Activists now speculate that Carnogursky and Kusy will in fact be convicted, but that their prison sentences will be suspended. They believe such an approach will allow the regime to say that "justice" was done, but avoid the international condemnation actual imprisonment would bring.

Appeal hearing set in Devaty case

6. Activists are less sanguine about the prospects for Stanislav Devaty. His appeal of a twenty-month prison sentence imposed in late August (Prague 5960) will be heard in a regional court in Brno on October 11. One activist has said the regime in Devaty's case has put itself in a place from which it cannot extricate itself without losing face and that

---

a. Papal encyclical on human rights issued on April 11, 1963.

it would take a miracle for Devaty's sentence to be suspended. Most activists fear Devaty will undertake another life-threatening hunger strike if imprisoned again.

Pacem in Terris stops activity

7. An activist has told us that Pacem in Terris (PIT), the officially sponsored peace organization of Catholic priests, has decided to cease its activities. The organization, which will not formally disband, has been losing ground since 1982 when Pope John Paul II ordered that priests disassociate themselves from the organization. In a related matter, the regime has accepted Cardinal Tomasek's nomination of a priest not associated with PIT to edit *Katolicke noviny*, a weekly newspaper of Church news which previously has been controlled by editors associated with PIT.

Saint Wenceslas Day demonstration

8. Following a Saint Wenceslas Day (September 27) mass at Prague's St. Vitus Cathedral, a crowd estimated at several thousand gathered in the evening on Wenceslas Square near the statue of the old king. Police peacefully dispersed the gathering, but a crowd estimated at 2,000 gathered some thirty minutes later and shouted slogans such as "freedom," "human rights," and "long live Bishop Korec." (Note: Korec is a bishop of the underground church in Slovakia.) The second gathering was also dispersed peacefully.

Plans for October 28

9. Human rights activists have asked the National Committee in Prague for a place in which to hold an independently organized rally to commemorate the October 28 anniversary of the 1918 founding of an independent Czechoslovakia. The National Committee's response has been equivocal, and activists have been told to contact managers of sites to identify a building or open space which would be available. Most activists would be surprised if a permit were actually granted for the rally.

10. Some of the same differences which arose between independent organizations concerning last August 21 seem to be resurfacing with regard to October 28. Charter 77 would seem to prefer a quieter indoor rally, while the Movement for Civil Liberty prefers a noisier outdoor gathering.

Nekolik vet

11. Over 30,000 persons have now signed the petition. At least eighteen persons have been fined for collecting signatures for the petition. Petitioner organizer Jiri Krizan was detained by police for several hours on September 29 concerning his activities. A "chain hunger

strike" was started on September 30 to support those prosecuted for their Nekolik vet activities.

12. Michael Kocab, a popular Czech composer who has signed the petition, told EmbOff he believes (although he has not been directly told) that he will no longer be able to work "officially." Kocab, who has contacts with Western firms, is not worried about his own livelihood, but is concerned for actors who have signed the petition. Kocab believes such persons have been blacklisted and will not be permitted to work in larger theaters, although they may be able to find work in smaller theaters. Prague actors apparently plan to boycott radio shows during November to protest discrimination against colleagues who have signed the petition.

The Nekolik vet party?

13. Jiri Krizan and twenty-one other activists wrote Prime Minister Adamec in September and asked that the GOC start a dialogue with working groups representing those who have signed the Few Sentences petition. Activists say that more persons have signed the petition than belong to the Czechoslovak People's Party (30,000 members) or the Socialist Party (16,000). Following the activists' logic, that makes "Nekolik vet" the second largest interest group in Czechoslovakia after the Communist Party. Adamec has not formally replied, although a representative of the prime minister has told activists that he is sympathetic to their demands.

Two Czech Brethren ministers lose licenses

14. Two ministers of the Evangelical Church of Czech Brethren, Zvonimir Sorm and Pavel Pokorny, have had their state licenses to work as clergymen withdrawn. Both clergymen participated in last year's funeral for human rights activist Pavel Wonka and have had links with independent groups. Thirty-seven Church members have sent a letter to Czechoslovak authorities protesting the withdrawal of the licenses. **BLACK**

10 October 1989 1529Z
PRAGUE 07059

FM AMEMBASSY PRAGUE | **TO** SECSTATE WASHDC 0000 | **INFO** EASTERN EUROPEAN POSTS

SUBJECT: THE PERCEPTION GROWS OF CPCZ LEADER JAKES AS A TRANSITIONAL FIGURE

1. Confidential—entire text.

2. Summary. While CPCz leader Jakes' position looks secure going into this week's Central Committee plenum, the perception of him as a transitional figure now dominates the popular imagination. In the short term he can rely on the public's political apathy, a satis-factorily performing economy and votes in the Presidium to keep his position. A Soviet rejection of its role in 1968 and the stirrings within the CPCz pose longer term threats. Jakes' fate, barring some unforeseen circumstances, seems likely to be decided by the CPCz's grass roots delegates at the May Party congress. Election of these delegates starts in January. End summary.

A shift in perceptions

3. Political observers here—dissident and official—agree that there has been a shift in popular perceptions of the GOC leadership. For many it is now not a question of "if," but "when" CPCz leader Jakes will be removed to make way for more serious reform measures. This is not to say that Jakes' removal is imminent or that his immediate successor will be an ardent reformer. The factors that have supported the status quo for 20 years, while slowly being undermined, are still in place. At least for the short term Jakes appears secure. We place little credence in rumors that he will be seriously challenged or resign at this week's October 11–12 plenum on the environment, though other lower-level personnel changes may occur. But over the longer term he has become, at least in the public mind, a transitional figure.

4. Recent developments in East Germany are almost as acute an embarrassment to the Jakes regime as to Honecker's. Jakes would prefer not to see his principal conservative ally so publicly humiliated. He may even fear isolation if the GDR backs away from its hardline resistance to reform. But despite a shared orthodox ideology, the pressures facing the Honecker regime are not directly applicable here.

Encouraging popular apathy

5. The Czechoslovak leadership has shrewdly pursued a selective relaxation of controls on its citizens. Travel is one good example. Since early 1988 the average Czechoslovak has been free to travel to the West if he can obtain the hard currency, legally or illegally, to do so. Virtually all return. While this policy may rebound in the long term as travel to the West heightens popular expectations, the chance to travel has probably served as a deterrent to a broader range of political activism among the young, so far.

6. Further, while the regime has targeted political activists and tried to segregate them from the general public, it has shown moderation in areas that do not pose a direct threat to the Party's authority. The scope for cultural expression continues to expand. The government is trying to co-opt environmental issues. The regime has also sought to reduce frictions with the Church. After years of intransigence, agreement is being reached on the appointment of new bishops and recently the organization Pacem in Terris has been virtually de-activated. The GOC appears to be trying to remove issues around which an opposition could crystalize and thus to continue to encourage the political apathy that has marked Czechoslovakia for 20 years.

The economy, a mainstay for now

7. The economy remains a strong card for Jakes personally, and for those who resist radical reform. It continues to deliver that adequate standard of living which has kept the general population acquiescent. Two new factors could, though, produce dislocations in the longer term and threaten that standard of living.

8. The new economic rules will, by the government's own admission, result in losses in some 30 percent of enterprises when they go into effect next year. Many of these are expected to be traditional, high-employment sectors like mining and heavy industry. A decision to end state subsidies to cover these losses (something the economy's managers like Prime Minister Adamec seem to want), could provoke labor unrest, now absent from the local scene.

9. Second, sales to the Soviet Union have dropped in the important areas of armaments (a result of Gorbachev's disarmament initiatives) and machinery (a result of Moscow giving its enterprises greater freedom to choose suppliers). Some observers are concerned about the "multiplier effect" this could have on the wider economy. Local economists play this fear down. Admitting that this could pose problems for individual firms, they claim that a general hard currency shortage will lead Soviet enterprises to continue to buy Czechoslovak goods with their soft rubles. In any case, Czechoslovakia has a current

bilateral trade surplus with the Soviet Union, which has the unfortunate result of leaving the country with a lot of "dead rubles" not good elsewhere.

Party unity and 1968

10. Jakes' greatest potential threat comes from within the Party. But again it does not appear an immediate one. Much attention has been given to recent signs of internal differences within the CPCz and to what extent they are locally or Soviet-encouraged. Articles in *Izvestiya* by Prime Minister Adamec and Central Committee security chief Hegenbart calling for more decisive reforms in the economy are examples. Significantly, as far as this embassy can tell, these criticisms do not originate from Jakes' inner circle. This group constitutes the majority in the CPCz Presidium and divisions must emerge within it before Jakes could be ousted.

11. A large part of the shift of perception from "if to when" on Jakes' removal is based on an expected Soviet repudiation of its role in the 1968 invasion. This action, it is assumed, will produce a more open, and for Jakes, compromising debate on those events, which will encourage opposition within the Party.

12. While a Soviet statement could encourage opposition, in our view, Jakes' removal would not follow automatically. This would appear particularly true if the Soviet repudiation narrowly confines itself to the military intervention and permits the current CPCz leadership to hold to its position that a counter-revolutionary situation in the country justified the internal purges and other measures that followed.

13. Moreover, Jakes has been careful to have even younger members of the Presidium, like Miroslav Stepan, publicly and regularly tout the official version of the 1968 events. This will make it all the harder for them to challenge the "inner" Presidium on this. And an important point, the interest in retaining the official version of 1968 runs much deeper than the top leadership of the Party. Virtually every institution in the country is staffed by people who took their positions in the wake of 1968. Some can make the transition to new thinking, many cannot.

A possible scenario

14. If Jakes had a chance to earn the credibility and emerge as a long-term Party leader, the public perception seems now to be that he has lost it. But his present position remains firm and, barring unforeseen circumstances, he looks likely to retain power into the new year. It is hard to predict what those special circumstances might be—perhaps an environmental disaster, a serious economic setback or a police over-reaction at the

October 28 demonstrations—but they would have to both shock the public and point up the leadership's incompetence in a way that would crystallize opposition.

15. There are more plausible scenarios for Jakes' departure from the scene. Most involve a challenge to him and the conservative circle around him at the May 1990 Party congress. If that challenge is to happen, it will start with the process, which begins in January, of selecting delegates to the congress. The outcome of those individual delegate elections is likely to be a more immediate determinant of Jakes' future than downturns in the economy or the rise of a popular opposition. A Soviet embassy contact has told us that Jakes would receive his "report card" from the CPCz's grass roots in May. It now looks as if he is not going to get passing grades. **BLACK**

11 October 1989 1642Z
PRAGUE 07098

FM AMEMBASSY PRAGUE | **TO** SECSTATE WASHDC 1011 | **INFO** EASTERN EUROPEAN POSTS
SUBJECT: INFLUENCE OF NON-COMMUNIST PARTIES IN THE
   CZECHOSLOVAK NATIONAL FRONT IS STILL LIMITED

1. Confidential—entire text.

2. Summary. In a recent call on the Czechoslovak Socialist Party (CSS), one of only four authorized non-Communist parties, EmbOff explored what, if any, substance was behind GOC claims that it was "re-activating" the National Front (i.e., giving this Communist transmission belt more of a role in policy making). EmbOff found CSS leadership more ready to voice independent views, including on human rights, but still powerless to affect policy. The CSS continues to disavow any role for itself as an opposition party or a mass political movement. It has refrained from actively recruiting new members, though there are apparently signs of youth interest in membership. CSS leadership continues to accept the Communist Party's "leading role," even if it would prefer that this role be exercised in a more democratic fashion. End summary.

Facts on the CSS

3. When POLEC chief called on CSS General Secretary Jan Skoda last week, he found him very pleased to receive embassy attention. While the CSS leaders, such as party president Bohuslav Kucera, have been active in fronting for various Communist public diplomacy initiatives, this small 16,000-member party is virtually ignored by Western

diplomats, with good reason. It has had virtually no influence since the 1948 Communist coup. Skoda recounted the party's history which extends back to the 19th century. Known originally as the National Socialist Party, it was founded as an offshoot of a Vienna-based Social Democratic Party and was meant to pursue a more Czech-oriented program. The party's insufficiently active stand against fascism during the Second World War, as Skoda described it, lost it much popular support. The party was re-named after the war and in 1948 was essentially disbanded and then re-established under a new leadership. But Skoda pointed out, the CSS was not and never had been a Marxist party. It supported a socialist program.

4. Skoda spoke of the changing demographics of the CSS. It had accepted some 2,000, mostly young (under 30), new members since 1987. This influx had largely balanced attrition due to death. A large number of members remain at pension age. Skoda said the CSS had no plans to actively recruit new members. (In fact none of the five legal parties in the front, other than the CPCz, can do so.) The CSS has no ambitions to be a mass political movement. All new members have volunteered their interest in the party. There were now between 800–1,000 applications a year. Most were attracted by CSS publications, particularly its daily paper *Svobone slovo* (the *Free Word*) which has a circulation of a quarter million. (Note: some of the paper's large circulation comes from the fact that it runs commercial advertisements. End note.)

5. Asked how the party on such a thin membership base was able to support its spacious offices in central Prague and a network of district and regional organizations, Skoda said the party depended on its very profitable publishing house, Melantrich. This had developed a niche for itself in producing books and publications on Czech history which had wide popular appeal among the young. It also published a magazine on Czech history. He shared a copy with us of its latest issue devoted to Anezka Premyslovna, the Czech medieval princess who will shortly be canonized a saint. (Comment: the CSS almost certainly receives government subsidies to retain its extensive party infrastructure. End comment.)

CSS's program within the National Front

6. Skoda put a good face on the CSS efforts to try and take advantage of the National Front's "re-activation." Though the CSS held only 18 out of 350 seats in the Federal Assembly, he said, it hoped to play a more active role in the legislative process. Earlier this summer it had, for the first time in years, proposed a draft law. According to Skoda this proposal would have amended the current regulation of freedom of assembly, spelling out precisely what procedures needed to be followed to apply for a permit to demon-

strate and giving the citizen a right to appeal an administrative decision in the courts. The measure did not receive CPCz support. Skoda criticized an existing Prague ordinance which bans demonstrations in the city's center in order to preserve its historic old quarter. It was his party's position, said Skoda, that such restrictions were only justifiable if applied equally to official and independent assemblies. In fact, the ordinance is used only against independent demonstrations. Official manifestations, such as May Day, can take place in the center.

7. The CSS, said Skoda, is represented on the special drafting committee for a new constitution. He did not expect the committee's work to produce any changes in the basic law, as it concerned human rights. The more important issue in his view was amendment of implementing legislation on civil rights incorporated by reference in the constitution. He said the CSS would be making proposals, including a new draft law concerning the right of petition, to bring these laws into better conformity with the Vienna Concluding Document.

8. Skoda confirmed that the CSS district organization in Prague 6 had recently issued a publication challenging the Communist Party's leading role in the National Front. He said that this statement reflected only the opinion of individuals. The CSS itself did not dispute the CPCz's leading role in society, which he said was "rooted in history." But he added that the Communists' leading role should be expressed on the basis of democratic principles, implying this was not presently the case.

The future

9. Skoda acknowledged that the government's decision to permit multiple-candidates in the 1991 Federal Assembly elections created some uncertainty for his party's future. In the past it had a guaranteed number of seats in the Federal Assembly and Czech National Council. He thought it would continue to be represented under the new scheme, though new election details had to be worked out. In his opinion the new rules would provide that a ballot contain more names than positions up for election. A citizen would then have a chance to scratch out the names of candidates up to that extra number.

10. Skoda repeated that the CSS had no interest in becoming a mass party or a party of opposition. Its place was within the National Front, seeking gradual change. He spoke of one model having been applied in Czechoslovakia for 40 years, with no chance in more than 20 years for discussing its suitability. This was changing, he said, but he wanted the influence of CSS on that discussion to grow gradually within the National Front.

11. In response to a question Skoda said he could imagine his party in the federal government, but not in the near future. (It now has a single minister in the Czech Republic National Council.) The CSS had links with the Polish Democratic Party—now a coalition partner in the new government there—and would be hosting a visit from the Polish party's chairman in November. Skoda said that the CSS was looking to expand its links with socialist parties in the West, but at present most of its intra-party links were with socialist states.

Comment

12. While this conversation is tame by Hungarian or Polish standards, it is a change from what our contacts with the National Front were saying even a few months ago. Then, even an implication that the CPCz was not observing "democratic principles" in exercising its leading role would have been surprising. The undercurrent of what Skoda said was that the limits for CSS initiative remained narrow. While it is exploring them, it is not about to do so aggressively.

13. Biographic note: Skoda, who appears in his early-to-mid-50's, is a more open and seemingly sincere personality than his boss, CSS president Bohsulav Kucera. Kucera, with whom the embassy has had more frequent contact, is nothing more than a mouthpiece for CPCz policies. Skoda struck us as a man who would welcome a wider political role for the CSS, but not one who would fight for it.

A postscript

14. Since the meeting with Skoda we have seen a few signs that the CSS membership may be more willing than the party's leadership to push the regime to open up the system. The first is a report that the party's north Moravian regional committee applied to organize its own independent youth group, challenging the Union of Socialist Youth's[a] right to a monopoly on such organizations. Second, a Saturday edition of the party paper "Svobodne slovo" included a rather unusual interview with dissident writer and Charter signatory Zdenek Urbanek. The subject of that interview was the work and life of Vaclav Cerny, an original Charter 77 founder and a figure who acted as moral voice for human rights through the post-war period in Czechoslovakia. Both Urbanek and the deceased Cerny have been essentially non-persons in official literary circles. Urbanek, a close embassy

---

a. The Union of Socialist Youth (SSM), established in 1970 by the Communist Party of Czechoslovakia as part of the dismantling of Prague Spring reforms, was a centralized children's and youth group.

contact, was until just a few weeks ago denied travel permission to attend even literary conferences outside the country. **BLACK**

19 October 1989 1527Z
PRAGUE 07293

FM AMEMBASSY PRAGUE | **TO** SECSTATE WASHDC PRIORITY 1176 | **INFO** EASTERN EUROPEAN POSTS, AMEMBASSY BRUSSELS, DEPT PASS TO ERIKA SCHLAGER CSCE COMMISSION, BRUSSELS ALSO FOR USEC

SUBJECT: HUMAN RIGHTS UPDATE: REGIME INTENSIFIES CRACKDOWN ON
INDEPENDENT ACTIVITY

REF: PRAGUE 7042

1. Confidential—entire text.

2. Summary. The Czechsolovak regime appears to have begun a new crackdown against the activities of independents which is at least as intense as the crackdown which followed January 1989 demonstrations. The crackdown has featured detentions, arrests, and criminal trials, the most significant of these events perhaps being the initiation of criminal proceedings against the editors of the samizdat newspaper *Lidove noviny*. The crackdown is motivated by the specific desire to minimize the size of October 28 independent demonstrations commemorating founding of the independent Czechoslovak Republic and the general desire to reverse the trend of ever-increasing and ever-varied independent activities. Such a reversal, however, would require the imprisonment of tens (if not hundreds) of persons, and the current crackdown has thus far not reached such massive proportions. End summary.

A new crackdown against independents

3. Members of the dissident community say the regime has begun a new crackdown against the activities of independents. Examples cited as evidence of such crackdown include: (1) the initiation of criminal prosecution against the editors of the samizdat monthly *Lidove noviny* (para 6–10); (2) police detention and interrogation of Obroda and other activists (para 11–13). (3) continued criminal prosecution of dozens of persons connected with the Nekolik vet petition and other independent activities (para 14–18); and

(4) possible plans to seal off Wenceslas Square on October 28 to prevent an independent rally commemorating founding of an independent Czechoslovak state (para 19–20).

4. The current campaign is at least as intense as the flurry of criminal prosecutions and general repression which followed last January's demonstrations. The campaign in part is a series of reactions to established independent political activity (e.g., Nekolik vet, Obroda, *Lidove noviny*). It is as well a general attempt to reverse the tide of ever-increasing and ever-varied independent activity (para 21–25) and a special attempt to minimize the size of independent demonstrations on October 28 (the spontaneity and size of recent demonstrations in East Germany apparently has surprised Czechoslovak authorities and independents alike and led both sides to believe large turnouts for October 28 are a possibility).

5. Comment. The current campaign of repression, in the short run, has the potential to slow down or discourage independent activity. However, like the campaign of repression which followed the January demonstrations, the current campaign thus far is not so wide-spread that it can be expected to reverse the trend of increasing independent political activism. To effect such a reversal, the criminal prosecution and imprisonment of tens (if not hundreds) of persons would be required. Such a widespread campaign of repression, if it were to occur, would eliminate even the pretext that the GOC was taking its CSCE commitments seriously. End comment.

Lidove noviny editors face criminal charges

6. Jiri Ruml and Rudolf Zeman, editors of the samizdat monthly *Lidove noviny*, have been charged with incitement for their work with the newspaper. Ruml and Zeman were both detained and interrogated on October 12 and their apartments searched. The incitement charge is punishable by one to five years imprisonment. Both Ruml and Zeman are jailed awaiting trial.

7. *Lidove noviny*, now in its second year of publication, is probably the Czechoslovak samizdat publication with the widest readership. The publishers produce 500 copies of the newspaper each month, which are then xeroxed by others and distributed throughout Czechoslovakia. The newspaper's editorial board estimates that eventually eight to ten thousand copies of the paper are produced. One dissident told us the paper's "decent tone" was attractive to the common person, and that it had in fact become "fashionable" to read the newspaper.

8. *Lidove noviny* typically has 24 pages of approximately 800 words each, with cartoons and photos. It includes domestic and foreign policy comments, sections on the economy, culture and the arts, ecology, interviews, a regular column on language, letters from readers, and various documents published in full. Articles in the paper have generally focused on human rights and the need for a more democratic and open society in Czechoslovakia.

9. Czechoslovak authorities have been concerned about *Lidove noviny* since it began formal publication in January 1988, fining the editors 500 crowns (about USD 50) each month for publishing without permission of the authorities. *Lidove noviny* dissidents claim, is the main reason Czechoslovak authorities are now considering a press law revision which would raise the fine for publishing without a permit to 10,000 crowns.

10. *Lidove noviny*'s editorial board (which includes Vaclav Havel and Jiri Dienstbier among others) has vowed to continue publication. One embassy contact told us that he expects the next issue to be published on time.

Obroda and other activists detained

11. Activists of Obroda, the Movement for Civil Liberty, the Independent Peace Association, and the Democratic Initiative attempted to meet on October 12 at the Cerny pivovar restaurant. After 20 minutes state security forces raided the meeting. Those present were taken into custody, interrogated and released. Questions during the interrogations focused on potential October 28 demonstrations. One of those present, Venek Silhan, was charged with a misdemeanor for having a draft proclamation concerning October 28 with him.

12. Police also detained Democratic Initiative members who attempted to meet in Prague and Brno last weekend. About 20 persons were questioned by police. Possible October 28 demonstrations were once again of principal interest to police.

Czechoslovak Helsinki Committee members detained

13. Six members of the Czechoslovak Helsinki Committee were detained, questioned, and released the evening of October 17. Jiri Hajek was among those detained. The detentions coincided with the visit to Prague of Jeri Laber, executive director of the U.S. Helsinki Watch Committee.

Nekolik vet

14. Over 33,000 persons have signed the Nekolik vet petition. One activist associated with the petition drive advised us over 70 persons have now been charged with criminal offenses for collecting signatures for the petition. Thus far no one in Slovakia is known to face charges for working with the petition drive.

Cibulka trial now expected in January

15. The mother of Petr Cibulka told EmbOff that it is now expected that the trial of her son will not be held until January 1990. October 14 marked one year that Petr Cibulka has been in jail awaiting trial on illegal enterprising charges (Prague 6076).

16. Mrs. Cibulka, who was allowed to visit her son in jail for the first time in September, stated that he complained of aching over his entire body. She also mentioned that her son's face was so swollen that she had trouble recognizing him. Mrs. Cibulka reported police have harassed Cibulka's lawyer, but that other members of the lawyer's "law firm" had intervened with authorities in an effort to stop the harassment.

Movement for Civil Liberty activists arrested

17. A meeting of the steering committee of the Movement for Civil Liberty (HOS) was broken up by police on October 17. Two of the HOS activists detained, Ivan Masek and Pavel Naumann, have been charged with incitement for carrying printed political leaflets with them.

Member of Czech Children avoids imprisonment

18. Lucie Vachova, a 22-year-old nurse and activist with the Czech Children, was convicted of incitement in Prague on October 18 in connection with the preparation and distribution of leaflets in August 1988/1988. Vachova was fined 4,000 crowns (about USD 400), but avoided the prison sentence (up to five years) which could have been imposed.

Official and independent plans for October 28

19. Czechoslovak authorities will not provide permission or a place for Charter 77 and other independent groups to gather on the anniversary of October 28, 1918 founding of Czechoslovakia. Charter 77 and others in response have issued a joint proclamation which underlines that the Czechoslovak Constitution guarantees the right of citizens to assemble. As of today neither Charter 77 or any other independent movement has chosen to endorse an independent demonstration or to specify a place where those wishing to

demonstrate might gather. One dissident told EmbOff that no one was anxious to take the lead on the issue given the current campaign of repression.

20. Czechoslovak authorities have announced their own plans for Wenceslas Square, traditional site of demonstrations, for October 28. A mass loyalty oath ceremony for military officers will take place in the square. Some dissidents speculate authorities might attempt to shut the square off to regular pedestrian traffic, but that if that were the case those wanting to demonstrate would find an alternative site, most likely Prague's Old Town Square.

Stirrings in the Socialist and People's Parties

21. A group of young members of Prague's Fifth District Socialist Party are in open conflict with the party's leadership. A few weeks ago those present at a meeting of the district five party voted and rejected the concept of the leading role of the Communist Party. There is also a report that the Socialist Party in Prague 5 has now begun publication of a newsletter called "The Demokrat," which is critical of Communist policy and calls for a more representative Socialist Party.

22. A reformist wing of the Czechoslovak People's Party called Obrodny Proud (or Living Stream) has been formed. Some 70 delegates met in Prague on October 14. Apparently the current leadership of the party attempted to prevent the caucus from taking place, and even asked police to help stop the meeting. At least two persons who wanted to attend were detained by police. The Obrodny Proud group has called for: (1) a religious re-orientation of the party's program, (2) resignation of the party's current leadership and (3) the early convening of an all party congress to debate the future of the party.

Independent publishing house in Brno

23. Atlantis, an independent publishing house, organized as a cooperative, has been established in Brno. The cooperative is seeking official registration with Czechoslovak authorities. Atlantis plans to publish exiled and independent authors, as well as various Czechoslovak independent publications (including *Lidove noviny*). Vaclav Havel has waived a 25,000 Deutschmark award which accompanies the German booksellers peace award Havel recently received, and asked that the 25,000 DM be given to Atlantis instead to support its activities.

Circle of independent intellectuals

24. A member of the organizing committee of the Circle of Independent Intellectuals told EmbOff that the group's members (who are predominately social, physical and biolog-

ical scientists) continue to not have any significant problems with authorities. A few members have been required to discuss their membership with supervisors, but no other actions have been taken by authorities. The organizer said he is satisfied with the group's progress in Prague, but that the response in Brno and Bratislava has been less than he hoped.

Environmental group opposes coal mill

25. A group calling itself the Northern Moravian Ecological Club is opposing the efforts of Czechoslovak authorities to construct a coal mill in Karvina near the Polish border. The group has issued a protest concerning the mill's construction (also signed by SPUSA, Movement for Civil Liberty, Czechoslovak-Polish Solidarity and others) and has promised public rallies (in both Czechoslovakia and Poland) in opposition to construction of the mill. **BLACK**

20 October 1989 1018Z
PRAGUE 07342

FM AMEMBASSY PRAGUE | **TO** SECSTATE WASHDC 1222 | **INFO** EASTERN EUROPEAN POSTS, AMEMBASSY BRUSSELS, DEPARTMENT PASS TO ERIKA SCHLAGER CSCE COMMISSION, BRUSSELS ALSO FOR USEC

SUBJECT: CZECHOSLOVAK HELSINKI COMMITTEE MEMBERS DETAINED

1. Confidential—entire text.

2. Fourteen members of the Czechoslovak Helsinki Committee were detained on Thursday morning, October 19, as they attempted to meet at Prague's U Piarstu restaurant. Also detained at the restaurant was Jeri Laber, executive director of the New York based Helsinki Watch, who was in Prague and had intended to attend the meeting. Laber's arrest apparently was provoked by her attempt to take pictures of the incident.

3. All those detained were taken to a police station, where Laber was released. The others were held for questioning about potential October 28 demonstrations. Ms. Laber told EmbOff yesterday that she believed all those who had been detained were now released.

4. The detentions are just the latest event in what is a stepped-up campaign against independent activities (Prague 7293). Although meetings of the Czechoslovak Helsinki Committee are often disrupted by police, recent meetings of the committee with foreign

visitors have not been disturbed, and yesterday's events mark another step backward by the Czechoslovak regime. **BLACK**

Note: not passed to Erika Schlager.

24 October 1989 1625Z
PRAGUE 07419

FM AMEMBASSY PRAGUE | **TO** SECSTATE WASHDC IMMEDIATE 1283

SUBJECT: EMBASSY REQUEST FOR DEPARTMENT STATEMENT ON CZECHOSLOVAK HUMAN RIGHTS SITUATION

REF: (A) PRAGUE 7342 (8) PRAGUE 7293 (C) PRAGUE 7042 (D) PRAGUE 6223

1. Confidential—entire text.

2. Summary/recommendation. The embassy recommends that the Department consider a short but strong statement this week on the deteriorating human rights situation in Czechoslovakia. The objective of the statement would be: (1) to show support for human rights groups at this period and (2) to give a signal to the GOC to exercise restraint over this weekend's expected demonstrations on the anniversary of the founding of the Czechoslovak Republic. Suggested points for inclusion in such a statement are contained in para 6. End summary.

3. As REFTELs record, the GOC has stepped up its repression of independent and human rights groups in recent weeks. The leadership of virtually every independent and opposition group has been touched by these actions. Dozens of persons face criminal charges and/or are under detention. Editors Jiri Ruml and Rudolf Zeman of the country 's major samizdat periodical *Lidove noviny* are now facing prosecution and a state investigation of the journal continues with the possibility that further charges will be filed against its staff. The GOC has shown no readiness, despite numerous demarches by Western governments, including the U.S., to remove longstanding charges against such prominent human rights activists as Jan Carnogursky, Miroslav Kusy and Stanislav Devaty.

4. The latest round of GOC repression is explainable in part by the regime's nervousness over developments in the GDR and fear of a spill-over effect here. That anxiety is made more acute in view of the upcoming Saturday, October 28 anniversary of the founding of the first Czechoslovak Republic. The date has been the occasion for demonstrations in Prague's center for the past two years and can expect to be so again (see SEPTEL).

5. The purpose of this message is to recommend that the Department consider making a short but strong press statement this week to note the deteriorating human rights situation in the country. The objective of the statement would be twofold. It would be a show of USG support to independent and human rights initiatives at a particularly difficult time. It would also offer an opportunity to signal our interest in seeing that the GOC exercise restraint in its reaction to the expected weekend's demonstrations.

6. Below we offer some suggested points for inclusion in such a statement:

—The Czechoslovak government's record in meeting its CSCE obligations in the area of human rights has never been satisfactory.

—Over the course of the past few weeks, however, we have witnessed a sharp upsurge in the number of human rights violations. Literally dozens of individuals have faced harassment, detention and criminal charges.

—The independent publication *Lidove noviny* has been placed under investigation and two of its editors, Jiri Ruml and Rudolf Zeman, have been detained and charged for the criminal offense of incitement.

—When Secretary Baker met with Foreign Minister Johanes less than a month ago at the UN, he reiterated our interest in an improvement in bilateral relations with Czechoslovakia. The secretary noted that such an improvement was not possible until Czechoslovakia adhered to the human rights obligations which it freely assumed as part of the CSCE process.

—The crackdown of the past weeks on human rights groups inside the country is a matter of deep concern to the U.S. These actions call into question the seriousness of Czechoslovakia's stated interest in improving relations.

—Over the last two years Czechoslovak citizens, in a genuine expression of civic patriotism, have marked the October 28 anniversary of the founding of the First Czechoslovak Republic with independent commemorations.

—We would hope that if such commemorations are repeated on this year's anniversary, the Czechoslovak government will respect the right of its people to assemble. This is a basic human right guaranteed by the Vienna Concluding Document and other acts to which Czechoslovakia has adhered as part of the CSCE process. **BLACK**

25 October 1989 1457Z
PRAGUE 07442

FM AMEMBASSY PRAGUE | **TO** SECSTATE WASHDC 1295 | **INFO** EASTERN EUROPEAN POSTS, AMEMBASSY BRUSSELS, BRUSSELS ALSO FOR USEC

SUBJECT: GOC ADVISOR ON THE IMPACT OF NEXT YEAR'S "NEW ECONOMIC RULES"

1. Confidential—entire text.

2. Summary. In a conversation with a senior advisor to First Deputy Prime Minister Urban, EmbOff was told that the government is serious about pursuing the "new economic rules" next year and expects them to produce significant changes in enterprise management and shifts in workforce. If true, the government may be greatly underestimating their potential for stirring labor unrest, something so far absent from the local scene. End summary.

3. In a lunch with Emilian Vosicky, foreign economic relations advisor to First Deputy Prime Minister Bohumil Urban, POLEC chief discussed the impact of next year's new economic rules on the Czechoslovak economy. While Vosicky does not deal directly with these reforms, his boss is the minister principally responsible for their implementation and EmbOff believes Vosicky offered a faithful presentation of Urban's thinking on them.

4. Throughout the lunch Vosicky stressed two points:

—Urban and other members of the government, particularly Prime Minister Adamec, are serious about enforcing the new economic rules as of 1 January. If unclear on their full impact, the government would try to make them work and then modify policy in light of this experience; and

—Inflation remains an overriding concern. To avoid the "Hungarian mistake,"[a] the government would retain control of total investments, wage growth—while allowing greater wage differentiation, and prices. This was essential to keep in check the monopolistic position of some enterprises in the domestic market. The foreign exchange position made it impossible to increase import competition as a counterweight to monopolistic tendencies and the government would not borrow to finance a current account deficit.

5. According to Vosicky the immediate impact of the new "self-financing" rules for enterprises would be to put pressure on incompetent managers to resign. Urban had no faith

_____

a. The Communist regime had ended in Hungary in October 1989 following the decision to introduce free market reforms.

in the new system of management elections by workers to accomplish this. The idea of enterprise democracy, as incorporated in the new state enterprise law, had been based on a false analogy between workers and shareholders in a Western corporation. Vosicky, and presumably Urban, believe the government will step in to replace "political" factory directors as enterprises run up losses, perhaps as part of a "consolidation" program as provided in the state enterprise law. At an appropriate time the provisions for management elections in the law would be withdrawn.

6. Vosicky gave a qualified yes to the question of whether the government would allow firms to go bust. There would be a transitional period (up to five years). During this time the government might create a support fund for enterprises whose poor performance resulted from past management mistakes or factors outside an enterprise's control (i.e., unrealistic state prices for its inputs or production).

7. Vosicky argued that a majority of firms would achieve profitability by removing the substantial featherbedding in their workforce and raising productivity. The new labor code, giving managers wider discretion to hire and fire, would be enforced. While the government would put a cap on total wage growth, managers would be free to distribute the aggregate wages in a way that encouraged performance. And if there were staff cutbacks, fewer workers could share the wage pie.

8. According to Vosicky, the government has no special plans for worker adjustment programs, other than in the mining industry where some retraining and job placement will be offered. In other sectors released workers will be pretty much on their own to find a new job, essentially using the want ads. The government places considerable confidence in its own statistics showing a labor shortage. It assumes jobs can be had for those who look for them. Moreover, Vosicky denied worker mobility would be a problem. Most workers would stay within their own republic, if not region, and could rely on the use of their new employer's guesthouse/worker dormitories until families relocated.

9. Vosicky agreed with EmbOff's assessment that the measures, as he was describing them, appeared designed to make existing firms profitable, not restructure the economy. The government, Vosicky said, believed there was room to exploit Czechoslovakia's traditional competitive advantage in sectors like textile machinery, glass and porcelain, and some machine tools. Investment in new or sunrise sectors would continue to be directed by the state planning commission and federal ministries, known in reconstruction parlance as the "unified center." Cooperatives might play a role here, but the space for free enterprise would remain limited essentially to privately-leased shops and restaurants employing family members.

10. At this point EmbOff voiced some skepticism about the way in which Vosicky under-stated the problems of labor adjustment (particularly in view of the fact that the country has no equivalent of unemployment insurance) and overstated the center's ability to pick industrial winners and losers. Those points aside, Vosicky was presenting a scenario that offered considerable economic discomfort for workers, not just management. As the joke went, Czechoslovak workers were currently satisfied to be half as productive as Austrians for a quarter the wages, because they knew that they had job security. Wasn't, EmbOff asked, the government ignoring such a program's potential for labor unrest and politiciza-tion of the workforce, something so far absent on the local scene.

11. Vosicky's reply was not convincing. He said there would be winners and losers under the new rules, the point being that one would cancel out the other. Vosicky implied the government could rely on the basic apathy of the Czechoslovak worker until the new rules began to produce positive effect on the economy and salaries. Special attention over the transition period would be given to the internal market to keep the consumer satisfied and offer the better paid worker goods to spend his salary on.

12. Vosicky discounted the possibility of labor's politicization. The potential for widespread popular opposition had peaked in January this year during the Palach demonstrations. The government had acted since then to defuse issues around which the opposition could coalesce. The August anniversary demonstrations had been a small affair, said Vosicky.

13. Vosicky conceded that this weekend's October 28 demonstration might be a better guide to popular dissatisfaction since it will be a patriotic holiday. He doubted more than a few thousand, at most 5,000 mostly young persons, would participate. If numbers were substantially larger than that, Vosicky said he might have to review his assumptions about the Czechoslovak national character. He clearly did not think that would be the case.

14. Comment. We offer Vosicky's thoughts as representative of what some of the more pragmatic, Western-oriented members of the government are thinking. Some of his ideas on labor mobility strike us as naive. To be fair to Vosicky, however, he would be the first to admit that what the government is doing in terms of reform next year is meant only as a first step, preparing the ground for more fundamental changes in price formation, etc. But if the government is as serious about cuts in workforce at unprofitable enterprises as he makes out, it is greatly underrating their potential to stir up labor unrest.

15. Biographic data. Vosicky, who is in his mid-40s, is not an economist. He probably owes his job with Urban in part to the fact that he is a polyglot. He speaks excellent English, French, German and Russian. His background is in the foreign trade ministry which he left

a little more than a year ago when he ran afoul of Deputy Foreign Trade Minister Nemec[a] over how to proceed in negotiations with the EC on a trade protocol. Vosicky travels widely in the West and has spent long periods in Brussels negotiating with the EC. His wife is the manager of a popular restaurant in downtown Prague. Vosicky's comment on a limited role of the private sector in Czechoslovakia is a personal view as well as official policy. It seems to be drawn from his wife's insider view of the restaurant trade where she sees few incentives for Czechs starting up their own business. **BLACK**

25 October 1989 1604Z
PRAGUE 07451

FM AMEMBASSY PRAGUE | **TO** SECSTATE WASHDC 1306 | **INFO** EASTERN EUROPEAN POSTS, AMEMBASSY BRUSSELS, BRUSSELS ALSO FOR USEC, DEPT PASS TO ERIKA SCHLAGER CSCE COMMISSION

SUBJECT: INDEPENDENT GROUPS CALL FOR OCTOBER 28 DEMONSTRATIONS

1. Confidential—entire text.

2. Summary. Charter 77 and five other independent groups have called for independent rallies on Saturday, October 28, to commemorate the 71st anniversary of the founding of Czechoslovakia. An independent rally on Prague's Wenceslas Square is scheduled for Saturday afternoon. The only official commemoration thus far announced for the holiday is a mass loyalty oath ceremony for the military at 10:00 a.m. on Wenceslas Square. Dissident contacts believe that turnout for the October 28 independent rally will exceed the 3,000 persons who demonstrated on August 21. The one significant factor which might reduce the turnout is a recent widespread crackdown on human rights and opposition groups. End summary.

3. Charter 77 and five other independent groups have issued a proclamation calling for peaceful and independent rallies throughout Czechoslovakia on Saturday, October 28, to commemorate the 71st anniversary of the country's founding. The declaration called such rallies "the most expressive form of statement in the current situation of the country." Dissidents have asked those in Prague to gather at 3:00 p.m. on Wenceslas Square.

4. Only one officially-sponsored event for October 28 has thus far been announced. Fifteen hundred recent recruits of the Czechoslovak People's Army, Border Guard, and Interior

---

a. Jiří Němec, Czechoslovak deputy minister of foreign trade.

Ministry forces will take a loyalty oath en masse on Wenceslas at 10:00 a.m. on Saturday. *Rudé Právo* indicates that only holders of tickets will be allowed on the square for the ceremony, but did not indicate if and when the square would be re-opened for regular pedestrian traffic.

5. Dissident contacts believe the independent October 28 rally will be larger than the demonstration in Prague on August 21 when some 3,000 persons gathered on Wenceslas Square (Prague 5726), but refuse to guess how large crowds may be. Factors encouraging a larger turnout include: (1) recent events, including massive and peaceful demonstrations, in East Germany; (2) the relatively peaceful nature of the August 21 demonstration in Prague; (3) the lack of threats by the regime to use violence against demonstrators; (4) the less political and more nationalist nature of the October 28 holiday (as opposed to August 21); and (5) an unambiguous and united call for demonstrations by independent groups (in contrast with August 21 when Charter 77 did not call for demonstrations).

Counterbalancing the above factors has been a widespread crackdown on human rights and opposition groups which has resulted in numerous arrests and detentions in recent weeks. This crackdown has not been accompanied by an anti-opposition and threatening propaganda campaign as was the case in August but may have an effect of deterring the youthful membership of the new independent initiatives. **BLACK**

25 October 1989 1612Z
PRAGUE 07455

FM AMEMBASSY PRAGUE | **TO** SECSTATE WASHDC 1312 | **INFO** EASTERN EUROPEAN POSTS, DEPT PASS TO ERIKA SCHLAGER CSCE COMMISSION

SUBJECT: A VISIT TO BRATISLAVA: SLOVAKS AWARE OF REGIONAL CHANGES, BUT NOT YET READY TO LEAD CHANGE IN SLOVAKIA

1. Confidential—entire text.

2. Summary. A visit to Bratislava by EUR/EEY desk officer for Czechoslovakia and EmbOff left the impression that while Slovaks are certainly aware of the changes in Eastern Europe and the possible implications for Slovakia, it is unlikely that Slovaks will lead any dramatic changes in Czechoslovakia. Martin Libiak, press spokesman for the Slovak prime minister's office, provided cautious and conventional responses to questions, showing emotion only when attacking Alexander Dubcek and the Slovak dissident and former Communist Miroslav Kusy. Juraj Janosovsky, chairman of the Slovak Union of Youth,

also provided responses tracking Party policy, but his remarks implied his readiness to accept changes should they come, although he personally will not be in the forefront of those advocating change. A visit with Bratislava dissidents found them believing Jan Carnogursky and Miroslav Kusy will never be brought to trial, but also believing that the ever-growing and ever-varied independent activities seen in the Czech lands will not soon be seen in Slovakia. The one exception may be the Hungarian minority in Slovakia, amongst which dissident groups with links to non-Communist groups in Hungary (para 19) are now functioning. End summary.

3. EUR/EEY desk officer for Czechoslovakia and EmbOff visited Bratislava on October 20. The visit included day calls on two Slovak officials as well as an evening with the core members of the dissident movement in Slovakia. The conversations with apparatchiks and dissidents alike left the impression that while Slovaks are certainly aware of the changes in Eastern Europe and the possible implications for them, it is unlikely that the Slovaks will lead any dramatic changes.

The cautious director of Press and Information

4. Mr. Martin Libiak, chairman of the Department for Press and Information of the Slovak prime minister's office, proved the most cautious of all those visited, generally providing conventional and sterile responses to questions. Libiak downplayed any conflict between Slovaks and Czechs, indicating that any animosity between the two ethnic groups had been all but eradicated years ago. With regard to the process of drafting a new constitution, Libiak believed that the new constitution will not provide for guaranteed Slovak positions in Party or government institutions, but that positions will be filled on the basis of ability.

5. Libiak was even cautious in his description of economic reforms. He acknowledged the need for and inevitability of such reforms, but offered no particular praise for the reforms being implemented in January 1990, saying only that the results of the reforms will be known after one year and "we'll be wiser." Libiak admitted that Slovakia has an economic advantage over the Czech lands because its industrial plant in some respects is more modern, but termed the industrial base in Bohemia and Moravia stronger overall. He cited tourism as an area where foreign investment in Slovakia would be especially welcome (to build hotels and other infrastructure in the high and low Tatras[a]), but also indicated a recent French proposal had been rejected because it failed to provide sufficient protection for the environment. The press spokesman also stated that at the present moment, Slovakia in fact has "too many tourists, especially from Hungary and Poland."

---

a. A mountain range in Slovakia.

6. Libiak stated that serious problems exist in the relationship between Czechoslovakia and Hungary. He indicated that Czechoslovakia did not want to take a confrontational path in the relationship and did not want to sharpen differences between the two. The GOC, in its dealings with Hungary, will be guided by the principle that one should forgive his neighbor if he makes a mistake.

7. Apparently there is no room for forgiveness for Slovak dissidents, such as Jan Carnogursky and Miroslav Kusy (Prague 5830), who take what Libiak described as unfriendly positions toward the state. According to Libiak, although the government encourages an open dialogue, there will be no dialogue with those who would "drown the regime in a little spoon of water." Kusy drew the greatest wrath from Libiak, it apparently being especially galling for Libiak that a former Party official like Kusy would be a dissident.

8. Another former Communist, Alexander Dubcek, also drew heavy criticism. Libiak pronounced Dubcek "a tourist," and "an old man who in his old age learned to speak like an orator." Libiak rejected the possibility that Dubcek might return to the political scene, saying Dubcek was too old and that even those who supported Dubcek in 1968 did not now support him. As for Libiak, he stated that in 1968 he lived in a small village and did not even know about Dubcek.

A more flexible view at the youth union

9. A visit to the Slovak Union of Socialist Youth found its chairman, Juraj Janosovsky, to be a more pragmatic and flexible apparatchik than Mr. Libiak. Janosovsky stated that the young in Slovakia are participating in the process of reform. While most young people in principle support reconstruction, there are those who are afraid of the discipline which such a program will require, and there are others who have no interest in the program, thinking it only a "tactical move."

10. Janosovsky declared that groups outside the National Front damage the process of reconstruction. Nonetheless, he admitted that "in the end, these groups can be a positive element, they enrich the environment." Janosovsky also proclaimed himself to be personally sympathetic in part to changes in Hungary, especially to the "democratization of public life" and to pluralism, although Janosovsky's view of pluralism did not necessarily envision an increase in the number of political parties in Czechoslovakia.

11. Janosovsky also offered his capsule opinion concerning Slovakia, Slovaks and Slovak-Czech relations. He called Slovakia a "small nation" and a nation without national heroes. Slovaks he declared a small minority, more sensitive on some issues than other ethnic

groups. Nonetheless, any conflicts between Czechs and Slovaks were small compared with ethnic strife in other unnamed countries. He also finds Czechs more inventive, but Slovaks more spontaneous. Finally, in an uncharacteristic remark for a Slovak, Janosovsky stated the obvious—that the Czech standard of living today is lower than it might be as a result of the program of the last twenty years to bring economic conditions in Slovakia to the level of those in the Czech lands.

12. Although Janosovsky carefully avoided saying anything which would contradict current Party dogma, he nonetheless provided us with two intriguing statements. First, he stated that "every nation has the government it deserves," and second that "people often behave as they must." By these statements Janosovsky seemed to be signaling his own willingness to accept changes should such changes come, but that he personally will not be in the forefront advocating them.

The dissidents' view

13. EmbOff and desk officer's first unofficial call on the evening of October 20 was at the apartment of Jan Carnogursky, the imprisoned Catholic activist. Hoping to find Carnogursky's wife, we found instead his elderly father, who described his own 27 months in prison many years ago and accused the Czechoslovak regime of state terrorism in its action against his son. Carnogursky's father also implied that his son's refusal to sign a statement like that signed by the former Communist Kusy (Prague 7058 and para 17 below) demonstrated a kind of moral superiority on the part of his son. U.S. visitors described the actions already taken by the USG in support of Carnogursky (Prague 6040) and pledged continuing support.

14. The apartment of Milan Simecka, Slovak dissident and philosopher, was the second stop of the evening. The small apartment's living room was already filled with three members of a visiting Helsinki Watch delegation, as well as Mrs. Carnogursky and other dissidents. Mrs. Carnogursky said that her husband is allowed one visit a month, and that she and his parents were alternating visits, meaning she could in effect see her husband only once every two months. Mrs. Carnogursky also complained that no more than three persons may be included in any visiting group, and that she had been denied permission to bring all four of her children to the next visit because of the limit. She also verified that her son had been denied admission to law school in apparent retaliation for his father's activities. Mrs. Carnogursky, despite her husband's imprisonment, displayed an incredibly genuine cheerfulness which impressed all those who were visiting her.

15. Simecka predicted that Carnogursky will eventually be released from prison and that neither Carnogursky nor Kusy will ever face trial on the charges now pending against them. Simecka told us he had learned that he was originally on the list of those to be charged in the "Bratislava Five" case[a] (Prague 5830), but that it had been decided that indicting all three of the most prominent Slovak activists would have been "too much." Simecka called the regime's indictment of the Bratislava Five a mistake because the five represented a "coalition of Slovak democrats" and that the spectrum of protests (e.g., Alexander Dubcek, underground bishop Korec, Slovak intellectuals) indicated the wrong choices had been made. In particular, Simecka felt the imprisonment of the Catholic Carnogursky sent the wrong signal to Slovak Catholics, the strongest segment of the Slovak population according to Simecka.

16. All those present at the Simecka apartment then visited the home of Miroslav Kusy, recently released from prison. Unlike Simecka and Carnogursky (who live in cramped apartments in socialist-style high rises), Kusy lives in a relatively spacious, two-story single family dwelling in a nice Bratislava neighborhood. The house is a perquisite from Kusy's days as Slovak Party ideologist during the 1968 Prague Spring which he has been allowed to retain.

17. Kusy seemed mildly defensive about having signed a declaration not to engage in further "criminal activities" pending his trial. He took care to show his visitors a statement which had been broadcast over Radio Free Europe explaining why he had signed the declaration. Kusy told us he was uncertain whether he would resume his RFE work pending his trial. No trial date has been set.

18. In addition to Simecka and Kusy, a few other Slovak activists (including Simecka's son and Anton Selecky, one of the Bratislava Five) were present for the pork roast and potato pancake supper Kusy and his wife offered. Although representing different segments of the Slovak dissident community, and at times differing on details, those present offered the following assessment concerning dissent in Slovakia. With regard to October 28, nothing will happen on that day in Slovakia, not only because the readiness of Slovaks to engage in open dissent is considerably less than in the Czech lands, but because the creation of Czechoslovakia in 1918 is regarded with ambiguous feeling by Slovaks. The ever-growing and ever-varied independent activities seen in the Czech lands (Prague 7293) are not yet present in Slovakia, and may be a while in coming. The most commonly

---

a. Five Slovak dissidents were arrested after signing a letter describing planned protests. Their trial in the fall of 1989 was highly publicized and united the Slovak opposition against the Communist regime.

cited reasons for the general lack of open dissent are Slovak economic progress since 1968, the gentler and kinder process of "normalization" which occurred in Slovakia after 1968, and 1968 federalization of the GOC. Most do not see the Catholic Church as being a fount of dissent in Slovakia, and believe regime tactics to placate Catholics—such as the filling of empty bishoprics—have a reasonable chance of succeeding.

19. One possible source of future dissent does exist, however, that being the Hungarian minority in southern Slovakia. (Note: official statistics count 600,000 Hungarians in Czechoslovakia, but several of those present claim 800,000 is a more accurate figure. End note.) One dissident present advised that small groups of Hungarian dissidents exist in Slovakia, and that these groups have established contacts with non-Communist reformers in Hungary. We accepted this individual's offer to put us in contact with some of the leaders of these groups during an upcoming November trip to Slovakia.

20. (Note: a subsequent *Rudé Právo* report of an interview with west Slovak Party leader Ondrej Kvak confirmed official concern over illegal and antisocialist activity by the Hungarian minority. The article quoted Hungarians as composing 21 percent of the region's population. But Hungarian political activity can cut both ways. Many Slovaks remember 1000 years of Hungarian domination as a national tragedy and may not be sympathetic to "uppity" Hungarian activism. End note.)

Bratislava—general impressions

21. While Bratislava does not have the architectural character of Prague, it does have a small Old Town section which is being attractively restored. One contact, however, told us that the city government has not always shown respect for the historical past, and that a portion of the city's Jewish ghetto was destroyed to make way for a new bridge which now spans the Danube.

22. On the day of our visit the air seemed relatively clean. Our dissident contacts, however, assured us that the day was not typical, and that some pollutants from the region's chemical industry are not visible to the naked eye. They also emphasized that pollution in Slovakia is not limited to Bratislava and is a source of concern for the common citizen and the regime.

23. The public transportation system gave an impression of being adequate, and auto traffic moved with ease through the city. U.S. visitors encountered gas lines on Saturday morning on the approach to the Bratislava-Prague freeway, as Bratislavans gassed up for apparent weekend trips, but at times the modern freeway outside of Bratislava was virtually empty on the trip back to Prague. We were assured by Bratislavans that the

Slovak love of nature at least equals that of the Czechs, and that the mania to own a weekend cottage is as strong in Slovakia as in the Czech lands.

24. The highway leading into Bratislava is lined by high rise apartment complexes—mostly grey, but a few done in maroon or green to break the monotony. A deputy mayor of Bratislava told EmbOff on another trip that there is a shortage of at least 10,000 apartments in Bratislava, and that high rises are the fastest and cheapest way to ease the shortage. That same deputy mayor told us the apartment shortage is aggravated by a high Slovak divorce rate, meaning that a family hit by divorce will need at least two apartments.

25. Shops in Bratislava appeared to be as well stocked as in Prague. The only lines we witnessed were in Tuzex stores offering consumer electronics and Western style clothing. A number of those waiting in the lines were Poles. BLACK

27 October 1989 1324Z
PRAGUE 07490

FM AMEMBASSY PRAGUE | **TO** SECSTATE WASHDC IMMEDIATE 1342 | **INFO** EASTERN EUROPEAN POSTS, AMEMBASSY BRUSSELS, DEPT PASS TO ERIKA SCHLAGER CSCE COMMISSION, BRUSSELS ALSO FOR USEC

SUBJECT: REGIME DETAINS VACLAV HAVEL IN ANTICIPATION
    OF OCTOBER 28 DEMONSTRATIONS

REF: PRAGUE 7451

1. Confidential—entire text.

2. Summary. Vaclav Havel and a number of other independent activists have been detained by Czechoslovak police to prevent their participation in independent demonstrations scheduled for October 28. Havel was transferred to a hospital after complaining of difficulty breathing, where he remains under guard. We anticipate these arrests may be similar to arrests prior to August 21 demonstrations, when a number of activists were detained and then released without criminal charges being filed after conclusion of the demonstrations. End summary.

3. We have learned that Vaclav Havel was picked up by police Thursday evening, October 26, and taken to a Prague police station. Havel, who is a heavy smoker, complained of difficulty breathing and was transferred to a Prague hospital, where he remains at this time under guard.

4. Havel, in an earlier Radio Free Europe interview, announced that he planned to stay in Prague on Saturday, October 28 and go about his normal business. Havel added that if he was still free at 3:00 p.m. he planned to go to Wenceslas Square and observe any independent demonstration commemorating the 1918 founding of an independent Czechoslovakia, which might occur.

5. In addition to Havel, Eva Kanturkova of the Czechoslovak Helsinki Committee was detained and jailed on Thursday afternoon, October 26. Also detained Thursday was Charter 77 activist Jaroslav Sabata and John Bok of the Independent Peace Association. Five other human rights activists, including Jan Chudomez of the Independent Peace Association, were detained on Tuesday, after an interview with Austrian police, and remain jailed.

6. We have also learned that the activist Ladislav Lis was told by Czechoslovak police to leave town or face a weekend in jail. Lis has left Prague. Calls to Charter 77 spokesperson Dana Nemcova and religious activist Vaclav Maly Friday morning, October 27, found both at home and thus far free of detention.

7. Prior to the August 21 anniversary of the Warsaw Pact invasion of Czechoslovakia police detained at least six activists to prevent their participation in demonstrations. All those detained in August were released shortly after the demonstrations, and none were charged with violations of criminal law (Prague 5830 and 5960). We would suspect the current detention of Havel and the others will follow the August pattern of no criminal charges being filed. BLACK

29 October 1989 1720Z
PRAGUE 07534

FM AMEMBASSY PRAGUE | TO SECSTATE WASHDC NIACT IMMEDIATE 1375 | INFO EASTERN EUROPEAN POSTS, AMEMBASSY BRUSSELS, DEPT PASS TO ERIKA SCHLAGER CSCE COMMISSION, DEPT ALSO FOR OPS CENTER, BRUSSELS ALSO FOR USEC

SUBJECT: PRAGUE'S OCTOBER 28 DEMONSTRATION AND OCTOBER 29 DETENTION OF AMERICAN JOURNALISTS

REF: PRAGUE 7541

1. Confidential—entire text.

2. Summary. Although an independent demonstration by some 10,000 persons this weekend in Prague is a sign of increasing activism, the relatively small turnout in

comparison to recent demonstrations in East Germany indicates that the wider population here is yet unwilling to risk direct confrontation with the regime. The GOC has blamed foreigners and foreign media, particularly RFE and VOA, for instigating the demonstrations and has detained some 350 persons, including 17 foreigners, in connection with them. A repeat demonstration called for October 29 failed to materialize, but Czechoslovak police reportedly detained several American and other journalists who turned up to film it. The journalists have since been released. End summary.

3. A crowd of some 10,000 gathered on Prague's Wenceslas Square on Saturday afternoon, October 28, in response to a call for demonstrations by Charter 77 and other independent groups to commemorate the 71st anniversary of the founding of the Czechoslovak Republic. Riot-equipped police dispersed most of the crowd within a half hour, although small groups of demonstrators were still moving through the city several hours after the start of the demonstration. Generally, the demonstration itself and police action to break-up the rally were peaceful, although isolated instances of violence occurred. Official Czechoslovak media reported ten injured, including three police officers. Official media also indicated that 355 demonstrators were arrested. We understand most were held overnight and then released.

4. The GOC has blamed the demonstrations on foreign provocation. Radio Free Europe, the Voice of America and foreigners who participated in the demonstrations were singled out for special criticism. Short local media coverage of the demonstration focused on the presence of Western news crews on the square. Seventeen foreigners from different countries were among those detained.

5. Interestingly, among the many slogans shouted by demonstrators, EmbOffs heard none supporting Gorbachev. The predominantly young crowd shouted for "freedom," "another government" and, at several points "long live Havel and the Charter." "We are not isolated" and the "world is watching" were also frequently voiced.

6. On October 29 several Western journalists were detained by the Czechoslovak police when they assembled on Wenceslas Square to film a rumored repeat demonstration. Two CNN technicians unable to present Czechoslovak press accreditation were taken away by the police, but were released after showing that they had valid Czechoslovak journalists' visas. Other journalists on the square, including an ABC film crew, were directed by the police to a nearby hotel on Wenceslas Square and kept there for approximately two hours. The embassy intends to protest these detentions with the MFA.

7. In a related incident, Vaclav Havel remained in a Prague hospital Sunday morning (SEPTEL). Police authorities apparently had sought to have Havel transferred back to jail, but the hospital's medical staff had refused to permit the transfer. We also have reports that besides those we already reported, additional activists were detained prior to October 28, including Martin Palous and Ladislav Lis.

8. Comment. The turnout for the October 28 demonstration was several-fold larger than that seen on August 21, and approached or exceeded the size of the week-long Palach demonstrations in January. Its size and the mood of the crowd is consistent with a trend of increasing activism (Prague 7293). Nonetheless, the crowd size in no way compares with recent demonstrations in East Germany and reflects what we believe to be the situation here—that is, that the wider population is not yet ready directly to confront the regime for change, nor has it fully shaken off the political apathy of the post-1968 period of normalization. BLACK

31 October 1989 1423Z
PRAGUE 07590

FM AMEMBASSY PRAGUE | TO SECSTATE WASHDC IMMEDIATE 1418 | FOR OIG-STATE DS/CL (YATES)

SUBJECT: POSSIBLE PROVOCATION OF SENIOR INSPECTOR,
    AMBASSADOR FERNANDO RONDON

1. Confidential—entire text.

Synopsis: The following is an account of an incident that I would suggest was a deliberate act of harassment by agents of the host government. This suspicion is reinforced by the seriousness of uncommon events which have occurred in the past 2 weeks, both to embassy personnel and members of the inspection team. In this incident, the inspector in charge of the team, Ambassador Fernando Rondon found the lens of his 35 mm camera extensively damaged. The events as they occurred in the time/date frame are as follows:

2. The senior foreign service inspector, Ambassador Fernando Rondon, a trained observer and analyst, is convinced, as is the writer, that these events are a part of deliberate harassments to this group of senior officers visiting this post.

3. On the afternoon of the 28th of October, Ambassador Black visited the inspectors at the Jalta Hotel which overlooks Wenceslas Square where anti-government demonstrations

were taking place on a Czechoslovakian holiday. The ambassador and her group watched the demonstrations from the window ledge of Inspector Perry Shankle's room. Both Shankle and Rondon photographed the ambassador watching the demonstrations during the afternoon.

4. While Foreign Service Inspector Rondon was not specifically photographing the demonstrations, but rather the ambassador and Mr. Shankle, some persons outside the room looking up may have concluded that there were photographs being taken of the demonstrators.

5. That evening after the demonstration, the two inspectors, Shankle and Rondon, went to a dinner at the Admin officer's home. Shankle took his camera with him for the social occasion and Rondon left his in his hotel room.

6. Later at 12:30 a.m. October 29th, Rondon is sleeping in his hotel room and is awakened by an unknown person who is trying unsuccessfully but not in a stealthy manner, to enter the room. The door had been locked with the double throw feature of the locking mechanism and the entry key of the occupant had been left in the interior lock keyway. The noise of the attempt awoke Rondon.

7. On the morning of October 29th at 7:00 a.m., Rondon discovered that his breakfast request which had been completed the night before and at that time hung on the exterior of the door, was on the floor of the hallway about 3 feet from the door to the room.

8. Mid-morning October 29th on an automobile trip to Bratislava, Rondon decided to take a picture and discovered that his camera lens was damaged. The camera was last known to be in perfect operating condition the afternoon before. Rondon does not recall any incident in which the camera could have been damaged while in his possession. The camera had been placed in the camera case from the afternoon before until the attempted use the following morning.

9. There is an attempt being made to have the film which was in the camera, developed on an expeditious basis to ascertain whether it had been exposed.

10. Rondon believes that the camera was damaged on purpose and was a deliberate harassment incident. **BLACK**

31 October 1989 1739Z
PRAGUE 07611

FM AMEMBASSY PRAGUE | **TO** SECSTATE WASHDC IMMEDIATE 1427 | **FOR** EUR/EEY ONLY—FOR SWIHART FROM RUSSELL

SUBJECT: OFFICIAL INFORMAL NO. 194

1. (C) October 28 reaction. As we have been reporting the human rights situation has been deteriorating for several weeks now, not just in the days leading up to October 28. That is why we went in front channel with Prague 7419 recommending a strong USG statement before the anniversary. We agree a response is in order and the HDM should be invoked on the suppression of the demonstration, even if charges are not pressed against the 150 or so demonstrators detained past the weekend. We understand the French, now in the EC presidency, have protested the GOC's action on the part of the twelve.

2. (C) October 28 cont'd. We do not agree that disinviting Fojtik is a good idea. The invitation came personally from USIA Director Gelb and we are pretty far along on planning. If we want to show our displeasure over October 28, it would be better to keep his program tailored to the IV format,[a] restrict unnecessarily high access in Washington and repeat a strong human rights message to him. Canceling it outright might produce the sort of reaction from their side which would make it more difficult to obtain what we want: a super HAWG with GOC representation from Prague in December.

3. (C) October 28 cont'd. Please let us know if you want us to come in front channel with these points. We suspect that if the idea of canceling the visit originates in USIA, it may be motivated more by a concern for the logistical complexity the visit is taking on now that Fojtik has indicated he will be accompanied by eight persons.

4. (U) To Cameron from Ed. I sent in my request for extension (Prague 7424) last week via the PER channel. I have discussed the extension with my CDO, Charles Ash, and he indicated PER most likely will oppose the request. Their rationale is that the position is an FS-04 position and PER needs the position for junior officers to get in-cone experience. I have discussed this with the front office. The ambassador is preparing to send a message to the DG, backed by the inspectors, recommending that my 04 position be upgraded to 03 and that I be extended until 7/92. Any support EUR can give me would also be appreci-

---

a. International visitor, category for a foreign visit facilitated by the State Department.

ated. Also, thanks for checking and confirming that our human rights reporting is getting to the appropriate audience in Washington.

5. (C) NED[a] visit. NED President Gershman left satisfied with his program over October 29–30. He and Ms. Diuk met a number of independents, including Jiri Hajek (Helsinki Watch), Emmanuel Mandler (Democratic Initiative), Jiri Dienstbier (*Lidove noviny*), Karel Srp (Art Forum), Vladimir Hunat (Unijazz), Ivan Gabal (Circle of Independent Intellectuals), Zdenka Gabalova (Prague-L.A. Art Exhibition), and Jana Petrova (Independent Peace Initiative). We also squeezed in official calls with two non-Communist parties, the People's Party and Socialist Party. So far there have been no adverse repercussions, but we are certain the breadth of the independent contacts was not lost on the local authorities.

6. (C) NED cont'd. In a talk with Cliff the evening before he left, Gershman said the endowment would probably expand its programs in Czechoslovakia. It would continue to use current intermediaries in London, Stockholm and West Germany to channel the funds. Gershman said that until the various initiatives were better coordinated and set some priorities for their work, NED support would be limited to two new areas. The first would be funding reproduction and printing equipment for the independent journal *Lidove noviny* so that the paper could increase its circulation. NED will also consider contributing to a "support fund" which is being created for samizdat publications. This will be used to assist the independents in paying an expected increase in fines (from KCS 500 to 10,000) to go into effect under a new press and publication law next year (see Prague 7293).

7. (C) NED cont'd. Gershman indicated less interest in supporting some of the independent cultural initiatives like Art Forum and Unijazz. He said he would work from his end in Washington to find funding for Zdenka Gabalova's Prague-L.A. Art exhibit and thought this sort of initiative could be funded through IREX[b] or similar private groups.

8. (C) NED cont'd. In our briefing with Gershman we were frank in telling him how the GOC would view his activities and the way they could potentially be used for propaganda purposes. He seems not to take this point seriously, preferring to stress the endowment's non-governmental nature. In all his appointments he emphasized the NED's independence from the USG, as much for these contacts as anyone else who might be listening. Gershman mentioned the possibility of a future NED visit. If that

---

a. National Endowment for Democracy, a U.S. government-funded nonprofit organization established in 1983 focused on democracy promotion abroad.

b. International Research and Exchanges Board, an international nonprofit working in education and development.

develops and now that Gershman has the local contacts he needs, we will recommend that he keep at arms-length from the embassy and set up his own appointments. FYI: Gershman said he was not aware that ambassador had recommended that he not come to Prague at this time.

9. (C) Harassments. In addition to the incidents cited in our OI 186 and your 188 and in DS channel, the local goons arranged or quite likely arranged the following:

—Evening of 28 October (demonstration) person(s) unknown stripped the threads from the lens of the inspection team leader's camera left in his hotel room.

—Evening of 28 October five nails driven into tire of RSO leased auto parked near embassy.

We plan to raise most recent incidents not only with MFA security/protocol contact but with political level government and Party contacts as examples of actions that undercut efforts to improve the relationship. BLACK

31 October 1989 1741Z
PRAGUE 07612

FM AMEMBASSY PRAGUE | TO SECSTATE WASHDC IMMEDIATE 1429, INFO EASTERN EUROPEAN POSTS, AMEMBASSY BRUSSELS DEPT PASS TO ERIKA SCHLAGER CSCE COMMISSION, BRUSSELS ALSO FOR USEC

SUBJECT: OCTOBER 28 DEMONSTRATION—ARREST REPORT

1. Confidential—entire text.

2. Summary. Most of those detained before and during the October 28 demonstration in Prague have been released. Vaclav Havel reportedly has been discharged from the hospital. Those detained before the demonstration most likely will not be charged, but activists anticipate most persons detained during the demonstration could be charged with "an offense against public order," a misdemeanor. The large number of those detained and disruption of phone service of members of the dissident community has made it difficult for independent groups such as VONS to gather information about the detentions. End summary.

3. At least 29 persons were detained prior to the afternoon of October 28 to prevent their participation in demonstrations. All are believed to have been released. Apparently none of those detained have been charged with violations of the criminal law. Among the

better known of those detained were Charter 77 spokespersons Vaclav Havel and Tomas Hradilek, religious activist Vaclav Maly, Brno activist Jaroslav Sabata, and Jan Chudomel of the Independent Peace Association.

4. According to a hospital source, Vaclav Havel was released from the hospital on Tuesday morning, October 31. He reportedly entered a cab at the hospital and intended to return to his Prague apartment. Our source indicated Havel's bronchial condition had cleared up, but that he still was not completely well.

5. Official sources continue to report 355 persons were detained during the October 28 demonstration in Prague. Of those detained, 206 were released within a few hours, but the remaining 149 were imprisoned for 48 hours under section 23 of the state security law. This provision of law allows Czechoslovak authorities to detain a person without pressing formal charges.

6. Most of the 149 detained for 48 hours have been released but activists fear they could be charged with "an offense against public order," which carries maximum penal ties of 20,000 crown fine (about USD 2,000) and six-month imprisonment. We, however, have been unable to confirm that any of those detained have been formally charged, and know of at least two cases where detainees were released without being told under what provision of the criminal code, if any, they would be criminally charged.

7. It has been difficult to obtain information about those detained on October 28 because many of those activists who would normally provide information to independent monitors were under arrest. A second cause of the problem has been disruption of telephone service of a number of activists, making it more difficult for the activists to communicate. Specifically, the disruption of the phone service of Petr Uhl of VONS over the weekend (service was restored on October 31) severely slowed the independent community's fact gathering capability. **BLACK**

07 November 1989 1418Z
PRAGUE 07790

FM AMEMBASSY PRAGUE | **TO** SECSTATE WASHDC 1545

SUBJECT: HANDLING ATTEMPTED SIT-INS AT U.S. EMBASSY/CONSULAR PREMISES
IN EASTERN EUROPE

REF: STATE 357095

PLEASE REPEAT STATE 320425 TO AMEMBASSY PRAGUE. **BLACK**

NOTE: STATE 320425 NO LONGER AVAILABLE IN IM.

SECRET

13 November 1989 1735Z
PRAGUE 07940

FM AMEMBASSY PRAGUE | **TO** SECSTATE WASHDC IMMEDIATE 1649 | **FOR** EUR/EEY ONLY—FOR
SWIHART FROM RUSSELL

SUBJECT: OFFICIAL INFORMAL NO. 202

(C) Fojtik visit. (State 196/4). Our latest information on the Fojtik visit is contained in
Prague 7879.

(LOU) Hornblow visit. We are doing a front channel on this very useful visit. We now look
forward to a Swihart[a] visit. As Ted discussed with Mike, ambassador hopes EUR and HA
can weigh in with FCA/JO on the Kaska extension request. As an 0-3, Ed is not a junior
officer and his extension (and upgrading the position to 0-3) will affect Prague's ability
to cover the human rights and overall political situation at a time of actual and potential
change here. Let us know if another front channel message from the ambassador appears
to be needed.

(C) HAWG agenda. In terms of agenda ideas for the HAWG we recommend that you look at
our reporting cable on Mike Hornblow's lunch with dissidents who noted four key areas:

---

a. James W. Swihart, director of the Office of Eastern European and Yugoslav
   Affairs in the Bureau of European and Canadian Affairs, U.S. Department of
   State.

—legalization of the activities of a local Helsinki Watch group as provided in the Vienna Concluding Document;
—a guaranteeing, not just liberalizing, of the right to travel;
—access to Western periodicals and information; and
—removing the political paragraphs of the penal code covering "incitement," "subversion," and "actions damaging the interests of the republic abroad," which are used to punish free expression.

(C) HAWG—cont'd. We would also recommend:
—a review of GOC plans to amend its law governing exercise of human rights: the new press law, draft law on right of assembly and petition and the new penal code. (We are working to obtain copies and more information on these drafts.)
—arbitrary abuse of the investigatory process (i.e., house searches, detentions and interrogations without cause) and the absence of any Miranda-style warning of a citizens' rights.
—the inability of a citizen to appeal bureaucratic or administrative decisions which deny one the right to travel or to get a permit to hold a demonstration. And
—discrimination, particularly in the area of education, based on political grounds.

(C) HAWG—cont'd. We can supply the Department illustrative examples on all of these areas and hope before long to also provide our own analysis of the GOC's inadequacies in these areas. We should put Michovsky[a] on notice that we will be raising specific human rights cases and requests for information and will give him such a list in sufficient time so that he can get answers from Prague.

(U) Background notes on Czechoslovakia (our OI 116). We are still passing out June 1987 background notes. Does EEY have an estimated date for publication of the revised background notes? **BLACK**

---

a. Jiří Michovský, deputy chief of mission of the Czechoslovak Embassy in Washington.

15 November 1989 1605Z
PRAGUE 08011

FM AMEMBASSY PRAGUE | **TO** SECSTATE WASHDC PRIORITY 1704 | **INFO** EASTERN EUROPEAN POSTS, AMEMBASSY BRUSSELS, AMEMBASSY STOCKHOLM, DEPT PASS TO ERIKA SCHLAGER CSCE COMMISSION, BRUSSELS FOR USEC

SUBJECT: HUMAN RIGHTS UPDATE

1. Confidential—entire text.

2. Summary. Students have formed two independent groups and plan a November 17 demonstration.[a] The Democratic Initiative has declared itself an opposition political party. A Czechoslovak branch of the Radical Party has been created. Local Socialist Party organizations continue to demonstrate an interest in a more independent role for the party. Activist Jiri Jelinek was convicted of incitement and sentenced to 12-months imprisonment. *Lidove noviny* editors and Movement for Civil Liberty activists remain in custody awaiting trial on incitement charges. Charter spokesperson Sasa Vondra has completed his two-month prison sentence and been released. A defense fund of 150,000 crowns (about USD 15,000) has been collected to pay the fines of persons fined for collecting signatures for the Nekolik vet petition. Religious activists have accused the regime of "parasitizing" the canonization of Agnes of Bohemia. A Bratislava chapter of the official human rights committee has been formed. Vaclav Havel believes the age of the "classic dissident" has ended but that Czechoslovakia has not yet entered an era in which a real political opposition with charismatic leaders exists. End summary.

Official and unofficial events to mark November 17 anniversary

3. Both official and unofficial ceremonies to commemorate the 50th anniversary of the death of Jan Opletal, a student killed by Nazis in 1939, are scheduled for November 17. The official ceremony, sponsored by the Union of Socialist Youth (SSM), is limited to a commemoration of Opletal's death, and its antifascist aspects. Czechoslovak authorities turned down a SSM request which would have allowed an official march through the

---

a. On November 17, 1989, students organized an on-campus demonstration in Prague to commemorate the fiftieth anniversary of a Nazi crackdown on universities. The students spontaneously marched toward Wenceslas Square, their numbers growing to nearly fifty thousand on the way. The police prevented them from continuing and ultimately used violence against a core of about two thousand demonstrators.

center of Prague and instead have shunted the official march to a part of town where one dissident says "no one will see it."

4. The non-official commemoration will be a march following the path originally proposed by the SSM. Brochures circulating in Prague urge that those participating in the march "bring a flower along." The non-official march will remember Opletal's death and the fight against totalitarianism. The non-official march is apparently sponsored by two recently-formed independent student groups, the Independent Student Association and the Independent Association of Youth.

5. Comment. The formation of these two independent student groups marks a new dimension in independent activity. University students especially have been politically quiescent because any unapproved political activity has the potential to lead to the expulsion of a student from his studies. The November 17 demonstration will be an early test of the new independent student organizations and their ability to interest students in independent political action.

Democratic Initiative declares itself an opposition party

6. The Democratic Initiative (DI)[a] has declared its intention to function as an opposition political party and has submitted a request to Czechoslovak authorities for official registration. Official recognition is unlikely as the DI is not part of the National Front. The DI has advised the GOC that legal obstacles preventing recognition of a political party outside the framework of the National Front are inconsistent with Principle 26 of the Vienna Concluding Document (which confirms that organizations have a positive role to play in contributing to achievement of the aims of the CSCE process). The political program of the DI is said to be based on the ideals of T.G. Masaryk and the First Republic.

Radical Party plans protest at Romanian embassy

7. The newly-formed Czechoslovak branch of the Radical Party plans a November 15 protest in front of the Romanian embassy in Prague. The protest concerns Romanian abuses of human rights. One of the party's organizers told EmbOff that he had been contacted by Radical Party representatives in Italy and had been asked to start a Czechoslovak chapter. The Czechoslovak branch at present numbers only a handful of members.

---

a. A political opposition group, later to become a party, founded by Charter 77 signatories.

Socialist Party continues search for new identity

8. Two recent activities of the Czechoslovak Socialist Party are illustrative of the ferment within the party. A November 6 meeting of the local party in Brno featured a discussion on the theme of political developments in the Warsaw Pact. The local National Front (NF) had refused the party's request that the meeting be open to the public. The party went ahead with the discussion (participants, including dissidents, received invitations to get around the NF restriction). EmbOff who was present saw about 75 persons engage in an open and free-wheeling discussion which focused on the lack of genuine reforms in Czechoslovakia. Local party leaders in a brief chat with EmbOff after the public discussion made it clear that in Brno at least Socialist Party leaders plan to break with their subservience to the Communist Party.

9. The regional committee of the Socialist Party in Prague District Ten on November 11 met to discuss Czechoslovak authorities handling of the October 28 holiday. A statement was approved condemning police action against demonstrators and urging authorities to abolish bans on public demonstrations.

Jiri Jelinek convicted of incitement

10. Jiri Jelinek, an activist from Tabor, was convicted of incitement charges on November 9 and sentenced to 12-months imprisonment. Jelinek's "crimes" included distribution of a brochure promoting a counter-demonstration on May Day and authorship of a letter criticizing the official campaign against the Nekolik vet petition.

Lidove noviny and HOS activists remain imprisoned

11. *Lidove noviny* editors Jiri Ruml and Rudolf Zeman and Movement for Civil Liberty (HOS) activists Ivan Masek and Pavel Naumann remain in detention awaiting trial on incitement charges (Prague 7293). On November 9 a small group of HOS activists attempted to deliver a petition in support of the four activists to the Ministry of Interior. After demonstrators unfurled a banner proclaiming "Stalinism is not dead" in front of the ministry, police broke up the demonstration and detained some 15 persons for questioning. All those detained were released later in the day.

Sasa Vondra released

12. Charter 77 spokesman and Nekolik vet petition organizer, Sasa Vondra has been released from two months of imprisonment. Vondra declared his imprisonment bearable, but complained that authorities confiscated letters Vondra's wife had sent to him.

Nekolik vet

13. Over 38,000 persons have thus far signed the petition. The entire membership of the Czech Union of Anti-Fascist Fighters of Prague District 4 is among recent petition signatories.

14. Some 150,000 crowns (about USD 15,000) have been collected as a fund to pay fines for individuals fined for collecting petition signatures. Petition organizers believe between 70 and 80 persons have been fined up to 5,000 crowns for collecting signatures.

Saint Agnes of Bohemia canonized

15. Official Czechoslovak media reported that 8,000 believers attended the November 12 canonization of Agnes of Bohemia. Church sources indicate that the 8,000 figure represents those who traveled through official channels, and that possibly another 2,000 persons traveled by other means to Rome. The canonization ceremony was broadcast live from St. Peter's Basilica by Czechoslovak television, but a homily by Cardinal Tomasek was not broadcast.

16. An official Czechoslovak delegation, headed by Milan Kymlicka, the Czech minister of culture, attended the canonization ceremony. Charter 77 issued a document criticizing the Communist Party for attempting to "parasitize" the canonization for its own purposes.

17. Cardinal Tomasek in a RFE interview cited St. Agnes as being an example of one who followed Christ but stood close to political and public life. The cardinal will officiate at a mass in Prague on November 25 to celebrate the canonization.

Bratislava branch of official human rights committee formed

18. A branch office of the official committee of the Czechoslovak Republic for Human Rights and Humanitarian Cooperation has been established in Bratislava. An official announcement stated the committee has received a growing number of complaints from citizens in the Slovak Republic and that a Bratislava office will allow the committee to accelerate handling of cases it has received.

Environmental protest in northern Bohemia

19. *Rudé Právo* reported that a crowd of about one thousand participated in an environmental demonstration in the north Bohemian town of Teplice on Saturday, November 11, and again on Sunday, November 12. The crowd shouted appeals for clean air. Apparently the demonstrators peacefully dispersed on Sunday when advised their assembly was illegal, but re-assembled and demonstrated again on Monday, November 13.

20. The northern Bohemian region is said to have the most polluted air in Europe. *Rudé Právo* reported that air pollution in northern Bohemia was so severe on Monday that regulations had been invoked which required power stations, heating plants, and large industrial concerns to reduce output in an effort to improve air quality.

21. Comment. The article in *Rudé Právo* and television reporting of the demonstration was remarkable in at least two respects. It forthrightly admitted the seriousness of the pollution problem in northern Bohemia and did not condemn what in the past would have been considered an antisocialist demonstration.

Vaclav Havel to receive Olof Palme Prize

22. The Swedish foreign minister will travel to Prague on November 23–24 to present the Olof Palme Prize[a] to Vaclav Havel. We understand that Havel continues to fear that if he traveled outside of Czechoslovakia that the regime might not allow him to return. As a consequence the award ceremony will be in Prague instead of Stockholm. It is not clear whether the GOC will be laying on an official program for the Swedish foreign minister.

Havel takes note of period of transition

23. Vaclav Havel in an interview in a Vienna newspaper took note of what he called an "intermediate stage" of political development in Czechoslovakia. Havel stated that totalitarian structures are beginning to crumble and that the era of "classic dissidents" had come to an end. On the other hand, the era of a real political opposition with charismatic leaders has not yet taken hold. According to Havel, the intermediate state in which Czechoslovakia now finds itself involves one in which "individual personalities embody certain symbols—as was the case with Walesa[b] in Poland." (Comment: somewhat reluctantly Havel has become just such an opposition symbol in Czechoslovakia, though in recent discussions with EmbOffs he has expressed an interest in seeing political life develop to such a stage that he could turn his human rights work over to real politicians. End comment.) **BLACK**

---

a. The Olof Palme Prize has been awarded annually since 1987 by the Olof Palme Memorial Fund for International Understanding and Common Security. The prize recognizes individuals and organizations for achievements in human rights. Havel won the prize in 1989 "for his consistent and courageous contributions to truth and democracy."

b. Lech Wałęsa, the leader of the Polish labor union Solidarity; awarded the Nobel Prize for Peace in 1983.

16 November 1989 1745Z
PRAGUE 08050

FM AMEMBASSY PRAGUE | **TO** SECSTATE WASHDC IMMEDIATE 1731 | **FOR** EUR/EEY ONLY—FOR SWIHART FROM RUSSELL

SUBJECT: OFFICIAL INFORMAL NO. 204

1. (U) East Germans in Prague (State 199/6). To Cameron from Cliff. Senator Lugar's[a] constituent seems to be confusing us with our mission in East Berlin where there was a big media flap over asylum seekers being ejected from the chancery there. During the several week period when East German refugees were camping out in Prague in the hopes of traveling to the West, the embassy received no requests for asylum. In any case, we certainly would never forcibly remove asylum seekers from the chancery and did not.

2. (U) EUR briefer on Czechoslovak travel controls (State 367436, para 10). We note that EUR's press guidance for November 15, which appears not to have been used, links obtaining a passport to possession of hard currency. That is not accurate. Passports are available without proof of possession of hard currency. But if a person wishes to travel, other than by invitation of relatives or friends, he must demonstrate possession of the necessary amount of hard currency. You may want to keep this in mind for future reference.

3. (C) For Cameron from Robert Kiene re Vacek visit.[b] Thank you for helping to obtain clearance for Vacek's trip to Washington after his entry on G-2 visa for UNGA. Let me know of any obstacles that may arise.

4. (LOU) Position candidates (State 198/1). Regarding bids on information systems manager position vice Booth, we have little knowledge of most of the candidates, but we do understand that Steve Lauderdale of Kingston and James Ditsworth of RAMC Bangkok are both quite good although Ditsworth may be "overqualified" for our relatively modest system according to our GSO and former Guangzhou systems manager Ken Yeager. All things being equal, we would lean towards Steve Lauderdale. **BLACK**

---

a. Senator Richard Lugar (R-IN).

b. Czechoslovak Deputy Foreign Minister Evžen Vacek was slated to attend the December 1989 meeting of the Humanitarian Affairs Working Group (HAWG) in Washington, D.C. Vacek would be coming from the UN General Assembly; the Czechoslovaks sought permission for Vacek to travel from New York to Washington.

PRAGUE 08117

FM AMEMBASSY PRAGUE | **TO** SECSTATE WASHDC IMMEDIATE 1780 | **FOR** EUR/EEY ONLY—FOR SWIHART FROM BOND

SUBJECT: OFFICIAL INFORMAL NO. 207

1. (C) Journalists' protest. We have delivered a diplomatic note protesting the police treatment of seven American journalists over the weekend. The text is contained in Prague 8087.[a] The ambassador has a request outstanding since this morning to meet with Foreign Minister Johanes on this matter personally. Despite the fact that the MFA's Protocol Department has confirmed that they passed this request on this morning to Johanes' secretariat, we still have no time for an appointment and it looks as if we will not have one today. Protocol tells us that Johanes is very busy with a visit by the Costa Rican foreign minister and an upcoming visit by the Belgian foreign minister. We understand the Canadians and British, who also had journalists injured, have also sent protests. We recommend, as we did in our weekend message (Prague 8082), that you call Houstecky as soon as convenient to hear our concerns.

2. (C) Update on demonstrations. As of 1630 Wenceslas Square is packed with demonstrators. An EmbOff who called in a report from the square says that there are probably 100,000 people assembled peacefully, waving flags and banners and chanting. The police are not intervening in any way but riot police, with water cannon and armored vehicles, are parked some distance from the square and are obviously ready to move if given order to do so. In view of the size of the assembly that seems unlikely.

3. (C) Demonstrations cont'd. One of the more interesting developments today was an independent news conference, that we have reported on, at which Vaclav Havel announced the creation of a "forum" of independent groups. The "forum" has the support, though not yet public, of leaders within the two non-Communist parties, the Socialist and People's Parties. The "forum" is demanding the resignation of all members of the CPCz leadership from 1968 and has said that it is ready to talk with anyone in the leadership except those people responsible for the post-1968 normalization. The official structures of

---

a. The U.S. Embassy in Czechoslovakia sent a diplomatic note to the Ministry of Foreign Affairs of Czechoslovakia protesting police brutality against American journalists during the November 17 demonstrations. This cable can be found in *Prague-Washington-Prague*, edited by Vilém Prečan (Prague: Václav Havel Library, 2004, 92–94).

power are beginning to creak and Jakes' chances of surviving this week are looking very unlikely. **BLACK**

21 November 1989 1312Z
PRAGUE 08137

FM AMEMBASSY PRAGUE | **TO** SECSTATE WASHDC IMMEDIATE 1792 | **FOR** CA/OCS/EMR, EUR/ EEY

SUBJECT: PROPOSED LANGUAGE FOR TRAVEL ADVISORY FOR CZECHOSLOVAKIA

1. Confidential—entire text.

2. In view of continuing mass demonstrations in Prague, and demonstrations now beginning in other major cities, the Department may wish to issue a travel advisory cautioning American citizens. It is the embassy's view that demonstrations are likely to cause major inconvenience rather than physical danger for travelers, but the potential for violent confrontations, such as occurred on November 17, cannot be ruled out. To the embassy's knowledge the only American citizens so far harmed are the American journalists reported in Prague 8087. A few, however, have been badly frightened.

3. Embassy proposes the following language for the Department's use:

—The Department of State wishes to advise American citizens that mass demonstrations in Prague, and to a lesser degree, other major cities in Czechoslovakia are likely to cause serious inconvenience to travelers, and that the possibility of detention or physical attack by riot police exists for those caught in the crowded downtown centers where demonstrations are occurring. American travelers are cautioned in particular to avoid Wenceslas Square and Old Town in Prague, and the university centers in Prague, Brno, Bratislava and possibly other cities. Travelers should be aware that many of the hotels frequented by foreign tourists are in these areas and that free movement to and from these hotels has been interrupted on occasion.

—American visitors to Czechoslovakia are urged to register with the American embassy in Prague. Additional up-to-date information may be obtained from the embassy, telephone: 536-641.

4. Recommend expiration date January 30. **BLACK**

21 November 1989 1717Z
PRAGUE 15045

FM AMEMBASSY PRAGUE | **TO** SECSTATE WASHDC 0000 **INFO** CSCE COLLECTIVE

SUBJECT: BELGIAN FOREIGN MINISTER CANCELS PRAGUE VISIT

REF: BRUSSELS 14807

1. Confidential—entire text.

2. MFA Political Director Hollants van Loocke confirmed to charge November 21 Belgian media reports that Foreign Minister Eyskens has canceled his November 22–24 visit to Czechoslovakia. Hollants van Loocke said that, before making his decision, Eyskens had telephoned the Belgian ambassador in Prague, who confirmed that the demonstrations place at risk Eyskens' ability to see the human rights activists and Charter 77 figures he had hoped to encounter. (FYI: Eyskens told the ambassador November 20 that he intended to see Vaclav Havel, Jiri Hajek, and Petr Uhl. End FYI.)

3. Also canceled was the visit to Prague shortly thereafter of Minister of Foreign Trade Urbain, who had planned to take with him a group of 30 Belgian businessmen.

4. Hollants van Loocke said that Eyskens will proceed with his November 28–30 visit to East Berlin. **MCCONNELL**

28 November 1989 1730Z
PRAGUE 08314

FM AMEMBASSY PRAGUE | **TO** SECSTATE WASHDC IMMEDIATE 1946, USIA WASHDC IMMEDIATE 7784 | **INFO** EASTERN EUROPEAN POSTS PRIORITY, AMEMBASSY BRUSSELS PRIORITY, USMISSION USUN NEW YORK PRIORITY, AMCONSUL MUNICH PRIORITY, BRUSSELS FOR USEC AMBASSADOR NILES, DEPARTMENT PASS TO ERIKA SCHLAGER CSCE COMMISSION, USIA— FOR EU (OLASON, PENDERGRAST, JORIA); INFO DD (KNOPP), C (PISTOR)

SUBJECT: CZECHOSLOVAK FOREIGN MINISTER GIVES CONCILIATORY RESPONSE
TO AMBASSADOR'S DEMARCHE ON NOVEMBER 17 DEMONSTRATIONS

REF: PRAGUE 8087

1. Confidential—entire text.

2. Summary and comment. In a meeting on November 28 with Foreign Minister Johanes, the ambassador followed-up on an earlier diplomatic note[a] protesting police activities to suppress November 17 demonstrations, including attacks on U.S. journalists. In line with recent changes in regime policy, Johanes was very conciliatory. He admitted that police actions had been an error and noted that they were under investigation. He stressed that the new Communist Party regime had understood the lesson of the demonstrations and was moving to speed up political and economic reform—including the goal of bringing other elements of society into the federal and state governments. He reiterated comments he had made in earlier meetings that turmoil and disruptions of order must be avoided, but the aggressive tone and unapologetic monologues that had marked these sessions was gone. Even his remarks about the need to avoid disruptions seemed to lack the past implicit threat of violent suppression if things went too far.

3. On another subject, Johanes confirmed that his deputy minister would go to Washington next month for the HAWG, though he hoped other subjects could be discussed given an improved climate of relations as a result of the recent internal political changes in Czechoslovakia. The ambassador also raised the recent expulsion of an RFE correspondent and the issue of PLO observer state status at the UN, but was told nothing new. End summary and comment.

4. Because of chaotic political events here, it took ambassador until November 28 to obtain an appointment with Foreign Minister Johanes to follow-up on the strong diplomatic note we had delivered November 20 (REFTEL), protesting brutal attacks on U.S. journalists and on the general population during peaceful November 17 demonstrations (Prague 8082). In addition to the ambassador and Johanes, the meeting included Johanes' secretariat head Zoubek, Third Department Deputy Director Rychlik and embassy EconOff Lampert. Johanes spoke partially in English and partially through an interpreter.

5. The ambassador began the meeting by re-emphasizing U.S. concern about the attacks. She noted that the journalists had clearly identified themselves as U.S. citizens and accredited reporters, but that this identification had seemed to provoke rather than deflect the police, making the attacks appear to be deliberately aimed at the journalists.

6. Johanes responded that, while he did not want to make excuses, it was difficult to distinguish between demonstrators and reporters "once these things started." On a

---

a. The diplomatic note delivered on Nov. 20 (REFTEL) is Prague 08087 and can be found in *Prague-Washington-Prague*, edited by Vilém Prečan (Prague: Václav Havel Library, 2004, 92–94).

more general level, however, he was quite conciliatory, pointing out that the government had already admitted that the actions of security forces against the demonstrators had been an error and were under investigation. He added that the government would also investigate charges of mistreatment of journalists at the demonstrations and would get us an answer.

7. Johanes went on to note that the regime was in the process of making many changes as a result of its past mistakes. He specifically said that not enough had been done in the area of democratization, and that the public "had paid back to us" for this failing. The government's number one priority was to speed up the already begun political and economic reforms. Necessary changes must not lead to confrontations or destabilization, however, and Czechoslovakia needed to avoid the disruptions of order that had plagued neighboring countries. On strikes, for example, he pointed out that Prime Minister Adamec had urged workers to "keep everything running" by avoiding work stoppages in such vital areas as electrical or coal production. Adamec was not trying to stop progress, but turmoil would have a negative impact in developments in Czechoslovakia and Europe in general.

8. According to Johanes, the government was determined on a very broad dialogue "with all those who have concern for our country." He noted that not merely was Adamec having a meeting that day with the newly-established Civic Forum, but was also conducting a dialogue with the other parties making up the National Front—parties which had revitalized themselves into independent forces. Along these lines, Johanes said Czechoslovakia appreciated the positive comments made by President Bush (sic) on new CP Secretary General Urbanek and the general developments in Czechoslovakia.

9. In terms of dialogue, Johanes contended that the new Party program already contained most of the demands voiced by the population during the recent demonstrations. The dialogue would also include the subject of how to restructure politically so that other elements could be represented in the federal and republic governments. He somewhat finessed the question of whether these elements could include the Civic Forum by noting that this was not a political party, but it did not sound like he was excluding this possibility. He also referred to the reform Communist group Obroda as a participant in this dialogue.

Other items

10. Ambassador took the opportunity of the meeting to raise several other subjects.

—HAWG: Johanes confirmed that Deputy Foreign Minister Vacek would come to Washington next month for the HAWG. He reiterated Czechoslovak hopes that Vacek could raise other issues in Washington besides human rights. Referring to the utility of his meeting in New York with Secretary Baker and the fact that some of the detainees discussed at that time had been released, Johanes thought that recent developments meant it was not too early for Vacek to participate in a review of the overall U.S.-Czechoslovak relationship. Among possible subjects was normalization of economic relations (presumably meaning granting of MFN) and Czechoslovakia's desire to rejoin the IMF. He indicated that he might give us more concrete proposals for discussion soon. The ambassador responded that she would pass on Johanes' ideas to Washington, but thought it still might be a little soon to raise some subjects.

—RFE expulsion: The ambassador noted our unhappiness that RFE correspondent Pechacek had had his visa revoked and then been detained at the border because he arrived there an hour later than instructed in the expulsion order (Munich 4656). Johanes said he knew nothing of the case. (A report on a lower level demarche will be sent SEPTEL.)

—PLO observer state status at UN: The ambassador followed up our lower level demarche (Prague 8268). Johanes again said that he was unfamiliar with the question. BLACK

01 December 1989 1523Z
PRAGUE 08415

FM AMEMBASSY PRAGUE | **TO** SECSTATE WASHDC IMMEDIATE 2029 | **INFO** EASTERN EUROPEAN POSTS IMMEDIATE, AMEMBASSY BRUSSELS IMMEDIATE, USMISSION USBERLIN IMMEDIATE, BRUSSELS FOR USEC - AMBASSADOR NILES, DEPARTMENT PASS TO ERIKA SCHLAGER CSCE COMMISSION, EAST BERLIN/USMISSION BERLIN PASS TO GEORGE ASHWORTH, ARMS CONTROL OBSERVER GROUP

SUBJECT: MEETING OF CIVIC FORUM REPRESENTATIVES AND AMERICAN SENATORS

1. Confidential—entire text.

2. Summary. A delegation of American senators visited with Civic Forum representatives in Prague on November 30. The Civic Forum representatives briefed the senatorial delegation concerning recent dramatic events, as well as presenting their views concerning future political and economic developments. The Civic Forum believes the most important support the USG can offer the Forum in the immediate future is political, in particular support which would minimize the possibility that force might be used to thwart democratic forces and processes now present. In the longer term, American assistance to

developing political parties, and educational exchanges, would be useful. The senatorial delegation also met with auxiliary bishop Antonin Liska during its visit. End summary.

3. A delegation of American senators met with representatives of the Civic Forum (CF) in Prague on November 30. The senators present were Claiborne Pell, Paul Sarbanes, John Chafee, and John Warner. Civic Forum participants were Vaclav Maly (Catholic priest and former Charter 77 spokesperson), Ivan Gabal[a] (sociologist and founder of the Circle of Independent Intelligentsia), Martin Palous (philosopher and former Charter 77 spokesperson), Pavel Bratinka (conservative dissident writer and a physicist by training), and Tomas Jezek (economist from the Forecasting Institute, Czechoslovak Academy of Science). During the one-hour session, the Civic Forum representatives reviewed the dramatic events of the past two weeks and gave their views concerning possible political and economic developments.

CF views concerning the new coalition government

4. The Civic Forum representatives indicated that Prime Minister Adamec[b] had offered the Forum a place in the coalition government now being formed, but the Adamec offer had been declined. The Civic Forum feels it is too soon to have a minister in the government and believes Communists might attempt to manipulate such a situation. The Forum representatives confirmed that they had made only two concrete demands concerning personnel in the new coalition government: (1) that the minister of interior be an uncompromised civilian who is not a member of the Communist Party; and (2) that the minister of defense be an uncompromised civilian who could be a Communist. (Note. The Civic Forum feels that the threat of a "military putsch" has passed. End note.)

5. The Civic Forum has demanded that the government being formed by Adamec reflect a plurality of interests. If the coalition government does not provide a program which guarantees free elections and fundamental freedoms (speech, association, press, religion), the CF will demand resignation of the government. The CF feels that the general strike of November 27 was a success, and that another general strike could be successfully called to pressure the government again. The CF indicated that it will give the coalition

---

a. Ivan Gabal was one of the founders of the Circle of Independent Intelligentsia, a Czechoslovak dissident organization.

b. Ladislav Adamec, Czechoslovak prime minister. He resigned on December 7, 1989. Marián Čalfa, a Slovak Communist, succeeded him with the agreement of Civic Forum and Public Against Violence. Negotiations over the following weeks led to the formation of a non-Communist government led by former dissidents and reformers.

government until the end of 1989 to demonstrate a concrete commitment to implement these reforms. The CF representatives admitted that a call for resignation of the coalition government could provoke a political crisis, but believed such a crisis would lead to political improvements.

Views on the development of democratic political structures

6. The Civic Forum representatives repeated that the Forum is not a political party. The Forum, however, does want to encourage the growth of political parties and clubs in Czechoslovakia and believes a variety of parties, with their different programs and ideas, is essential to the growth of democratic structures in Czechoslovakia. (Note. The CF representatives specifically ask that the National Endowment for Democracy support the various efforts at political party-building now going on in Czechoslovakia, although no one present could state whether such assistance would be legal. End note.)

7. The Civic Forum representatives present also stated that those participating in Forum activities represent a spectrum of views, but that a goal shared by almost everyone in the Forum is establishment of a Western-style parliamentary system for Czechoslovakia. Although the parliamentary system from the inter-war period could serve as a model for the future, the CF representatives noted that any future parliamentary system would need to take account of the current federalized system of separate Czech and Slovak republics. The CF reps noted that current events were contributing to a rise of national identity, and that citizens were beginning to think of themselves not only as Czechs or Slovaks but also as Czechoslovaks.

8. Although all the Civic Forum representatives present support free elections and parliamentary democracy, there was a division of opinion as to when elections should be held. Most of the Civic Forum representatives seemed to favor an election no later than May, and view such an "early election" as a means of maintaining the present momentum for reform. Dr. Gabal, however, indicated that he believes an election in the latter half of 1990 would allow more time for the building of political parties and other democratic structures.

9. The broad spectrum of opinion within the CF has made it necessary for the CF to avoid the use of "too strong words." In particular, the CF has not incorporated a statement into its principles concerning private property because much of the CF membership is of a socialist/leftist bent. Rather, by avoiding controversial statements and concentrating only on the common goal of establishment of a parliamentary democracy, the Civic Forum hopes to maintain a high level of support from the general population and thus maintain pressure on the GOC to undertake basic democratic reforms.

View on the economy

10. The CF representatives present seemed committed to the concept of a "market economy with good social programs." However, they indicated that many Czechoslovaks were slow to become disillusioned about socialism and that a consensus about so-called "liberal democratic principles" (such as the private ownership of the means of production), had not yet been achieved.

11. The CF spokespersons stated that the private ownership of the means of production had been abolished in its entirety in Czechoslovakia. (Comment. Exceptions exist, though in practical effect this is correct. End comment.) Many Czechoslovaks continue to associate "private ownership" with the ownership of large enterprises. Any program of restructuring the economy toward private ownership would have to take into account the large size of Czechoslovak industrial enterprises. (Comment. This may have been meant to imply that, at least initially, such enterprises would remain state-owned. End comment.) In addition, any shift to private ownership must be done in a way which does not encourage professionals to move "downward" in the economy. The specific example of Hungary was cited where opportunities in the service and agricultural sections apparently caused many professionals to leave their professions.

12. CF representatives believe that the Czechoslovak economic situation is deteriorating, and this has placed pressure upon the current leadership of the GOC to reach an accommodation with the opposition. Despite this deterioration, the CF does not believe a massive economic package, such as that fashioned for Poland, is necessary here. (Comment. In earlier contacts CF reps had rejected the idea of Western "aid" as necessary to help restructure the economy and would prefer a reliance on commercial credits, increased exports, and private investment to assist in the process. End comment.)

How the USG can help

13. Asked what the USG could do to assist those working for democracy in Czechoslovakia, those present stressed that in the short term the most important U.S. contribution would be simply to show political support in a way that would minimize the potential that force might be used to thwart the democratic forces and processes now present in Czechoslovakia.

14. The CF also asked that the USG not prematurely grant the GOC most favored nation (MFN) status. The CF expects the GOC will ask for MFN after some reforms have been undertaken. The CF asked that the USG consult with CF representatives before taking any action on this question.

15. The CF representatives also stated they are in need of an exchange of views with American experts and officials. Civic Forum reps complained they are so busy at present that they have little or no time to read the newspapers. Political and economic perspectives that American experts could offer would be useful for them. The CF asks, however, that the USG realize that the path to democracy in Czechoslovakia will be different from that in Poland and Hungary, and that the USG during any exchanges of opinion be sensitive to and sympathetic with these differences.

16. With regard to longer term assistance from the U.S., the CF reps believed it would be useful for the U.S. to provide educational opportunities in the U.S. for Czechoslovak students. Another useful program would be for American experts in a variety of fields to come to Czechoslovakia to teach in their fields of expertise.

The visit with Bishop Liska

17. The senatorial delegation also called on Antonin Liska, auxiliary bishop of the diocese of Prague, for his evaluation of the current situation. Liska termed the changes underway in Czechoslovakia a renewal of democracy and an opportunity for the more equal treatment of all Czechoslovak citizens. Liska pointed out that Cardinal Tomasek had supported the efforts of those working for democracy. Liska believes the movement toward democracy is irreversible. With regard to current Church affairs, the bishop indicated the Church had already seen a loosening of state controls, and expected such process to continue. (One CF source has indicated that the CF has demanded that the GOC enact a law guaranteeing separation of church and state.) **RUSSELL**

06 December 1989 1724Z
PRAGUE 07772

FM AMEMBASSY PRAGUE | **TO** SECSTATE WASHDC IMMEDIATE 1538 | **FOR** EUR/EEY ONLY—FOR SWIHART FROM RUSSELL

SUBJECT: OFFICIAL INFORMAL NO. 197

1. (C) Fojtik saga continued. The ambassador got through to the deputy secretary Monday afternoon our time and briefly reviewed our thinking on the Fojtik visit and why it should not be canceled. Eagleburger[a] said that he did not have background information or an

---

a. U.S. Deputy Secretary of State Lawrence Eagleburger.

action memo before him on the subject but as soon as he did he would contact the ambassador before taking a decision. The memo is probably between A/S Seitz's office and Eagleburger's. If EEY does have any additional opportunity for input, however, we think it might be useful for Eagleburger to be aware of the way French President Mitterand handled a visit to Prague last December. Faced with criticism that the timing of the visit might be inopportune (it followed last October's crackdown on demonstrations), he used his official meetings and press statements to deliver a strong human rights message which was well received within the dissident community here and the public in France. We think we could similarly turn the Fojtik visit to our advantage.

2. (LOU) Inspection. The OIG inspection went well overall, with a number of tightening up recommendations for Admin and CONS and an indication that Washington wants more economic and labor reporting (the labor unions here are, of course, a bad joke). Predictably but unfortunately, there was little receptivity to our plea for more Admin and POLEC staffing assistance. The inspectors felt they were doing us a favor by not suggesting that the Bratislava building be sold, although they felt that a USIS-only facility would be a good idea. They flew off to Budapest on Saturday.

3. (C) For Cameron from Ted. I note in my tickler file that we need to do our annual post reporting plan by November 30 based on Washington comment on our 1989 effort, due October 31. Could you please check the status of this, as embassy sections need plenty of lead-time to prepare our 1990 plan.

4. (LOU) For EEY-Cameron Munter and EUR/EX/PMO[a]-Rich Jaworski. Diplomatic and consular titles (Prague 181/ 2-4). Since we will soon be required to make some decisions on this issue, we would appreciate your thoughts or a status of your efforts to gather information on this issue as addressed ref 0-1. **BLACK**

---

a. Post Management Division, Office of the Executive Director, Bureau of European and Canadian Affairs, U.S. Department of State.

06 December 1989 0538Z

PRAGUE 08530[a]

FM AMEMBASSY PRAGUE | **TO** SECSTATE WASHDC IMMEDIATE 2139 | **INFO** USMISSION USBERLIN IMMEDIATE, USMISSION GENEVA IMMEDIATE, AMCONSUL STUTTGART IMMEDIATE, AMEMBASSY BUDAPEST IMMEDIATE, AMEMBASSY BONN IMMEDIATE, AMEMBASSY AMBBERLIN IMMEDIATE, AMEMBASSY VIENNA IMMEDIATE, PLEASE PASS TO CODEL BATEMAN

SUBJECT: CODEL BATEMAN - THREAT ASSESSMENT

1. Confidential—entire text.

2. Prague is considered a low threat post in regards to terrorist activity. Although in the past month, there have been large public demonstrations and political turmoil, it has been characterized after the first initial days, as a peaceful movement. There seems to be no immediate danger of either part of the public demonstrators nor the government elements, presently in place, to turn to repressive measures or violence. In any case, there is no animosity nor resentment directed against official Americans, embassy personnel or tourists. The Western news media in the early stages was assaulted by the government forces; this is not currently a threat.

3. However, Embassy Prague has for a long period been considered in the critical category as a hostile intelligence target which of course includes the embassy personnel and embassy visitors. CODEL should request specific threat information from Bureau of Diplomatic Security/Counterintelligence Staff and Threat Analysis Division.

4. Recently and as an addendum to this report, there have been reports in the past several months of thefts from hotel rooms, even in the top-rated hotels. There also seems to have been an unmeasured increase in street crime such as pickpockets and thefts perpetrated on targets of opportunity. **BLACK**

---

a. This text was duplicated in two additional cables sent by U.S. Embassy Prague, Prague 08600 and Prague 08565, in order to provide identical security information to other congressional delegations. Prague 08600 and Prague 08565 were addressed to CODEL Edwards and CODEL Gephardt, respectively.

PRAGUE 08850

FM AMEMBASSY PRAGUE | **TO** SECSTATE WASHDC IMMEDIATE 2403 | **INFO** EASTERN EUROPEAN POSTS PRIORITY, AMEMBASSY BRUSSELS PRIORITY, BRUSSELS FOR USEC— AMBASSADOR NILES, DEPT PASS TO ERIKA SCHLAGER CSCE COMMISSION

SUBJECT: CPCZ AND CIVIC FORUM CLASH OVER TIMING OF PRESIDENTIAL ELECTION

REF: (A) PRAGUE 8700 (B) PRAGUE 8788

1. Confidential—entire text.

2. Summary. The idea of direct election of a new Czechoslovak president now seems dead. A president should be elected by the Federal Assembly as stipulated in the constitution. The Communists and two of the other legal parties are proposing, however, that this vote be delayed until late January. The Civic Forum sees this tactic as an attempt to deprive Vaclav Havel of the presidency. Havel has made a nationwide speech proposing himself as president for only a transitional period until free Federal Assembly elections can be held in mid-1990. Havel has apparently come to an agreement with Alexander Dubcek whereby this main Slovak candidate will stand down in favor of Havel. The Civic Forum is calling for a public, televised election of the president and a mass rally in favor of Havel's candidacy when the assembly meets on December 19. The Communists and other parties in parliament claim these tactics are unconstitutional. It is unclear whether Communists and others will put their proposal on delaying the election to a vote when the assembly meets. End summary.

3. Despite reports at the end of last week to the contrary (ref b), the issue of the election of a new Czechoslovak president has not been settled. All sides now appear to have dropped the idea of conducting a direct popular election as first proposed by the Federal Assembly's Communist deputies (ref a). Such a measure would have required several amendments to the constitution and radically changed the president's relationship to the assembly. Even the Communists eventually came around to the impracticality of this proposal.

4. But if all are now agreed on the method of election (i.e., by the Federal Assembly), the question of timing is still open. The Communists and two of the other legal parties (Socialist and People's) are now calling for a delay in the election. This would be achieved by a change in the constitution to allow re-appointment of a new president within 40 days (not 14 as currently provided). This proposal is to be raised in the assembly when it meets again on Tuesday, December 19.

5. Presumably the Communists back the proposal because it may offer them a breathing space to put their house in order after their extraordinary Party congress later this week (December 20–21). The congress could produce a consensus on a CPCz presidential candidate, probably former Prime Minister Adamec. The Socialists and People's Parties are supporting the proposal for their own reasons. They have suggested using the extra time to hold by-elections to replace discredited members of the assembly. These by-elections might conceivably enlarge their current parliamentary representation.

6. The Civic Forum has reverted to its original position that a presidential election be held within 14 days. This would mean a new president before Christmas. On Saturday, December 16, Vaclav Havel appeared on nationwide television to announce his candidacy for president, but with certain qualifications. Havel said he wanted to serve only an interim term until free Federal Assembly elections could be held this summer. At that time, a truly representative assembly could elect a president with a full five-year term. He said he did not want to run for the office against Alexander Dubcek and that certain "dark forces" were trying to drive a wedge between himself and Dubcek, and by implication between Czechs and Slovaks. Havel also said he would only serve as president if Dubcek was at his side in a senior government position.

7. Civic Forum contacts tell us that Havel and Dubcek have now reached an agreement. According to these reports Dubcek will stand down from the presidency in favor of Havel. He will accept instead the position of chairman of the Federal Assembly. Some Western media are reporting that Dubcek has denied any such deal exists.

8. The Civic Forum has intensified its call for an early election by demanding that a public and televised vote be held when the assembly next meets on December 19. The Forum may also try to stage a mass demonstration outside the assembly building on that day to pressure the deputies to vote immediately on a president and not to accept the "40-day delay."

9. The Communists are calling these Civic Forum demands unconstitutional. A legal expert appearing on a television talk show Sunday evening claimed that the assembly's election had to be by secret ballot. He also said that a mass assembly to influence the vote was a violation of the constitutional immunity deputies have from coercion.

10. Most observers agree that Havel's chances of election remain good, particularly if Dubcek is out of the way, even if the Forum may not be able to force a vote before Christmas. We understand roundtable discussions involving the Communists, Civic Forum and other parties on this issue will be held tonight. Communist stalling is clearly linked

to the importance of the Czechoslovak presidency which is more than a symbolic office. The president will have great influence over the progress and course of political reform in the coming months. Under the constitution, the president is commander and chief; he selects a person to form a new government; he approves a number of diplomatic and academic appointments; and he has the power to grant pardons and amnesties. The latter could be particularly important if the current investigations of Communist officials widen to include claims of high level CPCz corruption. In short, even for a transitional period the president could play a key role. The Communists will do everything they can to prevent Havel winning it. **BLACK**

19 December 1989 1730Z
PRAGUE 08891

FM AMEMBASSY PRAGUE | **TO** SECSTATE WASHDC IMMEDIATE 2444 | **FOR** EUR/EEY ONLY—FOR SWIHART FROM RUSSELL

SUBJECT: OFFICIAL INFORMAL NO. 225

1. (C) CODEL Edwards. Congressman Edwards[a] and his wife, Edith Wilke, were very happy with their December 16–19 visit to Prague. They had an excellent schedule. We will be reporting front channel on the visit, but in broad outline they had a good exchange with about 70 journalism students at Charles University on Sunday, followed by participation in a 20 kilometer march/demonstration. On Monday, after an embassy briefing, they met with a pair of "reform" Communists (Jaromir Sedlak and Rudolf Hegenbart) and a self-described "old Communist" (former ambassador to the U.S. Dusan Spacil). The reformers talked about a need to purge the Party, while Spacil blamed the regime's "mistakes" of the last 40 years on political leaders who had "warped" genuine Communism in order to get personal power—and then used the power "stupidly." They also met with Civic Forum representatives and the new minister of labor, Petr Miller. At several points during the visit, Edwards expressed support for restoring MFN to Czechoslovakia and relaxing or removing CoCom restrictions—of particular interest to him since he represents "Silicon Valley" in California. He also appeared favorable to the idea of reopening the consulate in Bratislava and opening a cultural center in Prague.

---

a. Rep. William Donlon "Don" Edwards (D-CA).

2. (LOU) Arnulf I. Simmon, head of Micro Processing Technologies, Inc., came to the embassy to speak with Janet.[a] He is a U.S. citizen of Czechoslovak origin and he claimed to have close contacts in the Civic Forum and the new government. He showed Janet a document, valid until December 31, 1989, purporting to be from Civic Forum and authorizing him to provide them information on office equipment systems. Civic Forum has raised with us its interest in acquiring office and telecommunications equipment to improve its links around the country. He also said he had contacted AT&T and planned to lead a delegation from AT&T to Czechoslovakia in January to negotiate sales of equipment. But before he arranges such a visit he wanted assurances that there would not be any CoCom problems. Janet advised him to contact the Departments of State and Commerce in Washington, so he may soon be stopping by. Please pass this information to Shelley Galbraith and the Office of Technology Assessment at Commerce.

3. (LOU) DG[b] visit. For Mike from Ted. Visit went well and DG was supportive on Kaska extension. He will pursue the matter in Washington, as well as the issue of continued access by our international school U.S. teachers[c] to our embassy commissary. The issue of onward assignments for Cliff and Steve was discussed in encouraging fashion. Thanks for your support at that end and for keeping us informed. **BLACK**

---

a. Janet G. Speck, commercial section officer, U.S. Embassy Prague.

b. Director general of the U.S. Foreign Service.

c. U.S. embassies typically have a commissary providing diplomats with duty-free access to food and other goods. In some cases where these goods are not easily accessible on the local market, access to the commissary is also provided to U.S. teachers at international schools.

29 December 1989 1618Z

PRAGUE 09118[a]

FM AMEMBASSY PRAGUE | **TO** SECSTATE WASHDC IMMEDIATE 2615 **INFO** EASTERN EUROPEAN POSTS IMMEDIATE

SUBJECT: CODEL LA FALCE

1. Confidential—entire text.

2. Prague remains a low threat in relation to international terrorist activity. Although in the past two months there have been large public demonstrations against the previous repressive government which for 40 years dominated the political scene in Czechoslovakia, it has been characterized as a continuing peaceful revolution. After the first two days of the public demonstrations in November when a number of Czechoslovak citizens and members of the foreign media were assaulted by security forces, there has been no further violence either on the part of the demonstrators nor the government police units. There is no projection of further violence. In any case there has not been any animosity or resentment against official Americans, Western tourists nor the international news media after those first days.

3. The embassy in Prague has for a long period been considered within the critical category as a hostile intelligence target which of course includes the embassy personnel and embassy visitors. Embassy officers are observing and assessing with interest some relatively recent incidents involving the typical old-style harassments against American staff. At this point it is difficult to make a positive assessment as to the future of harassments against American staff. While the embassy looks forward with optimism, there is current evidence that optimism may be replaced or in any event premature. There is no reason to believe that hotel rooms are not continuing to be monitored by electronic devices nor will visiting official personnel be exempt from baggage searches while it is unattended in hotel rooms. It must be assumed, at least during this immediate period, that this Eastern European phenomenon[b] is still intact.

---

a. This text was duplicated in three additional cables sent by U.S. Embassy Prague, Prague 09119, Prague 09120, and Prague 09121, in order to provide identical security information to other delegations. Prague 09119, Prague 09120, and Prague 09121 were addressed to Staffdel (staff delegation) Tucker, CODEL Torrecelli, and CODEL Solarz, respectively.

b. Intelligence officers of the notorious *Státní bezpečnost* (StB) regularly bugged rooms in hotels frequented by foreign diplomats. The Cold War–era surveillance technology allowed spies to listen in on phone calls and conversations between guests.

4. Moreover, since the American intervention in Panama,[a] the embassy has had several relatively minor demonstrations instigated by Latin American persons and held directly in the front entrance to the chancery. As of this writing, they are diminishing in size and fervor. However, further demonstrations by the Latin student element in Prague is expected but it is not anticipated that these demonstrations will include any numbers of Czechoslovak nationals nor other large sympathetic, aggressive groups. Some other Third World students have been identified with the Latin American demonstrators.

5. Finally as an addendum to this report there have been continuing incidents in the past months of thefts from hotel rooms, even in the top-rated hotels. This has been serious since in several cases persons have entered the room while the occupant has been sleeping. Also there has been an unmeasured increase in street crimes such as pick pockets, thefts and even some assaults including a rape. These crimes have been perpetrated against targets of opportunity rather than selected national groups or foreigners.

6. CODEL should request specific threat information from bureau of Diplomatic Security/ Counterintelligence Staff and Threat Analysis Division. **BLACK**

---

a. On December 20, 1989, U.S. forces invaded Panama, ousting military dictator Manuel Noriega following his indictment in the United States on charges of drug trafficking.

AFTERWORD

The Aftermath of Revolution

U.S. Support for Czech and Slovak
Liberal Democracy, 1989–Present

KELSEY LANDAU | NORMAN EISEN | MIKULÁŠ PEŠTA

The years following the events of 1989 were eventful for Czechoslovakia and its successors, the Czech Republic and Slovakia, which were created on January 1, 1993, as part of the "Velvet Divorce." Starting in 1990, American aid to Czechoslovakia assisted with the transition to a liberal democracy.[1] Assistance through organizations such as the United States Agency for International Development (USAID) included funding, training, and technical support for political, business, military, and civil society institutions. By 2000, the Czech Republic and Slovakia "graduated" from aid assistance by transitioning to liberal democratic systems and their relationship with the United States shifted to a different footing.

We argue here that the successes and failures of American assistance are reflected in the complex realities of liberal democracy in both the Czech Republic and Slovakia of today, realities that endure in the face of significant challenges in both countries. The two nations are on the one hand weighed down by illiberal trends and persistent corruption that we trace in part to the rapid economic privatization the United States prioritized and supported in the 1990s. On the other hand, the strong civil societies and independent media that the United States has assisted in both nations today help fight corruption and otherwise promote democratic governance.

U.S. DEMOCRACY ASSISTANCE POST-1989

The Czechoslovak Context

The new Czechoslovak democracy led by ex-dissident President Václav Havel proved energetic from the start, gratifying its observers in U.S. Embassy Prague. As the diplomats reported to Washington shortly before Havel's inauguration, Ambassador Shirley Temple Black expressed in a cable to the U.S. Department of State that his election "symbolically confirms in the minds of average Czechs and Slovaks that the democratic process here is irreversible and free elections guaranteed. The next phase of this revolution will be to institutionalize political reforms."[2] Political parties formed and consolidated rapidly despite Havel's antipathy to them (his feelings in part rooted in the divisions they fostered),[3] and preparations for the first free election in the summer of 1990 proceeded briskly.

The two leading Velvet Revolution civil society umbrella organizations—the Civic Forum (OF) in the Czech Republic and the Public Against Violence (VPN) in Slovakia—dominated the June election and united disparate political currents. In addition, the Social Democratic Party re-emerged after having been subsumed under the former regime, and the Czechoslovak People's Party separated from the Communist-controlled National Front. The Communist Party of Czechoslovakia was allowed to continue to exist (unusual for the former Soviet Bloc) but delivered poor results.[4] The next election in 1992 featured a full complement of political parties—the ballot so transformed that the last remnants of the OF, which had faced internal divisions, did not even get into parliament.[5]

Newly democratic post-November Czechoslovakia oriented itself toward the West, a consensus shared across the political spectrum from conservatives to liberals to social democrats; only the Communists opposed this alignment. Although Czechoslovaks debated a wide array of political scenarios at the beginning of the 1990s—including neutrality, preservation of the alliance with the Soviets, and dissolution of both the Warsaw Pact and (more improbably) the North Atlantic Treaty Organization (NATO)—integration into NATO and the European Economic Community soon emerged as the most popular option.[6]

In terms of economics, a variety of Western ideologies flourished in the new Czechoslovakia, not the least of which was the neoliberalism of Reaganomics and Thatcherism. Neoliberalism held that "economic development could be achieved by relying on the power of market forces and private property, unleashed by a radical curtailment of the state."[7] The neoliberal approach, which was in its global heyday in the 1980s and 1990s, found devout admirers in Czechoslovakia after 1989. One notable supporter of the approach was Finance Minister (and later Prime Minister of the Czech Republic) Václav Klaus. These and other ideas from the United States and the United Kingdom loomed large. As historian Martin Myant puts it, "the dominant trend in the making of the economic policy was the effort to deny the relevance of any other economic thinking than the 'orthodox' one that developed in the USA."[8] The "Anglo-Saxon way" was not the only option for urgently needed economic transformation; other voices promoted the Scandinavian social democratic model and Western European–style highly-regulated capitalism. But the strong free-market approach won the day.[9]

Influenced by the Washington Consensus, Czechoslovakia transitioned to a market economy through large-scale privatizations and deregulations in the form of "shock therapy."[10] Officials pursued rapid economic transformation based on three key components: macroeconomic stabilization, market liberalization, and privatization.[11] Economists understood well that the first two components entailed "raising interest rates, limiting monetary emissions, freeing prices, and opening up trade," which stabilized and liberalized economies.[12] However, the mass attempt at privatizing an entire economy was uncharted terrain. Czechoslovakia, and its successor governments, relied on three interlocking policies to transfer the nationalized economy into the hands of private citizens: auctioning off state-owned enterprises (SOEs), implementing a mass voucher program, and offering restitution (returning nationalized property to original owners or their heirs).[13]

A U.S. Focus on Free Markets

American aid to Czechoslovakia emphasized supporting economic transformation over direct funding for other democracy mechanisms.[14] In the principal U.S. assistance program, 75 percent of aid focused on economic restructuring, while only 5 percent directly promoted democratic institutions in the Czech part of the country (then to the Czech Republic) from 1990 to 1996. In Slovakia, approximately 66 percent of aid focused on economic restructuring and 9 percent on strengthening democratic institutions.[15] For a more detailed breakdown, see figures 1 and 2.

The structure of U.S. funding reflected a widespread viewpoint in both the scholarly community and the political realm that free markets were necessary for democratization.[16] According to historian Hal Brands, as "America's favored liberal model was racing forward economically as well as po-

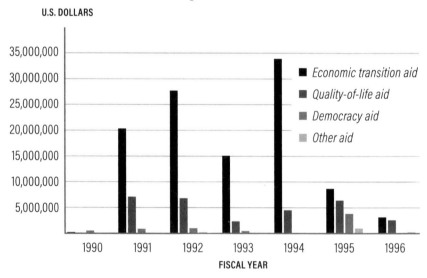

FIGURE 1. SEED Act Obligations to Czechoslovakia/ Czech Republic, 1990–1996

litically" around the world, American policymakers came to believe "that the global order was remaking itself to reflect America's core preferences, and that energetic engagement was integral to keeping the process going."[17] Both Republican and Democratic policymakers adopted the idea that capitalism was a precondition for democracy, and pursued the two together to consolidate America's leading role in the international system. A week after the Soviet Union officially dissolved, President George H. W. Bush remarked that, "Despite a potential for instability and chaos, these events clearly serve our national interest . . . [W]e will only succeed in this interconnected world by continuing to lead the fight for free people and free and fair trade," as "a free and prosperous global economy is essential for America's prosperity—that means jobs and economic growth right here at home."[18] By connecting the need to build and integrate the economies of the former Soviet Bloc and

FIGURE 2. SEED Act Aid Obligations to Czechoslovakia/ Slovak Republic, 1990–1998

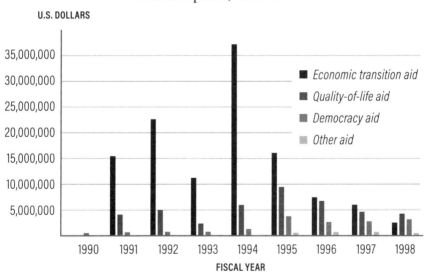

U.S. DOLLARS

- Economic transition aid
- Quality-of-life aid
- Democracy aid
- Other aid

FISCAL YEAR

Note: "Quality of life" aid includes emergency and humanitarian assistance for housing, the environment, the social safety net, and healthcare. "Other" aid primarily composes auditing and evaluation costs. Since aid was given separately to both the Czech and Slovak parts of Czechoslovakia even when the country was unified, the Velvet Divorce caused a minimal amount of disruption to American aid programs. Numbers are not adjusted for inflation.

the creation of American jobs, Bush both emphasized his belief in a liberal world order driven by American ideals and justified policies intended to help America's former enemies. James Baker, Bush's secretary of state, was even more explicit: "By furthering the development and integration of market economies within the international system, we strengthen the collective force of those that share our principles."[19]

Bush's Democratic successor, President Bill Clinton, continued the promotion of economic and political transformation. As historian Rasmus Sinding Søndergaard has argued, the Clinton administration "made a direct connection between the advance of democratic government abroad and American national security." The administration worked to achieve this advance by "integrat[ing] democracies into foreign markets" and "help[ing to] strengthen civil society, market institutions, and good governance."[20]

U.S. support for Czechoslovak consolidation of democracy through economic transformation took several forms.[21] The most notable was the Support for Eastern European Democracy (SEED) Act of 1989, which over time provided the Czech Republic with approximately $170 million and Slovakia with approximately $150 million in assistance. Through the SEED Act, the United States helped transfer state-owned assets to the private sector, establish a policy framework for private-sector development, and create a competitive financial sector.[22] Some support came through monetary assistance in the technical planning of privatization; the United States provided $7 million for technical assistance through fiscal year 1992 and $4 million more to "support large-scale privatization."[23]

In April 1991, the SEED Act created the Czech and Slovak-American Enterprise Fund (CSAEF) for Czechoslovakia. The goal of CSAEF was to encourage private corporations to make loans to or invest in small- and medium-size businesses in which other financial institutions were "reluctant to invest."[24] An initial $63.9 million of investment capital was approved for this enterprise fund.[25] Two years later, following the Velvet Divorce, the CSAEF created two country-specific funds—the Czech-American Enterprise Fund (CAEF) and the Slovak-American Enterprise Fund (SAEF), which worked under separate management teams but shared a common board of directors.[26] These two funds took different courses following their separation, with the SAEF finding greater success than its Czech counterpart, the CAEF. However, neither were hugely successful at bolstering sustained development due to incurred costs and a focus on high-risk investments.[27]

Together, the CSAEF, the CAEF, and the SAEF invested in fifty-one small business loans totaling $4.5 million between 1996 and 2008. They also offered technical assistance and training programs for small businesses.[28] In the beginning, this worked particularly well for Slovakia, including because it filled a void for small business loans. As a result, the SAEF program satisfied a need for the economy that was otherwise not met. In cooperation with local banks, SAEF trained both bank staff and small business borrowers, promoted good accounting practices, and advised on managing and growing small businesses.[29]

Meanwhile, the board of directors experienced considerable management turnover, both at the local level and with staffers from the United States, which aggravated investment challenges in those early years. Doubts emerged about the level of competence of some of the board members and of the American managers based in the country. The split of the Czech and Slovak components of the fund also caused problems—there was a string of poorly-performing investments from 1992 to 1996 and dishonesty and fraud in several cases, which led to subsequent prolonged court activity.[30]

Most critically, both funds, but especially the CAEF, experienced substantial losses with their investments in small start-ups and other high-risk sectors.[31] By 1996, a serious crisis had emerged. Their losses led the board and USAID to decide to terminate activity in the Czech Republic and to devote the remaining grant money exclusively to Slovakia. They also decided to sell the CAEF portfolio at a discount, liquidate the investment portfolios of SAEF, and then rebuild the SAEF investment portfolio in Slovakia.[32]

Another, more successful example of how the United States provided assistance toward economic transformation was the Center for International Private Enterprise (CIPE), an arm of the U.S. government–funded National Endowment for Democracy (NED). As its then mission statement declared, CIPE aimed to "promote principles and policies of private enterprise which strengthen democratic development."[33] CIPE provided financial support to the Association of Czechoslovak Entrepreneurs (ACE), an organization established in December 1989 to create a strong business environment. One of ACE's CIPE-supported programs worked to offer intensive training courses for aspiring Czechoslovak entrepreneurs, and another took the form of a legislative advisory service that worked to promote business-friendly policies at the governmental level.[34]

Additional support to the Czech Republic and Slovakia came in the form of expert advice from American economists and consulting firms. Throughout the 1990s, for example, hundreds of privatization plans were reviewed by a team of bankers, accountants, and lawyers. Through 1994, the team advised more than 120 transactions valued at about $2 billion.[35] In other instances, the Czech and Slovak governments relied on the United States for help with regulatory policy. For example, in 1996, the chairman of the Prague Stock Exchange turned to USAID for assistance in drafting an "SEC [Securities and Exchange Commission]-type regulatory body for the Czech capital markets."[36]

Another form of assistance—and one that bridged the divide between economic and democracy aid—came not from experts, but from ordinary Americans. Post–Cold War economic and democracy programs were implemented by the Peace Corps, an independent agency of the U.S. government that sends American volunteers to serve in interested countries for two years. Representative programs include teaching English, assisting business owners, overseeing environmental projects, and establishing libraries.[37] As an organization that, since its founding, has served in part to further both international development goals and American foreign policy goals in host countries—and that has widespread positive name recognition—the Peace Corps was well equipped to take advantage of the fall of the Iron Curtain and begin sending volunteers to Czechoslovakia in 1990.[38]

Testifying before Congress in 1990, Sargent Shriver, the agency's first director and by then an elder statesman of the Peace Corps, called for the Peace Corps to stand at the vanguard of a new foreign policy dedicated to "mak[ing] peace preparedness as much as military preparedness the most important need in our Nation today and in the world."[39] Observing how poorly prepared the United States was for the Soviet Union's collapse, Shriver noted that "no one calls for $100 million to extend the Peace Corps behind the Iron Curtain," and he asked why not, given that "the nations of Central Europe need teachers, not only of English, but of political science, accounting, economics, history, business organization, yes, even advertising, to help them start an open economy."[40] Shriver proposed that the Peace Corps could fill this need and that "nothing would surpass an offer by the U.S.A. to send 10,000 Peace Corps volunteers to Central Europe and to the U.S.S.R. in the 1990s. Make that offer and scores of thousands in the U.S.A. would volunteer—65,000 persons in the U.S.A. volunteered for Peace Corps service in the first few months after Kennedy called for their help in the Third World. Just as many, maybe more, would volunteer to help Central Europe and the citizens of the U.S.S.R."[41] Shriver was proposing that the Peace Corps play a central role in helping Central Europe transition to a capitalist and democratic system. However, his vision was never considered as a serious policy proposal.

In the end, Peace Corps volunteers did enter Czechoslovakia and other Central and Eastern European countries, but in numbers far from those that Shriver had envisioned. From 1990 to 1997, the Peace Corps sent at least 223 volunteers to the Czech Republic, and from 1990 to 2002 more than 320 volunteers were sent to Slovakia.[42] Their accomplishments were, without a doubt, substantive and tangible—albeit a far cry from Shriver's call for 10,000 volunteers flooding behind the Iron Curtain.

U.S. Democracy Aid

Funding allocated to democracy aid constituted just 4.7 percent of total SEED assistance to the Czech Republic and 8.8 percent of funding to Slovakia.[43] The funding largely followed three main categories, as described by Thomas Carothers, a leading authority on democracy aid assistance: (1) support for institutions fundamental to democratic contestation, notably including the promotion of free and fair elections and the formation of political parties; (2) support for and the reform of "key state institutions, especially those checking the power of centralized executives, such as parliaments, judiciaries, and local governments"; and, above all, (3) support for civil society.[44] It was on this latter category that the United States focused the most, and, indeed, civil society remains a key component of Czech and Slovak democracy to this day.[45]

Below, we review American democracy aid programs in both the Czech Republic and Slovakia, tracing this support through the categories identified by Carothers as well as through a fourth category, that of military reform. While not exhaustive, this list provides a representative overview of American democracy aid programs throughout the 1990s.[46]

Support for Institutions of Democratic Contestation   Controversy ensued immediately upon the commencement of American aid to support democratic contestation. In the 1990 Czechoslovak election, the NED provided nine grants totaling $842,485 to the OF, and provided further support to the VPN.[47] Support included office equipment, seminars on party organization and civic engagement, assistance with drafting election laws, and a team of international election observers.[48] However, representatives from other Czechoslovak parties quickly questioned why American aid had gone to only two of twenty-three parties competing in the elections, with one calling it an "injustice."[49] The NED's president pointed out that the grants were not intended for campaign purposes, and that, at the time they were approved, neither OF nor VPN had been political parties. Nevertheless, the United States thereafter offered aid irrespective of party and publicly supported "both Prime Minister Klaus and President Havel, two political personalities with distinctly different sensibilities, approaches, and agendas."[50]

In other efforts that year, U.S. government–funded nonprofit organizations trained a wider array of party representatives. For example, at least 150 representatives of 24 different political groups attended workshops on campaigning and party formation organized by the National Democratic Institute (NDI) and National Republican Institute for International Affairs (NRIIA; later International Republic Institute, or IRI).[51] After the Czechoslovak parliamentary elections—deemed by an NDI observer delegation as "free and fair"—American support for political contestation institutions soon dwindled away.[52]

Strengthening Public Governance Institutions   American democracy aid to Czechoslovakia and its successor states in this second area was more wide-ranging and included support for the national parliament, the judicial system, and local governments. These initiatives, however, focused on strengthening capacity via mechanisms like technical training and providing office equipment, rather than on wholesale institutional reform.

U.S. assistance focused on the Czechoslovak parliament and judiciary systems. In April 1990, the U.S. House of Representatives created the Speaker's Special Task Force on the Development of Parliamentary Institutions in Eastern Europe, which received at least $15 million in SEED funds (spread across seven countries).[53] The Congressional Research Service (CRS), under the direction of a bipartisan group of members of Congress, provided technical assistance to legislators. This assistance included office equipment, books and CD-ROMs, and training for legislators and staff.[54] Under this initiative, by 1992 the Czechoslovak Federal Assembly had received approximately $2.1 million in technical and equipment assistance.[55]

With the goal of strengthening democratic governance at the local level, USAID embarked on a series of initiatives in Czechoslovakia and both successor states that included training city officials and coordinating programs run by the National League of Cities, the Urban Institute, the U.S. Information Agency, the International City/County Management Association (ICMA), and the Meridian International Center. One program sent Czech mayors and deputy mayors on a five-week study tour of American cities and included a three-day training seminar on urban management.[56] In addition, the National League of Cities and ICMA provided technical assistance to the Union of Towns and Communities (UTC) during a tour of city associations in Eastern Europe. This tour enabled UTC to facilitate greater communication and collaboration between local officials.[57] In Slovakia, American advisors similarly worked with "city mayors and managers to improve public administration and financial management," and the American Bar Association/Central and East European Law Initiative (ABA/CEELI) provided technical legal assistance to organizations like a "judges' association" that promoted an "independent judiciary and working to develop a new judicial code."[58]

USAID-funded advisors also worked directly at the local level to train Czech municipal officials on improving their management and accounting practices and to train Slovak officials on enhancing their technical, managerial, and interpersonal skills.[59] In the Czech Republic, USAID funding led to the establishment of municipal credit courses for bank staff that reached more than 700 public administrators, municipal managers, and infrastructure professionals.[60] Additionally, the USAID-funded Housing Guaranty municipal finance program established a credit system designed to strengthen city governments and facilitate urban infrastructure development. Under the program, the Czech Municipal Finance Company borrowed up to $60 million to finance over 260 municipal infrastructure projects benefiting more than 70,000 households.[61] The program led to the development of a robust market-driven municipal credit market.[62] In Slovakia, meanwhile, the USAID-funded Local Self-Government Program promoted decentralization, democratic pluralism, and transparent management of municipal affairs.[63]

Support for Civil Society and Independent Media[64]   From the Velvet Revolution onward, American support for Czechoslovak civil society groups formed a key part of aid initiatives. In his Communist-era essay "The Power of the Powerless," Havel emphasized the idea of civil society as a structure parallel to traditional political organizations:

> They would be structures not in the sense of organizations or institutions, but like a community. Their authority certainly cannot be based on long-empty traditions, like the tradition of mass political parties, but rather on how, in concrete terms, they enter into a given situation. Rather than a strategic agglomeration of formalized organizations, it is better to have organizations springing up *ad hoc*, infused with enthusiasm for a particular purpose and disappearing when that purpose has been achieved. The leaders' authority ought to derive from their personalities and be personally tested in their particular surroundings, and not from their position in any *nomenklatura*.[65]

The *ad hoc*, context-responsive organization of civil society had worked to topple the Communist regime in 1989 and thereafter remained a powerful force supported by American democracy aid.[66] U.S. officials and leading academics (such as Robert Putnam, Francis Fukuyama, and Larry Diamond) believed that civil society together with "empowered ordinary citizens and grassroots social movements working collectively from below" would form "a parallel democratic polis to that which represented the official Communist totalitarian system and party-state."[67] In short, civil society could act as the antithesis of Communist statism.[68] As scholars Paula Newberg and Thomas Carothers argue, this focus on civil society tended to equate—somewhat contradictorily to Havel's vision of *ad hoc* gatherings of like-minded individuals—"civil society with nongovernmental organizations (NGOs), which provide an avenue for channeling funds without expanding the power of the state."[69] Thus, officials believed that NGOs could act as another check and balance on the concentration of official power.

In the Czech lands, USAID granted $1.5 million to the Foundation for a Civil Society to administer a two-year program dubbed the Democracy Network (DemNet) Program.[70] With an eye toward building a strong civil society, DemNet aimed to make the public aware of the importance of NGOs and stimulate philanthropic and corporate interest in funding them. DemNet's Czech-focused initiatives included the Small Grants Program, which provided $440,000 in grant money to NGOs to help them improve internal capacity and expand operations; 28 percent of these grant awardees focused explicitly on democracy building.[71] The Third Sector Image Campaign aimed to improve the image of NGOs in order to ensure lasting interest, support, and funding; under that umbrella, DemNet's journalism programs placed twenty-four students in journalism internships with NGOs, supported civil society lectures at two universities, and created a writing contest for the best student article on the NGO sector.[72] DemNet also sponsored a public relations agency to run a campaign promoting the Third Sector, and implemented a regional initiative called the Legal Framework Program, which worked to improve the legal environment for NGOs. USAID further provided funding to the International Center for Nonprofit Law to facilitate the creation and implementation of NGO laws in the Czech Republic. A law clarifying NGO regulations and recognizing NGOs as private providers of services was drafted (and passed) with SEED assistance.[73] The law proved important to establishing an environment favorable to a robust sector of interest groups and NGOs.[74]

In Slovakia, DemNet similarly worked to strengthen NGOs. NDI implemented a "train-the-trainers" program in community organizing and a Professional Media Program that worked to "strengthen independent media."[75] The program did so by improving the media's "technical and professional capabilities; assisting with the development of media associations, especially their ability to advocate and represent the interests of their sector; and strengthening the legal and regulatory environment in which independent media operate."[76] The program also supported the efforts of a Slovak journalism trade union to monitor media coverage of Slovakia's parliamentary election as well as coverage of local elections.[77] In the run-up to the 1998 parliamentary election, an NGO voter education and get-out-the-vote initiative called the OK '98 Civic Campaign helped generate high voter turnout. OK '98 was organized by a coalition of Slovak NGOs, many of which received DemNet funding. DemNet further provided approximately $80,000 in grants directly to Slovak NGOs to conduct local election activities.[78]

Other examples of support for civil society abound. CIVITAS (which became CIVITAS International in 1997), a group funded by the U.S. government, initiated civic education initiatives throughout Central and Eastern Europe during the 1990s to spread the ideas and values of democratic citizenship. Initiatives included teacher exchange programs, conferences, collaborative efforts to create civic education school curricula, and research on the effects of civic education.[79] The United States also supported independent media. In the Czech Republic, the United States Information Service provided technical support and training for journalists, and the NED provided direct grants to independent Czech journals and newspapers.[80] NED also financially supported the Transatlantic Dialogue on European Broadcasting, which ran a consulting program to help governments and media organizations in Central Europe establish strong broadcasting sectors. In 1990, this organization helped the Czechoslovak parliament draft legislation to regulate broadcasting.[81]

The Path to NATO Accession   An additional form of assistance that Americans, Czechs, and Slovaks alike considered to be a part of democratization support fell outside the scope of the SEED Act's mandate: supporting Czech and Slovak accession to NATO through military reform.[82] While primarily a military alliance, NATO also requires all member countries to commit to "strengthening their free institutions."[83] As a result, the United States used NATO membership as an incentive for Central and Eastern European countries to democratize while at the same time reaping the benefits of collective security.[84]

In January 1995, the U.S. Department of State reported that the "overarching aim of our security assistance policy in Central Europe is to promote regional stability—through democratization of armed forces [and] expansion of contacts between Central European armed forces and NATO (especially U.S.) militaries" in order to enable states to better participate in multinational peacekeeping initiatives.[85] The following year, a SEED Act Implementation Report stressed that, since 1991, the United States had been the "driving force behind NATO's effort to reach out" to Central and Eastern European countries, and that in 1996 the United States planned to provide $100 million in security-related assistance to prepare the countries for their eventual accession to NATO.[86] The rationale for this form of aid was to "help erase Cold War lines of confrontation and bring former adversaries into a community of shared values, principles, and interests."[87]

A crucial component of this form of democratization was transforming NATO's relations with Central and Eastern European countries by helping them to regain civilian control of the military and integrate the armed forces into the democratic political process.[88] However, as scholar Marybeth Peterson Ulrich notes, U.S. efforts in the Czech Republic ultimately focused far more on military efficiency and professionalization than on ideological transformation.[89] Military contact programs overwhelmingly concentrated on training military personnel to meet NATO standards rather than the stated democratization aspects of the program. While the process of accession to NATO (which came in 1999 for the Czechs and 2004 for the Slovaks) served as an incentive for the countries to democratize, more might have been done. Tellingly, in U.S. congressional hearings held in 2000, American policymakers stated that U.S. national interests in the Czech Republic were simply to facilitate military transition to NATO and spur the country's economic growth, with no mention of democratic transition.[90]

Graduating from Transition

By 2003, eight post-Communist countries had "graduated" from USAID assistance, including the Czech Republic in 1997 and Slovakia in 2000.[91] U.S. officials designed democracy aid to be short term, a strategy criticized by some outside observers. In a book on democratic transitions, political scientist Larry Diamond pushes back against the "myth" that new democracies would require only a few years of support—a misguided view that shaped U.S. thinking. Instead, Diamond argues that full democratization requires a long-term commitment by donor countries.[92]

Some U.S. policymakers did, indeed, acknowledge the need for a longer-term commitment, but they did not carry the day. Testifying before Congress in 1992, Robert L. Barry, then special advisor to the deputy secretary for Eastern European Assistance at the State Department, predicted that democracy assistance programs in then Czechoslovakia would need to continue for "years"—past the end of economic assistance.[93] To fulfill that need, USAID administrator Brian Atwood in 1999 proposed the creation of the Trust for Civil Society in Central and Eastern Europe, which would have allowed grant money to continue past the end of the formal assistance program.[94] This program, however, never materialized.[95] Instead, USAID wound down aid programs in the Czech Republic and then in Slovakia. A minute amount of SEED funding went toward grants for Czech NGOs after 1997—for instance, $268,000 in grant money in 2003—but that too ended in 2004.[96] In Slovakia, final programs included funding for Transparency International Slovakia's anti-corruption work and for the ABA/CEELI program.[97]

That is not to say, of course, that all forms of U.S. government assistance ended. The American embassies in both countries have provided financial support to initiatives in areas like voter education, minority outreach, and anti-corruption efforts.[98] For example, the American embassy in the Czech Republic has used its convening power to bring together such disparate groups within Czech society as businesspeople, civil society advocates, media representatives, and government officials (often including visiting American counterparts or dignitaries); has served as an outspoken public voice in support of strengthening the elements of democracy; has initiated or partnered in starting programs and projects; and has continued to provide financial, logistical, moral, and other support for liberal democracy within both countries.[99]

Several factors explain the U.S. government's unwillingness to devote more long-term resources toward democracy promotion in the Czech Republic and Slovakia. First and foremost, America no longer considered those nations a priority. USAID's focus had shifted to less-developed and less-stable countries in the Balkans, Southeast Europe, Central Asia, and, after 9/11, the Middle East.[100] Further, in 1995, USAID faced challenges from within the government, as conservative members of Congress pushed for the abolition of the agency.[101] Though a bill doing so passed the House, it never became law. Nonetheless, several foreign affairs offices found their duties curtailed and subsequently absorbed into the State Department during the Clinton administration.[102] Ultimately, USAID emerged from this era diminished, with its operating budget slashed and its staff cut by 29 percent between 1995 and 2000.[103] The situations in the Czech Republic and Slovakia therefore highlight a recurring challenge of U.S. limits on funding for democracy promotion: too many countries compete for USAID's attention, resulting in resources that are at times widely dispersed and spread thin.[104]

Some U.S. policymakers also believed that, given the imminent accession of the Czechs and Slovaks to the European Union (EU), responsibility for further reforms rested with the EU.[105] The European Economic Community, and later the EU, supported the post-Communist countries in Central Europe from the beginning. The EU's PHARE initiative (Poland and Hungary: Assistance for Restructuring their Economies)—which despite its name expanded to cover ten countries, including Czechoslovakia—was the first program intended for administrative reforms and the development of democratic institutions. PHARE poured $100 million into Czechoslovakia in 1991 alone.[106] Since the mid-1990s, development aid from the EU rose steadily and systematically prepared the Czech Republic and Slovakia for membership in the union.[107] Both countries became EU members in 2004. The EU thus became one of the most important external actors in creating legal transformation and rule of law.[108]

THE PRICE OF SUCCESS

Privatization and Corruption

Liberal democracy took hold in both countries in the 1990s and remains in place today despite challenges posed by the trend of populism and illiberalism sweeping Europe and beyond.[109] Political and market freedom endure, and the space for civil society and independent media remains open. Indeed, the two countries are faring better than some of their close neighbors, including the other members of the Visegrád Four (Hungary and Poland).

Post-1989 U.S. democracy promotion efforts—which emphasized a rapid transition to a market economy and the building up of civil society—

had both advantages and disadvantages. America undoubtedly deserves some credit for the state of affairs in the Czech Republic and Slovakia, although the exact amount is all but impossible to determine. But the U.S. focus on economics over the strengthening of political governance came at a cost with respect to both economic and democratic liberalization. The hasty privatization process, deemed successful at the time, allowed for widespread corruption, which in turn has undermined the liberal project. On the plus side, civil society, which was also a focus (admittedly a secondary one) of U.S. aid, has remained strong and today leads the fight against corruption.

It is important to note that the corruption evident in the privatization process did not spontaneously materialize in 1989. Rather, it may be traced back at least in part to the Communist period. Corruption benefitting the ruling class was an endemic feature of Communist regimes, and, after the Velvet Revolution, there was no definitive legal exclusion of powerful and often corrupt elites from positions of economic power, thereby exacerbating patterns of existing corruption and allowing them to endure into the new democratic era.[110] Laws such as the Czechoslovak Great Lustration Act of 1991 prevented certain categories of individuals (such as former officers of the State Security Service) from holding positions in state administration; however, these regulations did not apply to all categories of Communist-era elites.[111] In the newly democratic Czechoslovakia, those who held elected positions (such as mayors and members of parliament) or who were involved in foreign trade corporations remained unaffected by these laws.[112] Furthermore, even those Communist-era elites who were barred from holding public office still maintained their social networks spanning the administrative and business sectors.[113] The relative lack of alternative social networks in the immediate aftermath of the Velvet Revolution therefore gave Communist-era elites a comparative economic advantage once the regime fell.[114]

The legacy of Communist corruption resonated particularly strongly when it came to the issue of privatization, though Communist-era elites were far from the only ones who took advantage of the new system. Clientelism and bribery, two practices that had been well established in Communist society, continued to plague post-Communist privatization.[115] Compared to average citizens, former Communist elites were better positioned to take advantage of the voucher system by rigging auctions of privatizing companies and bribing officials to falsify documents or approve questionable loans.[116] In some instances, the elites were able to exploit spontaneous privatizations to their own benefit by securing purchases of state property at less than their actual value.[117] While rapid privatization certainly allowed for corruption in some instances to worsen, certain structures from the Communist era formed the foundation upon which corruption was able to persist.

In considering the ways that corruption continued in both nations after the Velvet Revolution, the phenomenon of "tunneling" (*tunelováni*) is instructive. The term refers to the "illicit, large-scale liquidation of the capital and holdings" of formerly state-owned entities, hollowing them out for the disproportionate benefit of owners over the public interest.[118] During the transition to capitalism, a lack of regulations coupled with massive sell-offs and the quick pace of privatization provided ample opportunity for, as scholar David Altshuler has noted, tunneling and other forms of "speculation and corruption."[119] Success in this period "flow[ed] from positions and connections established during the prior regime,"[120] and what emerged from the economic quagmire was a vast web of, as another scholar argues, "private fiefdoms serving the whims of entrenched lords."[121]

Tunneling was especially pervasive in the voucher privatization program, which aimed to reallocate state property directly to the people through coupons. According to World Bank economist John Nellis, voucher privatization was conceived as an efficient and fair solution to two serious problems facing post-Communist Czechoslovakia: "how to value firms and how to prevent 'dirty money' from buying up the assets."[122] The voucher program was launched in 1991, and the initial results were positive, especially compared to privatization in neighboring Poland and Hungary.[123] Indeed, the Czech Republic experienced rapid growth of the private sector share of GDP, low inflation, and low rates of unemployment. This led Prime Minister Václav Klaus to announce in 1996 that the transition to free-market capitalism was "more or less complete."[124] That same year, the World Bank declared the Czech Republic's mass privatization program to be the most successful to date.[125]

However, the tide soon receded. In 1996, the Czech GDP growth rate fell by 40 percent, and it would become clear that privatization had been inadequately regulated.[126] Klaus, known for his unshakeable trust in the free market and belief that there was "no such thing as dirty money," had refused to establish a regulatory agency to oversee the privatization process.[127] In November 1997, amid allegations that his Civic Democratic Party had access to a slush fund in Switzerland, Klaus was forced to resign.[128]

Without adequate monitoring, the Czech voucher approach had produced ownership structures that "impeded efficient corporate governance and restructuring."[129] Moreover, as Altshuler argues, mass privatization negatively impacted the newly formed Czech government in three areas: government inefficiency, unofficial payments, and protection of property rights.[130] As far back as 1991, 40 percent of Czechoslovak citizens polled thought that privatization was taking place "too fast."[131] This "Wild West capitalism," as it has been termed, therefore lent itself to various forms of rent-seeking. In this sense, some scholars view privatization as the root—at least in part—of contemporary corruption that continues to mar Czech democracy. A recent survey found that 95 percent of the Czech population considers corruption to be widespread and 71 percent of companies polled name corruption as a "major obstacle" to their business.[132]

The situation looked similar, though not identical, in the Slovak Republic. After splitting apart from Czechoslovakia in 1993, the newly independent country set out to define its "own way of transition" with an eye toward integration into the EU and NATO.[133] Integration was soon hindered, however, by the undemocratic behavior of Prime Minister Vladimir Mečiar, who "excluded political opposition from parliamentary committees, ignored Constitutional Court decisions, coopted security services and public media, attempted to reduce the independence and powers of the office of the president (a potential political rival), and severely limited transparency."[134] These democratic and human rights failures led to Slovakia's elimination from EU and NATO accession negotiations and delayed its membership in both institutions until 2004.[135]

Under Mečiar, domestic politics and national identity factored heavily into the Slovak privatization process, leading the fledgling government to pursue a so-called "Slovak capital stratum" controlled almost exclusively by Slovak entrepreneurs.[136] Another distinction from the Czech Republic came in the number of vouchers offered to Slovak citizens. While both republics employed a mass privatization scheme that allocated a majority of shares to citizens, the proportion of total shares for citizens was higher in Slovakia.[137] This left the country with a more diffuse corporate governance structure than the Czech Republic.

In the end, however, the focus on speed left the burgeoning Slovak economy—like that of the Czech Republic—lacking in powerful institutions that could regulate its transition. The dearth of regulation, combined with existing links between politicians and entrepreneurs, led to the phenomenon of tunneling in Slovakia as well. Political representatives regularly engaged in or supported "mafia-like criminal acts" that involved asset stripping during the privatization process.[138] For example, former Transport Minister Alexander Rezeš leaned on support from the Mečiar government to purchase a major steelworks company in the mid-1990s.[139] After channelling the profit back to other enterprises he controlled, Rezeš "ruined the company within a few years, and finally sold the steelworks to U.S. Steel."[140] Widespread tunneling led to the majority of the Slovak capital stratum enterprises declaring bankruptcy.[141] These sorts of behaviors, unchecked by any significant legal sanctions, created a climate of corruption that has persisted to this day.[142]

Slovak and Czech Democracy and Corruption Today[143]

Slovakia   A legacy of corruption continues to have an impact in Slovakia. Matters came to a head with the February 2018 murder of a Slovak journalist, Ján Kuciak, who had been investigating possible connections between Slovak politicians and an Italian crime network.[144] His assassination and that of his fiancée, Martina Kušnírová, prompted massive nationwide protests that led to the March 2018 resignation of then Prime Minister Robert Fico. But Fico and his government resisted other demands from the protestors who drove them out. The government refused to call new elections or make substantial personnel changes; the same three-party coalition led by Fico's party has remained in power; and the current prime minster, Peter Pellegrini, is Fico's close associate and hand-picked successor.[145] Fico has, moreover, disputed the legitimacy of the protests as expressions of actual Slovak discontent, claiming that they were instigated by foreign actors like George Soros.[146]

The press has also faced other threats. As prime minister, Fico pursued libel lawsuits against media organizations[147] and passed a law designed to restrict freedom of the press.[148] His nationalist allies in another party have sought to secure positions of influence over public radio and television.[149] Fico has also verbally attacked journalists over a period of many years. In 2007, he reportedly called members of the press "dirty scumbags";[150] in a December 2009 news conference, he compared journalists to the mafia;[151] in late 2016, he called them "dirty anti-Slovak prostitutes";[152] and in November 2018, he addressed a video message to "the clowns in the media . . . We will win the general elections again and I hope it hits . . . you really hard."[153] In Slovak, "hit" connotes "impact," but it can also mean "shoot."

Despite these concerns, the independent media sector—a former recipient of U.S. democracy aid—has played a critical role in revealing corruption. In Slovakia as elsewhere, public perception of corruption is largely shaped by "extensive media coverage of various corruption scandals."[154] In addition to the critical role of media in the Kuciak case, other scandals have garnered widespread attention and coverage from Slovakia's six daily newspapers.[155] In 2011, leaked information allegedly gathered by the Slovak Information Service outlined corrupt negotiations between politicians and an associate of a prominent financial group during the period of privatization.[156] The scandal received more than 5,400 mentions in Slovak media up to August 2014 and led to thousands of Slovaks protesting in Bratislava.[157]

There are multiple risks to the robust and independent coverage of future corruption scandals in Slovakia. First, as scholars have noted, the sheer number of alleged corruption scandals makes it "almost impossible to give each case the proper attention."[158] Second, significant challenges loom for the political independence of local media outlets due to *de facto* ownership by municipal authorities. For example, a mayoral candidate and newspaper owner in Bratislava "merged the election campaign with the advertising campaign for the local newspaper" and ended up winning the election.[159] This conflict of interest highlights a common example of the threat to impartiality and independent control of local media. For the moment, however, Slovak media remains strong and independent due in large part "to the active role of civil society and good legislative provisions that provide remedies for both the right to access to information and the protection of sources."[160]

Further reasons for optimism about the health of Slovak liberal democracy come from the same civil society sector that was once a locus of American transition support.[161] Public outrage in the months following the death of Kuciak and Kušnírová suggests that many Slovaks remain committed to democracy and are willing to push back against illiberal leaders to defend it. A nonpartisan movement called For a Decent Slovakia that emerged in the wake of the murders retains strong public support. On November 16, 2018—the day before the anniversary of the 1989 student protest that toppled the Czechoslovak Communist regime—up to 18,000 people participated in a protest organized by For a Decent Slovakia in Bratislava. Marchers called upon Pellegrini to prevent Fico from following Prime Minister Viktor Orbán's illiberal example in neighboring Hungary.[162] For a Decent Slovakia also continues to push for investigations into instances of alleged public corruption.[163]

While some lament the relative absence of Western support for Slovak democracy,[164] the current president, Zuzana Čaputová, is a champion of liberal-democratic causes.[165] Indeed, her March 2019 election was regarded as a referendum against corruption. Running on the slogan *"Postavme sa zlu, spolu to dokážeme"* ("let's stand up to evil together"), Čaputová has openly embraced anti-corruption rhetoric as part of Slovakia's history of peaceful resistance. In her inaugural address, she called for "the untouchability of selected persons" to "become history," and noted that the

> revolutionary change of the regime in 1989, the division of the federal state and other important changes in our society always occurred in a peaceful way, without violence and unrest. Even countries with a longer democratic tradition sometimes see people out on the streets in anger, showing their disagreement by causing damage. Nothing like that happened here. All the big public protests last year went down without violence, as people called for the return of decency to public life.[166]

While the office of the Slovak president is less powerful than that of the prime minister, Čaputová's election reflects widespread support for curbing corruption.

Czech Republic The same complicated legacies of U.S. aid—privatization and corruption on the one hand and a strong civil society and media on the other—are also central to the state of liberal democracy in the Czech Republic. The prime minister since December 2017, Andrej Babiš, worked for a state-owned enterprise in the pre-1989 Communist nation and was listed in secret police files as a collaborator (a role he vehemently denies).[167] He gained wealth by acquiring valuable state assets—including trade and petrochemical corporations—during the Czech Republic's period of privatization in the 1990s and early 2000s and merging them into the massive conglomerate Agrofert.[168] Babiš has translated that wealth into political influence through his political party Action of Dissatisfied Citizens (ANO), which positioned itself as anti-establishment and anti-corruption. ANO won a second-place showing in the 2013 parliamentary elections, earning 47 of the 200 seats and membership in the ruling coalition as a junior partner, with Babiš taking the post of finance minister, which he held from January 2014 to May 2017.[169] After the election, Babiš followed through on his campaign promise to support needed anti-corruption reforms advanced by civil society (with support from the U.S. Embassy in Prague).[170]

However, Babiš has since himself come under investigation in a major corruption scandal involving allegedly illegal EU subsidies to his businesses.[171] He strongly denied any impropriety.[172] He catapulted ANO to the top of the ballot in the 2017 parliamentary elections—winning roughly 20 percent more of the vote than the second-place Civic Democrats—partly by adopting populist anti-migrant rhetoric and policies.[173] In July 2018, Babiš denied that democracy in Hungary, Poland, and the Czech Republic faced any threats whatsoever; he also called press coverage of the investigation into his business holdings "bullshit."[174]

In addition, Babiš—like Fico in Slovakia—poses a risk to media independence. In 2013, Babiš purchased MAFRA, a Czech media company that publishes some of the nation's most influential newspapers. He subsequently acquired Radio Impuls, which boasts the country's largest radio audience.[175] These acquisitions prompted numerous resignations at the outlets and stoked fears that Babiš would seek to influence coverage to his benefit. These concerns were heightened in 2014 when Babiš fired a journalist who wrote critically of Agrofert,[176] and again three years later when leaked recordings revealed Babiš informing upper management when and how his newspapers should report on political rivals.[177]

In the wake of ANO's strong performance in the 2017 election—winning 78 of 200 seats of the Chamber of Deputies—Babiš initially failed to form a governing parliamentary coalition. The proposed government failed to secure the necessary coalition partners and lost a January 2018 parliamentary vote of confidence, primarily because opposition parties refused to associate with ANO while Babiš remained under police investigation.[178] In an even more distant echo of the country's troubled past, Babiš ultimately secured victory by relying on votes of the Communist Party of Bohemia and Moravia—the successor party to the Communists who controlled the nation during the Cold War.[179] In doing so, Babiš formed the first democratically elected Czech government to so rely on the Communists.[180] In his ascent, Babiš has found an ally in the unabashedly illiberal Czech President Miloš Zeman, who took office in 2013. Some even argue that Zeman is abusing his limited constitutional powers to favor Babiš.[181]

Since becoming prime minister, Babiš's legal controversies have continued. In April 2019, the Czech police recommended that he be prosecuted for misuse of EU subsidies.[182] Only the state prosecutor, who is appointed by the justice minister, can decide whether to accept the recommendation and file charges; the incumbent justice minister resigned the day after the police recommendation without citing a specific reason.[183] Babiš promptly installed Marie Benešová, a close ally of Zeman, as the new justice minister.[184] The unexpected switch led the media and the opposition to speculate that the prime minister had put Benešová in office to support him during the investigation.[185] Even though Benešová has yet to take action—and claims she does not intend to do so—she can theoretically remove public prosecutors, thus interfering with the charges against her boss, Babiš.[186] Separate from the police recommendation, a European Commission audit of Babiš's connection to certain EU funds found that, both as finance minister and prime minister, he had a fundamental conflict of interest. Despite recusing himself from daily operations of his businesses, Babiš maintained a financial interest and thereby stood to profit.[187] As of this writing, the Prague state attorney has re-opened an investigation into EU subsidies abuse, and another investigation by the European Commission also remains open.[188]

Despite these challenges, democratic energy in the Czech Republic endures. Zeman's 2018 victory over a pro-democracy candidate came by a narrow margin of just under 3 percentage points, suggesting that about half the nation rejected his views.[189] The media and judiciary remain largely independent,[190] and the ruling government has seen vibrant pushback from opposition political parties and the traditionally robust community of Czech civil society groups that received American support. The USAID-produced Civil Society Organization Sustainability Index for Central and Eastern Europe and Eurasia (which rates countries along seven dimensions of civil society sustainability) ranked the Czech Republic at 2.6, with a rank of 1 as the most developed and a rank of 7 as the most challenged—a better score than neighboring Slovakia.[191]

As in Slovakia, civil society in the Czech Republic has responded to Babiš's alleged corruption, and furiously so. Though Babiš's influence over Czech media and general antipathy toward the press undoubtedly pose a threat to media freedom, he has far from monopolistic control over Czech news. Indeed, the country has seen the creation of a flurry of independent news outlets, including from journalists fleeing Babiš's control.[192] The chief editor of *Mladá fronta DNES*, the second-largest newspaper in the Czech Republic, left the paper shortly after Babiš acquired it to start his own investigative media outlet. The new organization, *Reporter Magazine*, uncovered such stories as possible fraud involving advertisements paid by Babiš's businesses;[193] the media outlet Seznam Zprávy broke a noteworthy allegation by Babiš's son, who claimed to have been kidnapped in Ukraine to prevent him from testifying in his father's corruption case;[194] and the independent outlet Deník N has, among other stories, worked to expose Babiš's business interests.[195]

Allegations of corruption described in these stories have not gone unnoticed by the public. Civil protests erupted in Prague following Benešová's appointment—first on a relatively small scale, but then expanding into a broader indictment of Czech corruption. More than 100,000 people marched in early June 2019, followed by more than 200,000 a few weeks later—forming, as Havel had envisioned, an *ad hoc* civil society force parallel to political organizations. The latter protest took place in Letná Park, where a similar gathering had proved a turning point in the end of Communist rule three decades earlier. The protest was the largest seen in Prague since 1989.[196]

CONCLUSION

Before the Velvet Revolution, the United States focused on human rights as a strategy to end Communism in Czechoslovakia. That focus had a corollary in the post-1989 transition to liberal democracy: the U.S. concentration on economic liberalization and, to a lesser but still important extent, on building civil society. The contemporary state of Czech and Slovak politics, economics, and civil society reflects competing realities influenced by U.S. aid to these two fledgling democracies in post-Communist Europe. The same U.S.-supported privatization that created vibrant economies also contributed to an environment in which corruption continued to thrive. But a principal brake on that corruption—and more generally on democratic backsliding—is the strong civil society that was also fostered by U.S. aid. The protesters who took to the streets to defend democracy in recent years echo the demonstrations of 1989 and validate the importance of civil society that Havel long ago articulated. That thesis is shared by many generations of Americans, Czechs, and Slovaks who have subscribed to some variation of his ideas about its importance. As one of this volume's cables noted about protestors of that era, "they are less afraid than in the past."[197] That trend continues unabated.

Drawing precise causal connections between U.S. policymaking and the contemporary state of Czech and Slovak liberal democracy is beyond the scope of this afterword. But the evidence does suggest some lessons. As scholars and policymakers now increasingly recognize, economic liberalization is an important but insufficient condition for democracy. More American aid during the transition should have been devoted to the health of the political system, and in particular to checks on corruption. Even the economic dimension of that aid should have given consideration to hastening liberalization while also preventing tunneling and other forms of rent-seeking. "Graduation" should have come only after the strength of the new liberal democratic system had been demonstrated and stress tested.

Of course, the successes and failures of Czech and Slovak democratization were not determined by the level of American involvement alone; credit and responsibility alike ultimately rest primarily with the Czechs and Slovaks themselves. Nevertheless, American policymakers who guided support to the Czechs and Slovaks before, during, and after the Velvet Revolution can take some gratification in the endurance of liberal democracy in the Czech and Slovak republics today. It stubbornly continues despite daunting challenges.

NOTES

Introduction

1. January 2011 to August 2014.
2. Norman L. Eisen, *The Last Palace: Europe's Turbulent Century in Five Lives and One Legendary House* (New York: Crown, 2018).
3. Donald McNeil Jr., "Romania's Revolution of 1989: An Enduring Enigma," *New York Times,* December 31, 1999 (www.nytimes.com/1999/12/31/world/romania-s-revolution-of-1989-an-enduring-enigma.html).
4. Prokop Tomek, "Akce Zásah: Československá lidová armáda v listopadu 1989," *Historie a Vojenství* 4 (2015): 77–91.
5. The Mandatory Declassification Review (MDR) procedure is governed by Exec. Order No. 13526, 32 CFR 2001.33 (2005). For more information, see the State Department webpage on MDR requests at https://foia.state.gov/Learn/MDR.aspx.
6. Included as an appendix to this volume.
7. A household name in the United States owing to her time as a child actor, Black is today less well known for her second and also distinguished career in international affairs. She decided on that course partly as a result of her experiences in the Warsaw Pact invasion of Prague in 1968; she happened to be in the city at that time, and her outrage at the injustices she witnessed helped fuel her desire to become a diplomat. She went on to serve as a U.S. delegate to the United Nations in 1969, ambassador to Ghana from 1974 to 1976, and chief of protocol for the State Department from 1976 to 1977, before returning in 1989 to Czechoslovakia to represent the United States. Eisen, *The Last Palace,* 259–85. For more information about the life of Shirley Temple Black, see Patsy G. Hammontree, *Shirley Temple Black: A Bio-Bibliography* (Westport, CT: Greenwood Press, 1998), 143–88.
8. For a detailed assessment of U.S. Embassy Prague's activities in 1989, see Andrew Kenealy, "Best Supporting Actors: Shirley Temple Black, U.S. Embassy Prague, and the Velvet Revolution of 1989," *Journal of Cold War Studies,* forthcoming.

9. Daniel Thomas, *The Helsinki Effect: International Norms, Human Rights, and the Demise of Communism* (Princeton, NJ: Princeton University Press, 2001), 5–7.

10. Sarah Snyder, *Human Rights Activism and the End of the Cold War: A Transnational History of the Helsinki Network* (New York: Cambridge University Press, 2011), 233–34; Daniel Thomas, "The Helsinki Accords and Political Change in Eastern Europe," in *The Power of Human Rights: International Norms and Domestic Change*, edited by Thomas Risse, Stephen Ropp, and Kathryn Sikkink (Cambridge: Cambridge University Press, 1999), 221–22.

11. For more on the Helsinki negotiations, see John Fry, *The Helsinki Process: Negotiating Security and Cooperation in Europe* (Washington, DC: National Defense University Press, 1993).

12. Sarah Snyder, "The Foundation for Vienna: A Reassessment of the CSCE in the Mid-1980s," *Cold War History* 10, no. 4 (2010): 494 (https://doi.org/10.1080/14682740903460357).

13. John L. Gaddis, *The United States and the End of the Cold War: Implications, Reconsiderations, Provocations* (New York: Oxford University Press, 1992), 26.

14. For more, see William Korey, *The Promises We Keep* (New York: St. Martin's Press, 1993), 294–95.

15. Thomas, "The Helsinki Accords and Political Change in Eastern Europe," 222.

16. Thomas Risse and Kathryn Sikkink, "The Socialization of International Human Rights Norms into Domestic Practices: Introduction," in *The Power of Human Rights: International Norms and Domestic Change*, edited by Thomas Risse, Stephen Ropp, and Kathryn Sikkink (Cambridge: Cambridge University Press, 1999), 5.

17. Snyder, *Human Rights Activism and the End of the Cold War*, 8.

18. Gaddis, *The United States and the End of the Cold War*, 61.

19. Daniel Thomas, "Human Rights Ideas, the Demise of Communism, and the End of the Cold War," *Journal of Cold War Studies* 7, no. 2 (2005): 128 (https://doi.org/10.1162/1520397053630600).

20. For more on the CSCE process in the 1980s, see Fry, *The Helsinki Process*.

21. Speech by Ladislav Adamec at CC CPCz Extraordinary Session, November 24, 1989, in *Masterpieces of History: The Peaceful End of the Cold War in Europe, 1989*, edited by Svetlana Savranskaya, Thomas Blanton, and Vladislav Zubok (Budapest: Central European University Press, 2010), 609.

22. Thomas, "The Helsinki Accords and Political Change in Eastern Europe," 228–33.

23. Michal Pullman, "The Demise of the Communist Regime in Czechoslovakia, 1987–89: A Socio-Economic Perspective," in *The 1989 Revolutions in Central and Eastern Europe*, edited by Kevin McDermott and Matthew Stibbe (Manchester: Manchester University Press, 2015), 155.

24. For more on MFN status as a diplomatic tool, see Lincoln Gordon et al., *Eroding Empire: Western Relations with Eastern Europe* (Washington, DC: Brookings Institution Press, 1987), 110. In addition, the United States used its custody of Czechoslovak gold recovered from Nazi Germany as a tool of leverage until 1982. Henry Kamm, "Czech Ties to U.S. Still Cool Despite Agreement on Gold," *New York Times*, January 7, 1982 (www.nytimes.com/1982/01/17/world/czech-ties-to-us-still-cool-despite-agreement-on-gold.html).

25. Korey, *The Promises We Keep*, 294–95; John Tagliabue, "Czech Playwright Freed from Prison," *New York Times*, May 18, 1989 (www.nytimes.com/1989/05/18/world/czech-playwright-freed-from-prison.html).

26. Philipp Ther, *Europe Since 1989: A History* (Princeton, NJ: Princeton University Press, 2016), 72.

27. "U.S. Slams Czechoslovakia for Violence Against Protestors," Reuters, November 20, 1989.

28. Speech by Ladislav Adamec, November 24, 1989, in Savranskaya, Blanton, and Zubok, *Masterpieces of History*, 609.

29. In addition to the cables in this volume, this section draws on cables from November and December 1989 published in *Prague–Washington–Prague: Reports from the United States Embassy in Czechoslovakia, November–December 1989*, edited by Vilém Prečan (Prague: Václav Havel Library, 2004).

30. As one of Black's predecessors noted, these meetings served to "strengthen the sense of purpose and respectability among the Czechoslovak community of dissidents and, more important, to demonstrate to the Czechoslovak government and party the 'legitimate' role that the opposition groups were playing in promoting the rights guaranteed by the Helsinki Final Act and the Universal Declaration of Human Rights, both of which the government had signed." William H. Luers, "Czechoslovakia: Road to Revolution," *Foreign Affairs* 69, no. 2 (1990): 92 (www.foreignaffairs.com/articles/europe/1990-03-01/czechoslovakia-road-revolution).

31. For example, in one cable, the embassy reported that the government had begun a new crackdown in the run-up to a planned demonstration, providing rich details gleaned from meetings with the relatives of detained dissidents. Cable, Shirley Temple Black, U.S. Ambassador to Czechoslovakia, to U.S. Department of State, October 19, 1989, Prague 07293.

32. Cable, Black to U.S. Department of State, September 7, 1989, Prague 06136.

33. Cable, Black to U.S. Department of State, August 23, 1989, Prague 05736.

34. In one cable, Black writes about the possibility of the U.S. invoking the Human Dimension Mechanism in response to an imprisoned dissident's hunger strike. Cable, Black to U.S. Department of State, September 8, 1989, Prague 06223. In another cable, an embassy official writes, "While the GOC will take whatever actions it ultimately feels it must, it does have a concern for its reputation in the West. This is one reason its human rights policies have not fallen to the level of Romania or Bulgaria. . . . The Czechoslovaks consider themselves part of the West. They are very sensitive to criticisms that their behavior is not up to the standards of Western civilization, especially if this criticism comes from more than just the U.S. Secondly, the GOC desperately wants increased Western trade and investment. Strong criticism of the regime by Western governments may deter this trade and investment." Cable, Black to U.S. Department of State, August 15, 1989, Prague 05536.

35. Václav Havel, Speech to U.S. Congress, February 22, 1990 (www.vhlf.org/havel-quotes/speech-to-the-u-s-congress).

36. Robert K. Evanson, "Political Repression in Czechoslovakia, 1948–1984," *Canadian Slavonic Papers / Revue Canadienne des Slavistes* 28, no. 1 (1986): 1–21 (www.jstor.org/stable/40868539); Mary Heimann, *Czechoslovakia: The State That Failed* (New Haven, CT: Yale University Press, 2011).

37. Evanson, "Political Repression in Czechoslovakia, 1948–1984"; Heimann, *Czechoslovakia: The State That Failed*.

38. Ross Larsen, "Three Extraordinary Years for Temple Black," *Prague Post Magazine*, June 30, 1992.

39. Petition statement: "Several Sentences," June 1989, in *The Democratic Revolution in Czechoslovakia: Its Precondition, Course, and Immediate Repercussions 1987–89: A Chronology of Events and a Compendium of Declassified Documents*, edited by Vilém Prečan and Derek Paton (Prague: National Security Archive, Czechoslovak Documentation Centre, and Institute of Contemporary History, 1999), 99–100.
40. Prečan and Paton, *The Democratic Revolution in Czechoslovakia*, 29.
41. Cable, Black to U.S. Department of State, August 11, 1989, Prague 05480.
42. Cable, Black to U.S. Department of State, August 15, 1989, Prague 05547.
43. Cable, Theodore Russell, Deputy Chief of Mission, U.S. Embassy in Czechoslovakia, to U.S. Department of State, August 15, 1989, Prague 05536.
44. Cable, Black to U.S. Department of State, August 17, 1989, Prague 05614.
45. "370 Reported Held in Prague Protest," *New York Times*, August 23, 1989 (www.nytimes.com/1989/08/23/world/370-reported-held-in-prague-protest.html); Cable, Black to U.S. Department of State, August 22, 1989, Prague 05726.
46. Cable, Black to U.S. Department of State, August 22, 1989, Prague 05726.
47. Craig Whitney, "Prague Journal: Shirley Temple Unpacks a Bag of Memories," *New York Times*, September 11, 1989 (www.nytimes.com/1989/09/11/world/prague-journal-shirley-temple-black-unpacks-a-bag-of-memories.html).
48. Cable, Black to U.S. Department of State, August 30, 1989, Prague 05959.
49. Cable, Black to U.S. Department of State, August 17, 1989, Prague 05619.
50. Cable, Black to U.S. Department of State, August 23, 1989, Prague 05736; Whitney, "Prague Journal."
51. John Goshko, "U.S., Czechs Talk at Cabinet Level for First Time in 11 Years," *Washington Post*, September 28, 1989 (www.washingtonpost.com/archive/politics/1989/09/28/us-czechs-talk-at-cabinet-level-for-first-time-in-11-years/520312d5-9543-43b7-876d-cd5a9d314ec0).
52. Cable, Black to U.S. Department of State, September 21, 1989, Prague 06551.
53. Ibid.
54. Prečan and Paton, *The Democratic Revolution in Czechoslovakia*.
55. Cable, Black to U.S. Department of State, October 19, 1989, Prague 07293; Cable, Black to U.S. Department of State, October 24, 1989, Prague 07419.
56. Ibid.
57. Cable, Black to U.S. Department of State, October 19, 1989, Prague 07293.
58. Rob McRae, *Resistance and Revolution: Vaclav Havel's Czechoslovakia* (Ottawa: Carleton University Press, 1997), 94–97; Prečan and Paton, *The Democratic Revolution in Czechoslovakia*.
59. Edward Lucas, "Prague Rally Thwarted as Police Try New Tactics," *Independent*, October 30, 1989; Michael Kukral, *Prague 1989: Theater of Revolution* (Boulder, CO: East European Monographs, 1997), 40–43.
60. John Tagliabue, "Police in Prague Move to Break Up Big Protest March," *New York Times*, October 29, 1989 (www.nytimes.com/1989/10/29/world/police-in-prague-move-to-break-up-big-protest-march.html).
61. Cable, Black to U.S. Department of State, October 29, 1989, Prague 07534.
62. Edward Epstein, "From Hollywood to the Velvet Revolution: Shirley Temple Black—Who Once Out-hummed a Delegate from Cuba in a United Nations Ladies' Room—Says Her Years as a Film Star Were Good Preparation for Life as a Diplomat," *San Francisco Chronicle*, April 23, 1995.

63. Michael Wise, "Tens of Thousands Demand Reform in Prague," Reuters, November 17, 1989.

64. Eisen, *The Last Palace*, 309.

65. Joe Sommerlad, "Velvet Revolution: Czechs and Slovaks Celebrate Anniversary of Fall of Communism and Triumph of Vaclav Havel," *Independent,* November 16, 2018.

66. Cable, Black to U.S. Department of State, November 15, 1989, Prague 08011.

67. Eisen, *The Last Palace*, 309.

68. Eisen, *The Last Palace,* 310–11; Timothy Garton Ash, *The Magic Lantern: The Revolution of '89 Witnessed in Warsaw, Budapest, Berlin, and Prague* (New York: Vintage Books, 1993), 80.

69. Cable, Black to U.S. Department of State, November 18, 1989, Prague 08082 in Prečan, *Prague–Washington–Prague*, 91.

70. Michael Wise, "Army and Police Beat Prague Protesters After Over 50,000 March," Reuters, November 17, 1989; Prečan and Paton, *The Democratic Revolution in Czechoslovakia.*

71. Eisen, *The Last Palace*, 310–22.

72. Paula Butturini, "Prague, Czechoslovakia," *Chicago Tribune*, November 19, 1989.

73. Cable, Prague 08082 in Prečan, *Prague–Washington–Prague*, 91.

74. Cable, Black to U.S. Department of State, November 20, 1989, Prague 08117.

75. R. W. Apple, "Clamor in the East; Prague Opposition Mounts Huge Protest, Denouncing New Leadership as 'A Trick,'" *New York Times,* November 26, 1989 (www.nytimes.com/1989/11/26/world/clamor-east-prague-opposition-mounts-huge-protest-denouncing-new-leadership.html).

76. "Statement Announcing the Founding of Civic Forum and Its Plans," November 19, 1989, in Prečan and Paton, *The Democratic Revolution in Czechoslovakia.*

77. Cable, Black to U.S. Department of State, November 20, 1989, Prague 08117.

78. Tomek, "Akce Zásah," 77–91.

79. *Poslední hurá. Stenografický záznam z mimořádných zasedání ÚV KSČ 24. a 26. listopadu 1989* (Prague: Cesty, 1992): 68–70.

80. Ibid.

81. Daniel Forbes, "Champagne Corks Pop for the 'Prague Autumn' as Politburo Falls," Reuters, November 24, 1989; Prečan and Paton, *The Democratic Revolution in Czechoslovakia.*

82. Steven Greenhouse, "Hardliners Remain: Protesters Rejoice, but Moderate Premier Is Among Those Out," *New York Times*, November 25, 1989.

83. Michael Wise, "Czechoslovak Prime Minister to Put Opposition Demands to Party," Reuters, November 26, 1989.

84. Michael Wise, "Czechoslovaks Stage Nationwide Strike to End Communist Rule," Reuters, November 27, 1989; Prečan and Paton, *The Democratic Revolution in Czechoslovakia.*

85. Cable, Prague 08312 in Prečan, *Prague–Washington–Prague*, 173–76; Cable, Prague 08343 in Prečan, *Prague–Washington–Prague*, 186–89.

86. Cable, Prague 08415 in Prečan, *Prague–Washington–Prague*, 217.

87. Cable, Prague 08313 in Prečan, *Prague–Washington–Prague*, 177–78; Cable, Prague 08343 in Prečan, *Prague–Washington–Prague*, 186–89.

88. Serge Schemann, "Clamor in the East; Czechoslovakia's Moment in Time," *New York Times,* November 29, 1989 (www.nytimes.com/1989/11/29/world/clamor-

in-the-east-czechoslovakia-s-moment-in-time.html); Henry Kamm, "Clamor in Europe; Protest Rallies Resume in Prague in Effort to Oust New Government," *New York Times,* December 5, 1989 (www.nytimes.com/1989/12/05/world/clamor-europe-protest-rallies-resume-prague-effort-oust-new-government.html); Prečan and Paton, *The Democratic Revolution in Czechoslovakia,* 37–39.

89. Cable, Prague 08415 in Prečan, *Prague–Washington–Prague,* 217.
90. Cable, Prague 08315 in Prečan, *Prague–Washington–Prague,* 179–81.
91. Cable, Black to U.S. Department of State, November 28, 1989, Prague 08314.
92. "Negotiations to Start to Form New Czech Government," Reuters, December 8, 1989.
93. Cable, Black to U.S. Department of State, December 19, 1989, Prague 08891; Cable, Prague 08930 in Prečan, *Prague–Washington–Prague,* 307–12; in addition, a series of cables in this volume contain security information addressed to prospective congressional delegations, including Prague 08565, Prague 08600, Prague 08893, Prague 09118, Prague 09119, Prague 09120, and Prague 09121.
94. Cable, Prague 08415 in Prečan, *Prague–Washington–Prague,* 217; Cable, Black to U.S. Department of State, December 19, 1989, Prague 08891; Cable, Prague 08930 in Prečan, *Prague–Washington–Prague,* 307–12.
95. Václav Havel was elected president by the Federal Assembly on December 29, 1989, and took office upon the vote. He delivered an inaugural address to the nation three days later on New Year's Day. See Václav Havel, "New Year's Address to the Nation," speech, Czechoslovakia, January 1, 1990, Czech Republic Presidential website; Prečan and Paton, *The Democratic Revolution in Czechoslovakia.*
96. Michael Wise, "Vaclav Havel Inaugurated as Czechoslovak President," Reuters, December 29, 1989.

Afterword

1. By "liberal democracy," we are referring to a broad basket of political and economic freedoms, notably including, as William Galston outlines, popular sovereignty, equality of all citizens, a robust "sphere beyond the rightful reach of government in which individuals can enjoy independence and privacy," and a "commitment to economic growth and prosperity" via a suitably regulated market economy (William Galston, *Anti-Pluralism: The Populist Threat to Liberal Democracy* [New Haven, CT: Yale University Press, 2018], 28, 30–31). As we discuss, views differ on the role and necessity of free markets to the overall health of liberal democracy. For the purposes of this afterword, we include them together with the institutions of democratic contestation, civil society, and independent media, but acknowledge the wider array of elements that contribute to the health of liberal democratic systems.
2. Cable, Black to U.S. Department of State, December 29, 1989, Prague 09083, in *Prague–Washington–Prague: Reports from the United States Embassy in Czechoslovakia, November–December 1989,* edited by Vilém Prečan (Prague: Václav Havel Library, 2004), 357.
3. Václav Havel, "The Power of the Powerless," in *The Power of the Powerless: Citizens Against the State in Central-Eastern Europe,* edited by John Keane (New York: Routledge, 2015), 23–96.

4. James Kirchick, "Return of the Czech Communists," *Foreign Policy*, October 12, 2012 (https://foreignpolicy.com/2012/10/12/return-of-the-czech-communists). For election results, see: "Czechoslovakia: Parliamentary Elections Chamber of Nations, 1990" (http://archive.ipu.org/parline-e/reports/arc/2084_90.htm).

5. Jan Křen, *Čtvrt století střední Evropy: Visegrádské země v globálním příběhu let 1992–2017* (Prague: Karolinum, 2019), 131–35. For more on the political parties in post-revolution Czechoslovakia and the Czech Republic, see Adéla Gjuričová et al., *Rozděleni minulostí. Vytváření politických identit v České republice po roce 1989* (Prague: Knihovna Václava Havla, 2011).

6. Šárka Waisová, "Between Atlanticism, Anti-Americanism and Europeanization: Dilemmas in Czech Foreign Policy and the War on Terrorism," in *Czechoslovakia and Czech Republic in the World Politics,* edited by Ladislav Cabada and Šárka Waisová (Plzeň: Aleš Čeněk, 2006), 111–25.

7. Patrick Hamm, Lawrence P. King, and David Stuckler, "Mass Privatization, State Capacity, and Economic Growth in Post-Communist Countries," *American Sociological Review* 77, no. 2 (April 2012): 296–97 (doi.org/10.1177/0003122412441354).

8. Martin Myant, "Podoby kapitalismu v České republice," in *Kapitoly z dějin české demokracie po roce 1989,* edited by Adéla Gjuričová, Michal Kopeček (Prague: Paseka, 2008), 265–87.

9. Jan Bureš, *Občanské fórum* (Plzeň: Aleš Čeněk, 2007), 223–32; Křen, *Čtvrt století střední Evropy,* 94–146. See also Philipp Ther, *Europe since 1989: A History* (Princeton, NJ: Princeton University Press, 2016).

10. Petr Pithart, "Svobodné volby 1990: Jaké režimy od sebe oddělují?" in *Svobodné volby v Československu 1990. Referendum o dalším směřování státu a společnosti,* edited by Pavel Krákora (Prague: Epocha, 2010), 18–32; Lubomír Mlčoch, *Úvahy o české ekonomické tranformaci* (Prague: Vyšehrad, 2000), 85–89. The term "Washington Consensus" was developed by economist John Williamson in 1989 to summarize what most policymakers in the United States believed Latin American countries ought to undertake to improve their economies and quickly developed a much broader and more controversial usage. As Williamson, reflecting on the term in 2002, noted, "Audiences the world over seem to believe that [the Washington Consensus] signifies a set of neoliberal policies that have been imposed on hapless countries by the Washington-based international financial institutions and have led them to crisis and misery." The original ten—and less controversial—principles of the Washington Consensus are, according to Williamson's original conceptualization: fiscal discipline, reordering public expenditure priorities, tax reform, liberalizing interest rates, a competitive exchange rate, trade liberalization, liberalization of inward foreign direct investment, privatization, deregulation, and property rights. See John Williamson, "Did the Washington Consensus Fail?" *Peterson Institute for International Economics,* November 6, 2002 (www.piie.com/commentary/speeches-papers/did-washington-consensus-fail).

11. Pavel Mertlík, "Czech Privatization: From Public Ownership to Public Ownership in Five Years?" *Eastern European Economics* 35, no. 2 (March–April 1997): 64–83 (www.jstor.org/stable/4380082).

12. Hamm, King, and Stuckler, "Mass Privatization, State Capacity, and Economic Growth in Post-Communist Countries," 297.

13. Mertlík, *Czech Privatization*; Nemat Shafik, "Making a Market: Mass Privatization in the Czech and Slovak Republics," *World Development* 23, no. 7 (July 1995): 1143–56 (doi.org/10.1016/0305-750X(95)00037-D); Saul Estrin, "The Impact of Privatization in Transition Economies," in *The New Palgrave Dictionary of Economics, 2nd edition*, edited by Steven N. Durlauf and Lawrence E. Blume (London: Palgrave MacMillan, 2008) (doi.org/10.1057/978-1-349-95121-5_2547-1); Tomáš Ježek, "The Czechoslovak Experience with Privatization," *Journal of International Affairs* 50, no. 2 (Winter 1997): 477–88 (www.jstor.org/stable/24357627).

14. Paula R. Newberg and Thomas Carothers, "Aiding—and Defining—Democracy," *World Policy Journal* 13, no. 1 (1996): 97–108 (www.jstor.org/stable/40209465).

15. U.S. Department of State, "SEED Act Implementation Report: Fiscal Year 1998," March 1999 (https://pdf.usaid.gov/pdf_docs/PCAAB179.pdf).

16. Larry Diamond, *Promoting Democracy in the 1990s: Actors and Instruments, Issues and Imperatives* (New York: Carnegie Commission on Preventing Deadly Conflict, 1995), 38.

17. Hal Brands, *Making the Unipolar Moment: U.S. Foreign Policy and the Rise of the Post-Cold War Order* (Ithaca, NY: Cornell University Press, 2016), 222.

18. "End of the Soviet Union: Text of Bush's Address to Nation on Gorbachev's Resignation," *New York Times*, December 26, 1991 (www.nytimes.com/1991/12/26/world/end-soviet-union-text-bush-s-address-nation-gorbachev-s-resignation.html).

19. Brands, *Making the Unipolar Moment*, 326.

20. Rasmus Sinding Søndergaard, "Bill Clinton's 'Democratic Enlargement' and the Securitisation of Democracy Promotion," *Diplomacy & Statecraft* 26, no. 3 (July 3, 2015): 534–51 (doi.org/10.1080/09592296.2015.1067529).

21. The White House, *National Security Strategy of the United States,* January 1993 (http://nssarchive.us/national-security-strategy-1993); The White House, *National Security Strategy 1995: A National Security Strategy of Engagement and Enlargement,* February 1995 (http://nssarchive.us/national-security-strategy-1995); Steven W. Hook, "'Building Democracy' Through Foreign Aid: The Limitations of United States Political Conditionalities, 1992–96," *Democratization* 5, no. 3 (September 1998): 156–80 (doi.org/10.1080/13510349808403576).

22. U.S. Department of State, "SEED Act Implementation Report: Fiscal Year 1996," February 1997, 33 (https://pdf.usaid.gov/pdf_docs/PCAAA736.pdf).

23. U.S. Department of State, "SEED Act Implementation Report: Fiscal Year 1992," January 1993, 68 (https://pdf.usaid.gov/pdf_docs/PNABN454.pdf).

24. U.S. Government Accountability Office, *Enterprise Funds: Evolving Models for Private Sector Development in Central and Eastern Europe*, NSIAD-94-77, September 1994 (www.govinfo.gov/content/pkg/GAOREPORTS-NSIAD-94-77/html/GAOREPORTS-NSIAD-94-77.htm).

25. Albena Godlove et al., *Europe and Eurasia Enterprise Funds and Legacy Foundations Final Evaluation Report* (Washington, DC: USAID, 2017), 280 (https://pdf.usaid.gov/pdf_docs/PA00STKC.pdf).

26. U.S. Government Accountability Office, *Enterprise Funds.*

27. Godlove, *Europe and Eurasia*, 18.

28. Ibid.

29. Ibid., 281.
30. Ibid.
31. Ibid., 280.
32. Ibid.
33. U.S. Congress, House, *Central Enterprise Development Commission: Hearing Before the Committee on Small Business*, 102nd Cong., 1st sess., July 24, 1991 (statement of John D. Sullivan, Executive Director of the Center for International Private Enterprise), 54.
34. U.S. Congress, House, *Democracy Building in the Former Soviet Union: Hearing Before the Subcommittee on International Operations of the Committee on Foreign Affairs*, 102nd Cong., 2nd sess., March 18, 1992.
35. U.S. Department of State, "SEED Act Implementation Report: Fiscal Year 1994," January 1995, 37 (https://pdf.usaid.gov/pdf_docs/PCAAA701.pdf).
36. U.S. Department of State, "SEED Act Implementation Report: Fiscal Year 1996," February 1997, 35 (https://pdf.usaid.gov/pdf_docs/PCAAA736.pdf).
37. Grant Podelco, "The U.S. Peace Corps Teaches and Trains Throughout the East," *Radio Free Europe/Radio Liberty,* July 9, 1996 (www.rferl.org/a/1080933.html).
38. For more on the Peace Corps's role in advancing American foreign policy, see Kelsey Landau, "Under Humanitarian Cover: The Peace Corps as an Instrument of American Foreign Policy, 1961–1998," undergraduate thesis, University of Florida, 2017 (ufdcimages.uflib.ufl.edu/AA/00/05/79/45/00001/Kelsey%20Landau%20senior%20thesis.pdf), from which this discussion is adapted.
39. U.S. Congress, House, *Peace Corps: Meeting the Challenges of the 1990's* [sic]: *Hearing Before the Legislation and National Security Subcommittee of the Committee on Government Operations*, 101st Cong., 2nd sess., May 22, 1990, 16.
40. Ibid., 17.
41. Ibid., 18.
42. Podelco, "The U.S. Peace Corps Teaches and Trains Throughout the East"; Peace Corps, "Peace Corps Holds Discussion on the Slovak Republic," May 23, 2011 (www.peacecorps.gov/news/library/peace-corps-hosts-discussion-on-the-slovak-republic).
43. U.S. Department of State, "SEED Act Implementation Report: Fiscal Year 1998," March 1999.
44. Thomas Carothers, "Democracy Aid at 25: Time to Choose," Carnegie Endowment for International Peace, January 13, 2015 (https://carnegieendowment.org/2015/01/13/democracy-aid-at-25-time-to-choose-pub-57701).
45. USAID, "2017 CSO Sustainability Index for Central and Eastern Europe and Eurasia," September 2018 (www.usaid.gov/sites/default/files/documents/1866/2017_CSO_Sustainability_Index_for_Central_and_Eastern_Europe_and_Eurasia.pdf).
46. As noted above, American aid also focused on other indicators, especially the improvement of quality of life for citizens in both countries. These aid programs are beyond the scope of this afterword. For more details on those programs, see the SEED Act Implementation Reports from throughout the 1990s.
47. John K. Glenn, "International Aid to New Political Parties in the Czech Republic and Slovakia," *Voluntas: International Journal of Voluntary and Nonprofit Organizations* 11, no. 2 (2000): 161–79 (www.jstor.org/stable/27927681); U.S. Congress, House, *United States Public Diplomacy in*

Eastern Europe and the Soviet Union: Hearing Before the Subcommittee on International Relations of the Committee on Foreign Affairs, 102nd Cong., 1st sess., July 30, 1991 (Appendix 1: The National Endowment for Democracy's Programs in Eastern Europe and the Soviet Union).

48. U.S. Congress, House, *United States Public Diplomacy in Eastern Europe and the Soviet Union.*

49. Stephen Engelberg, "Evolution in Europe: U.S. Grant to Two Czech Parties Is Called Unfair Interference," *New York Times*, June 10, 1990 (www.nytimes.com/1990/06/10/world/evolution-in-europe-us-grant-to-2-czech-parties-is-called-unfair-interference.html).

50. Newberg and Carothers, "Aiding—and Defining—Democracy," 101.

51. U.S. Congress, House, *United States Public Diplomacy in Eastern Europe and the Soviet Union.*

52. National Democratic Institute for International Affairs, "Statement by the International Observer Delegation to the Czech and Slovak Federative Republic Elections," June 10, 1990 (www.ndi.org/sites/default/files/1369_sk_elec_5.pdf); U.S. Department of State, "SEED Act Implementation Report: Fiscal Year 1998."

53. William H. Robinson, "Parliamentary Development in Central and Eastern Europe," *Bulletin of the American Society for Information Science* 19, no. 4 (April/May 1993): 8.

54. Ibid. Technical assistance included training in parliamentary procedure, office automation, constituent services, and the establishment of a parliamentary research and information service similar to the CRS.

55. U.S. Congress, House, *U.S. Assistance to Central and Eastern Europe: Hearing Before the Subcommittee on Europe and the Middle East of the Committee on Foreign Affairs*, 102nd Cong., 2nd sess., June 3, 1992 (Appendix 1: U.S. Assistance to Central and Eastern Europe).

56. James Brooks, "Technical Assistance to Czech Mayors," National League of Cities, August 1993 (https://pdf.usaid.gov/pdf_docs/PNABW010.pdf).

57. Ibid.

58. U.S. Department of State, "SEED Act Implementation Report: Fiscal Year 1994," 80.

59. U.S. Department of State, "SEED Act Implementation Report: Fiscal Year 1998"; U.S. Department of State, "SEED Act Implementation Report: Fiscal Year 1995," February 1996 (https://pdf.usaid.gov/pdf_docs/PCAAA735.pdf).

60. U.S. Department of State, "SEED Act Implementation Report: Fiscal Year 1998"; U.S. Department of State, "SEED Act Implementation Report: Fiscal Year 1995."

61. U.S. Department of State, "SEED Act Implementation Report: Fiscal Year 1998."

62. Ibid.

63. U.S. Department of State, "SEED Act Implementation Report: Fiscal Year 1995."

64. While civil society and independent media are sometimes characterized as separate elements of society due to the differing mechanisms they use to hold governments to account, we follow the lead of Carothers (2015) and group them together here, as the civic space environment required to implement their work is similar for both, and both tended to be linked together in American democracy aid programs. See Carothers, "Democracy Aid at 25."

65. Havel, "The Power of the Powerless," 93; emphasis in original.

66. Some scholars have criticized what they term "the highly romanticized reading of the role of pro-democracy social movements in bringing about the demise of

Communism." See, for example, Omar G. Encarnación, "Assisting Civil Society and Promoting Democracy," in *The Oxford Handbook of Civil Society*, edited by Michael Edwards (Oxford, UK: Oxford University Press, 2011), 469. For a range of views on civil society aid promotion in the former Soviet Bloc, see, for example, Jessica Schmidt, *Rethinking Democracy Promotion in International Relations: The Rise of the Social* (New York: Routledge, 2016); Thomas Carothers, "Think Again: Civil Society," *Foreign Policy* (Winter 1999–2000), 18–29; and Robert L. Hutchings, *American Diplomacy and the End of the Cold War: An Insider's Account of U.S. Policy in Europe, 1989–1992* (Washington, DC: The Woodrow Wilson Center Press, 1997).

67. Omar G. Encarnación, "On Bowling Leagues and NGOs: A Critique of Civil Society's Revival," *Studies in Comparative and International Development* 36, no. 4 (December 2002): 117 (doi.org/10.1007/BF02686335).

68. This view has been criticized as turning "the concept of civil society into a magic cure for combating virtually all of society's ills." See Encarnación, "Assisting Civil Society and Promoting Democracy," 470.

69. Newberg and Carothers, "Aiding—and Defining—Democracy," 104. The focus on NGOs left behind a strong sector of indigenous organizations. However, as Adam Fagan has argued, the strategy left several aspects of NGO development unaddressed. In the Czech Republic, NGOs have at times lacked a grassroots focus and presence at the community level; their aims have at times aligned more with international donor concerns than with the concerns of local citizens; and, after the U.S. withdrawal of aid in 1997, many NGOs struggled to find local Czech donors. Slovak NGOs, too, struggled to develop local sources of funding once U.S. aid ceased, though USAID attempted to address this issue with the creation of the Donors Forum. See Adam Fagan, "Taking Stock of Civil-Society Development in Post-Communist Europe: Evidence from the Czech Republic," *Democratization* 12, no. 4 (2005): 528–47 (doi. org/10.1080/13510340500226077); and Sabina Crisen, "A Closer Look at the Slovak NGO Community," The Wilson Center, July 7, 2011 (www.wilsoncenter. org/publication/194-closer-look-the-slovak-ngo-community).

70. The Foundation for a Civil Society, "Democracy Network Program Czech Republic: Final Program Report," 1997 (https://pdf.usaid.gov/pdf_docs/ PDABQ053.pdf); The Foundation for a Civil Society, "Czech Republic Democracy Network Program: Quarterly Report for the Period of April 1 through June 30, 1995," 1995 (https://pdf.usaid.gov/pdf_docs/PDABM061.pdf).

71. The Foundation for a Civil Society, "Democracy Network Program Czech Republic: Final Program Report."

72. Ibid. In a symbolic note of the importance of civil society to American diplomatic efforts, the awards ceremony for the competition was hosted at the ambassador's residence.

73. U.S. Department of State, "SEED Act Implementation Report: Fiscal Year 1995"; U.S. Department of State, "SEED Act Implementation Report: Fiscal Year 1996."

74. U.S. Department of State, "SEED Act Implementation Report: Fiscal Year 1995."

75. U.S. Department of State, "SEED Act Implementation Report: Fiscal Year 1995," 104.

76. U.S. Department of State, "SEED Act Implementation Report: Fiscal Year 1998," 123.

77. Ibid., 124.

78. Ibid., 122–23.
79. Concepción Naval, Murray Print, and Ruud Veldhuis, "Education for Democratic Citizenship in the New Europe: Context and Reform," *European Journal of Education* 37, no. 2 (2002) (www.jstor.org/stable/1503793); Charles N. Quigley and Jack N. Hoar, "Civitas: An International Civic Education Exchange Program," in *Principles and Practices of Education for Democratic Citizenship*, edited by Charles F. Bahmueller and John J. Patrick (Bloomington, IN: ERIC/ ChESS 1999), 123–46 (https://files.eric.ed.gov/fulltext/ED434866.pdf).
80. U.S. Embassy Warsaw, "United States SEED Act Assistance Strategy Update for the Czech Republic," July 19, 1994 (https://pdf.usaid.gov/pdf_docs/PNABU147. pdf); U.S. Congress, House, *United States Public Diplomacy in Eastern Europe and the Soviet Union: Hearing Before the Subcommittee on International Relations of the Committee on Foreign Affairs*, House of Representatives, 102nd Cong., 1st sess., July 30, 1991 (Appendix 1: The National Endowment for Democracy's Programs in Eastern Europe and the Soviet Union).
81. U.S. Congress, House, *United States Public Diplomacy in Eastern Europe and the Soviet Union* (Appendix 1: The National Endowment for Democracy's Programs in Eastern Europe and the Soviet Union).
82. U.S. Department of State, "SEED Act Implementation Report: Fiscal Year 1994," 116.
83. North Atlantic Treaty Organization, "The North Atlantic Treaty," April 4, 1949 (www.nato.int/cps/en/natolive/official_texts_17120.htm).
84. Zbigniew Brzezinksi, "A Plan for Europe: How to Expand NATO," *Foreign Affairs*, January/February 1995 (www.foreignaffairs.com/articles/poland/1995-01-01/plan-europe-how-expand-nato).
85. U.S. Department of State, "SEED Act Implementation Report: Fiscal Year 1994," 116. For more on the United States' decision to enlarge NATO into Central and Eastern Europe, see James M. Goldgeier, *Not Whether But When: The U.S. Decision to Enlarge NATO* (Washington, DC: Brookings Institution Press, 1999).
86. U.S. Department of State, "SEED Act Implementation Report: Fiscal Year 1995," 156–57.
87. Ibid., 157.
88. Ibid.
89. Marybeth Peterson Ulrich, "U.S. Assistance and Democratic Militarization in the Czech Republic," *Problems of Post-Communism* 45, no. 2 (1998): 22–32 (doi. org/10.1080/10758216.1998.11655778).
90. U.S. Congress, House, *Foreign Operations, Export Financing, and Related Programs Appropriations for 2001: Hearings Before a Subcommittee of the Committee on Appropriations*, 106th Cong., 2nd sess., February 2000, 690–91.
91. U.S. Congress, House, *U.S. Assistance Programs in Europe: An Assessment: Hearing Before the Subcommittee on Europe of the Committee on International Relations*, 108th Cong., 1st sess., March 27, 2003 (testimony of Thomas Adams, Acting Coordinator, U.S. Assistance in Europe and Eurasia, Bureau of European and Eurasian Affairs, Department of State); USAID, "20 Years of USAID Economic Growth Assistance in Europe and Eurasia," July 2013 (www. usaid.gov/where-we-work/europe-and-eurasia/20-years-economic-growth-assistance).
92. Diamond, *In Search of Democracy*, 437.
93. U.S. Congress, House, *U.S. Assistance to Central and Eastern Europe: Hearing*

Before the Subcommittee on Europe and the Middle East of the Committee on Foreign Affairs, 11.

94. "Prepared Testimony of J. Brian Atwood, Administrator, U.S. Agency for International Development, Before the House International Relations Committee," *Federal News Service*, March 3, 1999.

95. The Trust for Civil Society in Central and Eastern Europe was instead privately funded, with no USAID involvement. See Andrew Milner, "The CEE Trust: A Job Well Done?" *Alliance Magazine*, December 2012 (www.alliancemagazine. org/analysis/the-cee-trust-a-job-well-done).

96. U.S. Department of State, "FY 2003 SEED Act Implementation Report: U.S. Government Assistance to Eastern Europe under the Support for East European Democracy (SEED) Act," January 2004 (https://pdf.usaid.gov/pdf_docs/ PCAAB336.pdf); U.S. Congress, House, *U.S. Assistance Programs in Europe: An Assessment: Hearing Before the Subcommittee on Europe of the Committee on International Relations.*

97. U.S. Department of State, "SEED Act Implementation Report: Fiscal Year 2003."

98. Ibid.; U.S. Embassy in Slovakia, "Joint Anti-Corruption Day Statement," December 7, 2018, https://sk.usembassy.gov/joint-anti-corruption-day-statement-4; U.S. Embassy in the Czech Republic, "U.S.-Czech Anti-Corruption Efforts," August 14, 2014, https://cz.usembassy.gov/wp-content/uploads/ sites/22/2015/11/Anti-Corruption-One-Pager.pdf; U.S. Embassy in the Czech Republic, "Small Grants Program" (https://cz.usembassy.gov/education-culture/ small-grants-program); U.S. Embassy in Slovakia," U.S. Embassy Bratislava PAS Annual Program Statement" (https://sk.usembassy.gov/wp-content/uploads/ sites/193/Annual-Program-Statement-FY-2019.pdf).

99. For example, the American embassy in the Czech Republic during the period in which one of the authors (Eisen) served as ambassador emphasized support for good governance and civil rights. The embassy broadened and deepened its preexisting pro-democracy and anti-corruption initiatives, including by supporting civil society through its Small Grants Program and helping to launch the World Forum on Governance, a conference series held in Prague from 2012 to 2014 that brought together representatives from the worlds of government, business, investment, media, and NGOs to "analyze the link between governance and corruption and to find practical solutions that can begin improving" the latter problem. (Stephen M. Davis, Thomas E. Mann, Norm Ornstein, and Nell Minow, "Prague Declaration on Governance and Anti-Corruption," The Brookings Institution, March 21, 2012 [www.brookings. edu/research/prague-declaration-on-governance-and-anti-corruption]). In Slovakia, too, the Small Grants program works to bolster civil society and other pro-democracy elements, with its priority program areas including initiatives that work to "strengthen the rule of law, government accountability, and anti-corruption efforts; promote human rights, support marginalized groups, and foster a culture of integration; [and] strengthen independent media, journalism, and counter disinformation" (U.S. Embassy in Slovakia, "Notice of Funding Opportunity" [https://sk.usembassy.gov/wp-content/uploads/sites/193/Annual-Program-Statement-FY-2019.pdf]).

100. Connie Veillette and Susan B. Epstein, *State, Foreign Operations, and Related Programs: FY 2008 Appropriations* (Washington, DC: Congressional Research Service, 2007), 2–4 (https://fas.org/sgp/crs/row/RL34023.pdf); USAID,

Monitoring Country Progress in Central and Eastern Europe and the Newly Independent States (Washington, DC: USAID, 1999) (https://pdf.usaid.gov/pdf_docs/PNADG905.pdf).

101. Susan B. Epstein, Larry Q. Nowels, and Steven A. Hildreth, *Foreign Policy Agency Reorganization in the 105th Congress* (Washington, DC: Congressional Research Service, 1998), 2 (https://pdf.usaid.gov/pdf_docs/PCAAA780.pdf).

102. Ibid., 13–17.

103. John Norris, "USAID: A History of US Foreign Aid Part 3: The Clashes of the 1990s," *Devex*, July 23, 2014 (www.devex.com/news/the-clashes-of-the-1990s-83341).

104. Barbara Ann J. Rieffer with Kristan Mercer, "US Democracy Promotion: The Bush and Clinton Administrations," *Global Society* 19, no. 4 (2005), 406 (doi.org/10.1080/13600820500242654).

105. U.S. Congress, House, *U.S. Assistance Programs in Europe: An Assessment: Hearing Before the Subcommittee on Europe of the Committee on International Relations* (testimony of Thomas Adams, Acting Coordinator, U.S. Assistance to Europe and Eurasia, Bureau of European and Eurasian Affairs, Department of State).

106. Petr Mareš, Jana Kreuzigerová, and Jan Marian, *Zahraniční pomoc v Česku a Československu po roce 1989: cíle, formy a výsledky* (Prague: Asociace pro mezinárodní otázky, 2006) (www.amo.cz/wp-content/uploads/2015/11/amocz-RM-01-08-05.pdf).

107. Anna Szczepańska, "The Czech Republic in the European Union," in *Obnova demokracie v Československu po roce 1989*, edited by Pavel Krákora (Prague: Epocha, 2010), 284–97.

108. Ivan Berend, *From the Soviet Bloc to the European Union: The Economic and Social Transformation of Central and Eastern Europe Since 1973* (Cambridge: Cambridge University Press, 2009), 79–106; Ther, *Europe Since 1989*, 144–59.

109. For an overview of democratic backsliding in Central Europe and Turkey, see Alina Polyakova et al., *The Anatomy of Illiberal States: Assessing and Responding to Democratic Decline in Turkey and Central Europe* (Washington, DC: The Brookings Institution, 2019), www.brookings.edu/research/the-anatomy-of-illiberal-states.

110. Roman David, "Lustration Laws in Action: The Motives and Evaluation of Lustration Policy in the Czech Republic and Poland (1989-2001)," *Law & Social Inquiry* 28, no. 2 (Spring 2003): 406 (https://jstor.org/stable/pdf/1215775).

111. Veronika Bílková, "Lustration: The Experience of Czechoslovakia/the Czech Republic" in *Conference on Past and Present-Day Lustration: Similarities, Differences, and Applicable Standards*, Strasbourg: Venice Commission, 2015), 2 (www.venice.coe.int/webforms/documents/default.aspx?pdffile=CDL-PI(2015)028-e).

112. "Czechs Approve the Purging of Ex-Communist Officials," *New York Times,* October 8, 1991 (www.nytimes.com/1991/10/08/world/czechs-approve-the-purging-of-ex-communist-officials.html).

113. David, "Lustration Laws in Action," 396.

114. Andras Sajo, "Corruption, Clientelism, and the Future of the Constitutional State in Eastern Europe," *East European Constitutional Review* 7, no. 2 (Spring 1998): 37–46 (https://heinonline.org/HOL/P?h=hein.journals/eeurcr7&i=137).

115. Irene McMaster, "Privatisation in Central and Eastern Europe: What Made

the Czech Republic so Distinctive?", *University of Strathclyde in Glasgow: European Policies Research Centre Regional and Industrial Research Papers*, no. 49 (November 2001), 29–30 (https://pureportal.strath.ac.uk/en/publications/privatisation-in-central-and-eastern-europe-what-made-the-czech-r).

116. David Altschuler, "Tunneling Towards Capitalism in the Czech Republic," *Ethnography* 2. no. 1 (March 2001), 120 (www.jstor.org/stable/24047721).

117. U.S. Congress, House, *Economic and Political Change in Eastern Europe: Report of Staff Study Mission to Poland, Hungary, Czechoslovakia, and the Former German Democratic Republic, August 1–12, 1990, to the Committee on Foreign Affairs*, 101st Cong., 2nd sess., November 1990.

118. Altshuler, "Tunneling Towards Capitalism," 116.

119. Ibid., 117.

120. Ibid., 132.

121. Rasma Karklins, "Typology of Post-Communist Corruption," *Problems of Post-Communism* 49, no. 4 (July 2002): 25 (doi.org/10.1080/10758216.2002.11655993).

122. John Nellis, *The World Bank, Privatization, and Enterprise Reform in Transition Economies: A Retrospective Analysis* (Washington, DC: The World Bank, 2002), 21 (http://documents.worldbank.org/curated/en/761441468758967175/pdf/multi0page.pdf).

123. Ibid., 22.

124. Ibid., 23.

125. World Bank, *World Development Report 1996: From Plan to Market* (New York: Oxford University Press, 1996), 23 (https://openknowledge.worldbank.org/handle/10986/5979).

126. Nellis, *The World Bank, Privatization, and Enterprise Reform in Transition Economies,* 25.

127. Leo Hockstader, "Czech's Downfall Shatters Hope for Economic Miracle," *Washington Post*, December 7, 1997 (https://www.washingtonpost.com/archive/politics/1997/12/07/czechs-downfall-shatters-hope-for-economic-miracle/2d2d9b1a-afcc-45eb-9b7f-66bd5e4d8307).

128. Paul Wilson, "Václav vs. Václav," *New York Review of Books,* May 10, 2007 (www.nybooks.com/articles/2007/05/10/vaclav-vs-vaclav); Václav Havel, "The Sad State of the Republic," *New York Review of Books*, March 5, 1998 (www.nybooks.com/articles/1998/03/05/the-sad-state-of-the-republic).

129. Organisation for Economic Cooperation and Development, *Czech Republic* (Paris: OECD, 1998), 49 (https://www.oecd-ilibrary.org/economics/oecd-economic-surveys-czech-republic-1998_eco_surveys-cze-1998-en;jsessionid=gstt2B3Twv85C5I0M5E59EKC.ip-10-240-5-161).

130. Hamm, King, and Stuckler, "Mass Privatization, State Capacity, and Economic Growth in Post-Communist Countries," 316.

131. U.S. Congress, House, *Central Enterprise Development Commission* (statement of John D. Sullivan, Executive Director of the Center for International Private Enterprise), 59.

132. Petra Koudelková, Wadim Strielkowski, and Denisa Hejlová, "Corruption and System Change in the Czech Republic: Firm-Level Evidence," *DANUBE: Law and Economics Review* 6, no. 1 (March 2015): 25–46 (doi.org/10.1515/danb-2015-0002).

133. Ivana Šikulová and Karol Frank, "The Slovak Experience with Transition to Market Economy," working paper, *Welfare, Wealth, and Work for Europe project*

(Bratislava: Ekonomický ústav SAV, 2013), http://ekonom.sav.sk/uploads/journals/229_wp_49_sikulova_frank_experience_with_transition.pdf.

134. Norman Eisen and Andrew Kenealy, "Slovakia," in Polyakova et al., *The Anatomy of Illiberal States*, 22.

135. Pavol Demeš, *A Collective Portrait: The U.S. Contribution to the Development of Civil Society in Slovakia* (Bratislava: Pavol Demeš, 2012), 30, 68; Milan Nič, Marek Slobodník, and Michal Šimečka, *Slovakia in the EU: An Unexpected Success Story?* (Berlin: Deutsche Gesellschaft für Auswärtige Politik, 2014), 4, https://dgap.org/en/think-tank/publications/dgapanalysis/slovakia-eu.

136. Demeš, *A Collective Portrait*, 27.

137. Shafik, "Making a Market."

138. Nicole Gallina, "Anti-Corruption Revisited: The Case of the Czech Republic and Slovakia," in *(Dys-)Functionalities of Corruption: Comparative Perspectives and Methodological Pluralism*, edited by Tobias Debiel and Andrea Gawrich (Wiesbaden: VS Verlag für Sozialwissenschaften, 2014), 201.

139. Gallina, "Anti-Corruption Revisited"; "Rezeš Link to Mečiar Villa Revealed," *Slovak Spectator*, October 6, 2008 (https://spectator.sme.sk/c/20030606/rezes-link-to-meciar-villa-revealed.html); "Alexander Rezeš, Politician and Privatizer, Dies," *Slovak Spectator*, July 8, 2002 (https://spectator.sme.sk/c/20016419/alexander-rezes-politician-and-privatiser-dies.html).

140. Gallina, "Anti-Corruption Revisited," 201.

141. Marian Virkovic, "Quasi-Effective Governance: Slovak Mass Privatisation 1991–1996," *Journal of Economic Studies* 30, no. 3 (2003): 294–350 (www.econstor.eu/bitstream/10419/125672/1/WWWforEurope_WPS_no017_MS23_Backgroundpaper1.pdf).

142. "Slovakia Corruption Index," Trading Economics (https://tradingeconomics.com/slovakia/corruption-index); Bertelsmann Stiftung, *BTI 2018 Country Report—Slovakia* (Gütersloh: Bertelsmann Stiftung, 2018), www.bti-project.org/fileadmin/files/BTI/Downloads/Reports/2018/pdf/BTI_2018_Slovakia.pdf.

143. This section and the following section on democratic backsliding in the Czech Republic were originally published by Norman Eisen and Andrew Kenealy in Polyakova et al., *The Anatomy of Illiberal States*. They have been adapted for incorporation here.

144. Rob Cameron, "Slovakia Grapples with Murdered Journalist's Last Story," *BBC*, February 28, 2018 (www.bbc.com/news/world-europe-43226567).

145. Miroslava Germanova and Marc Santora, "Slovaks Meet the New Bosses. They're Not Much Different from the Old Bosses," *New York Times*, March 22, 2018 (www.nytimes.com/2018/03/22/world/europe/slovakia-government-jan-kuciak.html); Tatiana Jancarikova, "Slovak President Accepts New Government to End Crisis over Journalist's Murder," *Reuters*, March 21, 2018 (https://af.reuters.com/article/worldNews/idUSKBN1GX28U).

146. "Fico novým zákonom pritvrdil: Hon na nepriateľov?!," *Nový Čas*, June 27, 2018 (www.cas.sk/clanok/711016/fico-novym-zakonom-pritvrdil-hon-na-nepriatelov).

147. See, for example, "Fico Sues 7 Plus Publisher," *Slovak Spectator*, September 16, 2013 (https://spectator.sme.sk/c/20048205/fico-sues-7-plus-publisher.html).

148. Michaela Terenzani, "Fico 'Replies' to Sme," *Slovak Spectator*, November 30, 2009 (https://spectator.sme.sk/c/20034596/fico-replies-to-sme.html); Michaela Terenzani, "Slovakia to 'Get Luckier' with Its Press Code," *Slovak Spectator*,

September 20, 2010 (https://spectator.sme.sk/c/20037431/slovakia-to-get-luckier-with-its-press-code.html).

149. See, for example, Daniel Milo and Katarína Klingová, "Vulnerability Index: Subversive Russian Influence in Central Europe," *GLOBSEC*, 2017, 24–25 (www.globsec.org/wp-content/uploads/2017/08/globsec-vulnerability-index. pdf).

150. "Fico Wins Lawsuit Over Magazine Article," *Slovak Spectator*, April 12, 2010 (https://spectator.sme.sk/c/20035831/fico-wins-lawsuit-over-magazine-article. html).

151. Beata Balogová, "PM Slams Media, Again," *Slovak Spectator*, December 21, 2009 (https://spectator.sme.sk/c/20034819/pm-slams-media-again.html).

152. U.S. Department of State, "Slovakia 2017 Human Rights Report," 9 (www. state.gov/wp-content/uploads/2019/01/Slovakia.pdf).

153. Chris Harris, "'We Want a Decent Slovakia,' Demand Protesters in Bratislava," *EuroNews*, November 17, 2018 (www.euronews.com/2018/11/17/we-want-a-decent-slovakia-demand-protesters-in-bratislava).

154. Andrej Školkay and Alena Ištoková, "Media Coverage of Corruption: The Role of Inter-Media Agenda Setting in the Context of Media Reporting on Scandals," *Środkowoeuropejskie Studia Polityczne* no. 2 (2016): 125–26.

155. Željko Sampor, "Media Pluralism Monitor 2016: Monitoring Risks for Media Pluralism in the EU and Beyond Country Report: Slovakia," *Centre for Media Pluralism and Media Freedom*, 2016 (https://cadmus.eui.eu/bitstream/ handle/1814/46810/Slovachia_EN.pdf).

156. Beata Balogová, "Slovak Politics Gripped by Gorilla File," *Slovak Spectator*, January 6, 2012 (https://spectator.sme.sk/c/20042075/slovak-politics-gripped-by-gorilla-file.html); K.M., "The Multi-Million Euro Gorilla," *Economist*, January 27, 2012 (www.economist.com/eastern-approaches/2012/01/27/the-multi-million-euro-gorilla); "Special Prosecutor: New Evidence in the Gorilla Case," *Slovak Spectator,* June 7, 2017 (https://spectator.sme.sk/c/20552887/ special-prosecutor-new-evidence-in-the-gorilla-case.html); Jan Cienski, "Slovaks Protest over Corruption Claims," *Financial Times*, February 10, 2012 (www.ft.com/content/6fc1858c-48cd-11e1-954a-00144feabdc0); "Slovak Politics Rocked by 'Gorilla' Corruption Scandal," *EURACTIV*, January 17, 2012 (www. euractiv.com/section/justice-home-affairs/news/slovak-politics-rocked-by-gorilla-corruption-scandal).

157. Školkay and Ištoková, "Media Coverage of Corruption."

158. Ibid., 126.

159. Sampor, "Media Pluralism Monitor 2016," 6.

160. Ibid., 4.

161. As mentioned above, civil society continues to receive support from the American embassies in both Prague and Bratislava.

162. Michaela Terenzani, "We Want a Decent Slovakia, People Chanted in Squares," *Slovak Spectator*, November 16, 2018 (https://spectator.sme. sk/c/20963805/we-want-a-decent-slovakia-people-chanted-in-squares.html).

163. Michaela Terenzani, "Abduction: Kaliňák Says He Is Ready to Take a Polygraph Test," *Slovak Spectator*, August 3, 2018 (https://spectator.sme. sk/c/20884543/abduction-kalinak-says-he-is-ready-to-take-a-polygraph-test. html).

164. Dalibor Rohac, "Central Europe's Identity Crisis," *The American Interest*,

August 13, 2018 (www.the-american-interest.com/2018/08/13/central-europes-identity-crisis).

165. Emily Tamkin, "Hailed by Liberals, Slovakia's First Female President Is Under a Lot of Pressure to Turn the Tide of Populism," *Washington Post*, April 1, 2019 (www.washingtonpost.com/world/2019/04/01/hailed-by-liberals-slovakias-new-female-president-is-under-lot-pressure-turn-tide-populism); Dalibor Rohac, "A Rebuke for Populism?" *The American Interest*, March 11, 2019 (www.the-american-interest.com/2019/03/11/slovakia-returns-to-normal).

166. "Inauguration Speech of President Zuzana Čaputová," *Slovak Spectator*, June 15, 2019 (https://spectator.sme.sk/c/22145941/inauguration-speech-of-president-zuzana-caputova.html).

167. Though Babiš was cleared by a Slovak court, historians have disputed the verdict, claiming that it relied too heavily on the flimsy testimony of former secret police agents. See Adam Drda, "Andrej Babis—Czech Oligarch," *Politico*, September 11, 2014 (www.politico.eu/article/andrej-babis-czech-oligarch).

168. Ibid.; Ola Cichowlas and Andrew Foxall, "Now the Czechs Have an Oligarch Problem, Too," *Foreign Policy*, April 10, 2015 (https://foreignpolicy.com/2015/04/10/now-the-czechs-have-an-oligarch-problem-too-andrej-babis).

169. Andrew Gardner, "Social Democrats Win Czech Elections," *Politico*, October 26, 2013 (www.politico.eu/article/social-democrats-win-czech-elections); Andrew Gardner, "Sobotka to Lead New Czech Government," *Politico*, January 29, 2014 (www.politico.eu/article/sobotka-to-lead-new-czech-government).

170. "Babiš dominuje, je to riziko pro demokracii, hlási Rekonstrukce státu. Dřív splu tepali korupci," *Aktuálně.cz*, April 22, 2018 (https://zpravy.aktualne.cz/domaci/kdysi-babis-prevzal-program-rekonstrukce-statu-nyni-ho-kriti/r~c90c388044b111e8b8310cc47ab5f122); Antonella Napolitano, "In Czech Republic, NGOs Launch Anti-Corruption Campaign," *TechPresident*, September 8, 2014 (http://techpresident.com/news/wegov/25252/czech-republic-ngos-anti-corruption-agenda).

171. "Czech Ministry Proposes to Scrap EU Subsidy for PM's Former Firm," *Reuters*, January 4, 2018 (www.reuters.com/article/czech-babis-eu/czech-ministry-proposes-to-scrap-eu-subsidy-for-pms-former-firm-idUSL8N1OZ1T6).

172. Marc Santora, "Scandal Around Billionaire Prime Minister Leaves Czechs in Limbo," *New York Times*, November 23, 2018 (www.nytimes.com/2018/11/23/world/europe/andrej-babis-czech-republic.html); "Czechs Protest After Babis Government Survives No-Confidence Vote," *Radio Free Europe/Radio Liberty*, November 24, 2018 (www.rferl.org/a/czechs-protest-after-babis-government-survives-no-confidence-vote/29618252.html).

173. David Frum, "The Toxic Politics of Migration in the Czech Republic," *Atlantic*, October 23, 2017 (www.theatlantic.com/international/archive/2017/10/czech-elections/543669); "Czech Election: Billionaire Babis Wins by Large Margin," *BBC*, October 22, 2017 (www.bbc.com/news/world-europe-41708844). For more on immigration fears and the populist response in Europe, see William A. Galston with Clara J. Hendrickson, *Anti-Pluralism*, 41–63.

174. ČTK, "PM Babiš Demands that EU Return Powers to National States," *Prague Daily Monitor*, July 20, 2018 (http://praguemonitor.com/2018/07/20/ft-pm-babi%C5%A1-demands-eu-return-powers-national-states).

175. "Nejposlouchanější stanicí zůstává rádio Impuls, potvrdil průzkum," *Lidovky. cz*, November 6, 2014 (www.lidovky.cz/byznys/media/nejposlouchanejsi-stanici-zustava-radio-impuls-potvrdil-pruzkum.A141106_194331_ln-media_hm).

176. "Local Oligarch Conflicts of Interest Dominate Czech Media," *Reporters Without Borders*, July 27, 2016 (https://rsf.org/en/news/local-oligarch-conflicts-interest-dominate-czech-media).

177. Michael Musil, "On Election Eve, Billionaire Czech Media Mogul Sparks Press Freedom Concerns," *International Press Institute*, October 17, 2017 (https://ipi.media/on-election-eve-billionaire-czech-media-mogul-sparks-press-freedom-concerns); "Nahrávka č. 2: Babiš domlouvá s redaktorem MF Dnes články proti Chovancovi," *Forum 24*, May 3, 2017 (www.forum24.cz/nahravka-c-2-babis-domlouva-s-redaktorem-mf-dnes-clanky-proti-chovancovi).

178. Hana de Goeij, "Czech Republic Faces Political Turmoil After No-Confidence Vote," *New York Times,* January 16, 2018 (www.nytimes.com/2018/01/16/world/europe/czech-andrej-babis.html). For more on Babiš's fraud charges, see Peter Laca and Ladka Mortkowitz Bauerova, "Billionaire Election Favorite Is Charged in Czech Fraud Case," *Bloomberg*, October 9, 2017 (www.bloomberg.com/news/articles/2017-10-09/czech-billionaire-charged-over-fraud-allegations-before-election).

179. Mary Stegmaier and Lukáš Linek, "The Communist Party Is Supporting the Czech Coalition Government. What Are the Implications?" *Washington Post,* July 26, 2018 (www.washingtonpost.com/news/monkey-cage/wp/2018/07/26/the-communist-party-is-supporting-the-czech-coalition-government-what-are-the-implications).

180. "The Enduring Influence of the Czech Republic's Communists," *Economist*, July 11, 2018 (www.economist.com/the-economist-explains/2018/07/11/the-enduring-influence-of-the-czech-republics-communists).

181. See, for example, Jiri Pehe, "Czech Democracy Under Pressure," *Journal of Democracy* 29, no. 3 (2018): 65–77 (doi.org/10.1353/jod.2018.0045).

182. Hana de Goeij and Marc Santora, "In the Largest Protests in Decades, Czechs Demand Resignation of Prime Minister," *New York Times,* June 23, 2019 (www.nytimes.com/2019/06/23/world/europe/czech-republic-protests-andrej-babis.html).

183. Daniela Lazarová, "Justice Minister's Resignation Raises Concerns about Possible Political Pressure on Judiciary," *Radio Praha*, April 23, 2019 (www.radio.cz/en/section/curraffrs/justice-ministers-resignation-raises-concerns-about-possible-political-pressure-on-judiciary).

184. Ibid.; "Marie Benešová se vrací jako ministryně spravedlnosti. Její jméno budí kritiku," *ČT24*, April 30, 2019 (https://ct24.ceskatelevize.cz/domaci/2801414-marie-benesova-se-vraci-jako-ministryne-spravedlnosti-jeji-jmeno-budi-kritiku).

185. "Ministryní spravedlnosti bude Marie Benešová. Opozice výměnu spojuje s Čapím hnízdem," *Aktuálně.cz*, April 18, 2019 (https://zpravy.aktualne.cz/domaci/ministr-spravedlnosti-knezinek-konci-ve-funkci-na-konci-dubn/r~8f35ceae61d011e9a049ac1f6b220ee8/).

186. Jaroslav Spurný, "Benešová pro Respekt: Nechystám se odvolat nejvyššího státního zástupce," *Respekt*, April 19, 2019 (www.respekt.cz/politika/benesova-pro-respekt-nechystam-se-odvolat-nejvyssiho-statniho-zastupce).

187. Jan Lopatka, "Czech PM Found in Conflict of Interest by EU Commission:

Report," *Reuters*, May 31, 2019 (www.reuters.com/article/us-czech-babis/czech-pm-found-in-conflict-of-interest-by-eu-commission-report-idUSKCN1T11FS).

188. Jan Lopatka, "Czech Attorneys Drop Fraud Charges Against Billionaire PM Babis," *Reuters,* September 13, 2019 (www.reuters.com/article/us-czech-babis/czech-attorneys-drop-fraud-charges-against-billionaire-pm-babis-idUSKCN1VY0U8); Jan Lopatka, "Top Czech Attorney Reopens Fraud Probe into PM Babis," Reuters, December 4, 2019 (www.reuters.com/article/us-czech-babis/top-czech-attorney-reopens-fraud-probe-into-pm-babis-idUSKBN1Y81JW).

189. Marc Santora, "Czech Republic Re-elects Milos Zeman, Populist Leader and Foe of Migrants," *New York Times*, January 27, 2018 (www.nytimes.com/2018/01/27/world/europe/czech-election-milos-zeman.html).

190. Pehe, "Czech Democracy Under Pressure," 72–3.

191. USAID, "2017 CSO Sustainability Index for Central and Eastern Europe and Eurasia," September 2018 (www.usaid.gov/sites/default/files/documents/1866/2017_CSO_Sustainability_Index_for_Central_and_Eastern_Europe_and_Eurasia.pdf).

192. Peter Ford, "How Do You Challenge the Mainstream Media? Czech Startups Are Finding Out," *Christian Science Monitor,* June 24, 2019 (www.csmonitor.com/World/Europe/2019/0624/How-do-you-challenge-the-mainstream-media-Czech-startups-are-finding-out).

193. Jiří Štický, "Další problém Babiše na Čapím hnízdě. Fígle s fiktivní reklamou," *Reportér*, July 14, 2019 (https://reportermagazin.cz/a/pv6e5/dalsi-problem-babise-na-capim-hnizde-figle-s-fiktivni-reklamou).

194. Sabina Slonková and Jiří Kubík, "Otec chtěl, abych zmizel. Drželi mě na Krymu. Reportéři Seznamu našli Babiše juniora," *Seznam Zprávy*, November 13, 2018 (www.seznamzpravy.cz/clanek/otec-chtel-abych-zmizel-drzeli-me-na-krymu-reporteri-seznamu-nasli-babise-juniora-ve-svycarsku-60222).

195. Eliška Hradilková Bártová, "Jeden nás krmí, druhý propojuje. Jak si Kellner a Babiš rozdělili Česko," *Deník N*, April 15, 2019 (https://denikn.cz/106525/jeden-nas-krmi-druhy-propojuje-jak-si-kellner-a-babis-rozdelili-cesko).

196. Marc Santora, "Protesters Fill Prague Square Again, in New Struggle for Country's Soul," *New York Times,* June 4, 2019 (www.nytimes.com/2019/06/04/world/europe/czech-republic-protests.html); de Goeij and Santora, "In the Largest Protests in Decades"; Redakce Seznam, "Na Letné chtělo Babišovu demisi čtvrt milionu lidí, další demonstrace bude v listopadu," *Seznam zprávy,* June 23, 2019 (www.seznamzpravy.cz/clanek/prahu-ceka-mozna-nejvetsi-demonstrace-od-roku-1989-74647).

197. Cable, Black to U.S. Department of State, Prague 05547, August 15, 1989.

BIBLIOGRAPHY

Altshuler, David S. "Tunneling Towards Capitalism in the Czech Republic." *Ethnography* 2, no. 1 (2001): 115–38. www.jstor.org/stable/24047721.

Berend, Ivan. *From the Soviet Bloc to the European Union: The Economic and Social Transformation of Central and Eastern Europe since 1973.* Cambridge University Press, 2009.

Bertelsmann Stiftung. *BTI 2018 Country Report—Slovakia.* Gütersloh: Bertelsmann Stiftung, 2018. http://www.bti-project.org/fileadmin/files/BTI/Downloads/Reports/2018/pdf/BTI_2018_Slovakia.pdf.

Bílková, Veronica. "Lustration: The Experience of Czechoslovakia/the Czech Republic." In *Conference on Past and Present-Day Lustration: Similarities, Differences, and Applicable Standards.* Strasbourg: Venice Commission, 2015. http://www.venice.coe.int/webforms/documents/default.aspx?pdffile=CDL-PI(2015)028-e.

Brands, Hal. *Making the Unipolar Moment: U.S. Foreign Policy and the Rise of the Post-Cold War Order.* Cornell University Press, 2016.

Brooks, James. "Technical Assistance to Czech Mayors." National League of Cities (August 1993). https://pdf.usaid.gov/pdf_docs/PNABW010.pdf.

Brzezinksi, Zbigniew. "A Plan for Europe: How to Expand NATO." *Foreign Affairs* (January/February 1995). www.foreignaffairs.com/articles/poland/1995-01-01/plan-europe-how-expand-nato.

Bureš, Jan. *Občanské fórum.* Plzeň: Aleš Čeněk, 2007.

Carothers, Thomas. "Think Again: Civil Society." *Foreign Policy* (winter 1999–2000), 18–29 (http://carnegieendowment.org/pdf/CivilSociety.pdf).

———. "Democracy Aid at 25: Time to Choose." Carnegie Endowment for International Peace (January 13, 2015). https://carnegieendowment.org/2015/01/13/democracy-aid-at-25-time-to-choose-pub-57701.

Cichowlas, Ola, and Andrew Foxall. "Now the Czechs Have an Oligarch Problem,

Too." *Foreign Policy* (April 10, 2015). foreignpolicy.com/2015/04/10/now-the-czechs-have-an-oligarch-problem-too-andrej-babis.

Crisen, Sabina. "A Closer Look at the Slovak NGO Community." *The Wilson Center* (July 7, 2011). www.wilsoncenter.org/publication/194-closer-look-the-slovak-ngo-community.

"Czechoslovakia: Parliamentary Elections Chamber of Nations, 1990." http://archive.ipu.org/parline-e/reports/arc/2084_90.htm.

David, Roman. "Lustration Laws in Action: The Motives and Evaluation of Lustration Policy in the Czech Republic and Poland (1989–2001)." *Law & Social Inquiry* 28, no. 2 (spring 2003): 387–439. www.jstor.org/stable/1215775.

Davis, Stephen M., Thomas E. Mann, Norm Ornstein, and Nell Minow. "Prague Declaration on Governance and Anti-Corruption." Brookings Institution (March 21, 2012). www.brookings.edu/research/prague-declaration-on-governance-and-anti-corruption.

Debiel, Tobias, and Andrea Gawrich, eds. *(Dys-)Functionalities of Corruption: Comparative Perspectives and Methodological Pluralism*. Wiesbaden: VS Verlag für Sozialwissenschaften, 2014.

Demeš, Pavol. *A Collective Portrait: The U.S. Contribution to the Development of Civil Society in Slovakia*. Bratislava: Pavol Demeš, 2012.

Diamond, Larry. *In Search of Democracy*. New York: Routledge, 2016.

———. *Promoting Democracy in the 1990s: Actors and Instruments, Issues and Imperatives*. New York: Carnegie Commission on Preventing Deadly Conflict, 1995.

Eisen, Norman. *The Last Palace: Europe's Turbulent Century in Five Lives and One Legendary House*. New York: Crown, 2018.

Encarnación, Omar G. "Assisting Civil Society and Promoting Democracy." In *The Oxford Handbook of Civil Society*, edited by Michael Edwards, 468–79. Oxford University Press, 2011.

———. "On Bowling Leagues and NGOs: A Critique of Civil Society's Revival." *Studies in Comparative and International Development* 36, no. 4 (2002): 116–31.

Epstein, Susan B., Larry Q. Nowels, and Steven A. Hildreth. *Foreign Policy Agency Reorganization in the 105th Congress*. Washington, DC: Congressional Research Service, 1998. https://pdf.usaid.gov/pdf_docs/PCAAA780.pdf.

Estrin, Saul. "The Impact of Privatization in Transition Economies." In *The New Palgrave Dictionary of Economics, 2nd edition*, edited by Steven N. Durlauf and Lawrence E. Blume. London: Palgrave MacMillan, 2008. https://doi.org/10.1057/978-1-349-95121-5_2547-1.

Evanson, Robert K. "Political Repression in Czechoslovakia, 1948–1984." *Canadian Slavonic Papers / Revue Canadienne des Slavistes* 28, no. 1 (1986): 1–21.

Fagan, Adam. "Taking Stock of Civil-Society Development in Post-Communist Europe: Evidence from the Czech Republic." *Democratization* 12, no. 4 (2005): 528–47. https://doi.org/10.1080/13510340500226077.

Fry, John. *The Helsinki Process: Negotiating Security and Cooperation in Europe*. Washington, DC: National Defense University Press, 1993.

Gaddis, John Lewis. *The United States and the End of the Cold War: Implications, Reconsiderations, Provocations*. Oxford University Press, 1992.

Gallina, Nicole. "Anti-Corruption Revisited: The Case of the Czech Republic and Slovakia." In *(Dys-)Functionalities of Corruption: Comparative Perspectives and Methodological Pluralism*, edited by Tobias Debiel and Andrea Gawrich, 183–218. Wiesbaden: VS Verlag für Sozialwissenschaften, 2014.

Galston, William. *Anti-Pluralism: The Populist Threat to Liberal Democracy.* Yale University Press, 2018.

Garton Ash, Timothy. *The Magic Lantern: The Revolution of '89 Witnessed in Warsaw, Budapest, Berlin, and Prague.* New York: Vintage Books, 1993.

Gjuričová, Adéla, Michal Kopeček, Petr Roubal, Jiří Suk, and Tomáš Zahradníček. *Rozděleni minulostí. Vytváření politických identit v České republice po roce 1989.* Prague: Knihovna Václava Havla, 2011.

Glenn, John K. "International Aid to New Political Parties in the Czech Republic and Slovakia." *Voluntas: International Journal of Voluntary and Nonprofit Organizations* 11, no. 2 (2000): 161–79. www.jstor.org/stable/27927681.

Godlove, Albena et al. *Europe and Eurasia Enterprise Funds and Legacy Foundations Final Evaluation Report.* Washington, DC: USAID, 2017. https://pdf.usaid.gov/pdf_docs/PA00STKC.pdf.

Goldgeier, James M. *Not Whether But When: The U.S. Decision to Enlarge NATO.* Washington, DC: Brookings Institution Press, 1999.

Gordon, Lincoln et al. *Eroding Empire: Western Relations with Eastern Europe.* Washington, DC: Brookings Institution Press, 1987.

Hamm, Patrick, Lawrence P. King, and David Stuckler. "Mass Privatization, State Capacity, and Economic Growth in Post-Communist Countries." *American Sociological Review* 77, no. 2 (2012): 295–324. https://doi.org/10.1177/0003122412441354.

Hammontree, Patsy G. *Shirley Temple Black: A Bio-Bibliography.* Westport, CT: Greenwood Press, 1998.

Havel, Václav. "New Year's Address to the Nation." Speech, Czechoslovakia (January 1, 1990). www.vhlf.org/havel-quotes/1990-new-years-speech.

———. "The Power of the Powerless." In *The Power of the Powerless: Citizens Against the State in Central-Eastern Europe*, edited by John Keane, 23–96. New York: Routledge, 2015.

———. "The Sad State of the Republic," *New York Review of Books* (March 5, 1998). www.nybooks.com/articles/1998/03/05/the-sad-state-of-the-republic.

———. Speech to U.S. Congress (February 22, 1990). www.vhlf.org/havel-quotes/speech-to-the-u-s-congress/.

———. "Václav vs. Václav." *New York Review of Books* (May 10, 2007). www.nybooks.com/articles/2007/05/10/vaclav-vs-vaclav.

Heimann, Mary. *Czechoslovakia: The State That Failed.* Yale University Press, 2011.

Hook, Steven W. "'Building Democracy' Through Foreign Aid: The Limitations of United States Political Conditionalities, 1992–96." *Democratization* 5, no. 3 (1998): 156–80. https://doi.org/10.1080/13510349808403576.

Hutchings, Robert L. *American Diplomacy and the End of the Cold War: An Insider's Account of U.S. Policy in Europe, 1989–1992.* Washington, DC: Woodrow Wilson Center Press, 1997.

Ježek, Tomáš. "The Czechoslovak Experience with Privatization." *Journal of International Affairs* 50, no. 2 (1997): 477–88. www.jstor.org/stable/24357627.

Karklins, Rasma. "Typology of Post-Communist Corruption." *Problems of Post-Communism* 49, no. 4 (2002): 22–32. https://doi.org/10.1080/10758216.2002.11655993.

Kenealy, Andrew. "Best Supporting Actors: U.S. Embassy Prague and the Velvet Revolution, 1989." *Journal of Cold War Studies*. Forthcoming.

Kirchick, James. "Return of the Czech Communists." *Foreign Policy* (October 12, 2012). www.foreignpolicy.com/2012/10/12/return-of-the-czech-communists.

Korey, William. *The Promises We Keep.* New York: St. Martin's Press, 1993.

Koudelková, Petra, Wadim Strielkowski, and Denisa Hejlová. "Corruption and System Change in the Czech Republic: Firm-Level Evidence." *DANUBE: Law and Economics Review* 6, no. 1 (March 2015): 25–46. https://doi.org/10.1515/danb-2015-0002.

Křen, Jan. *Čtvrt století střední Evropy: Visegrádské země v globálním příběhu let 1992-2017.* Prague: Karolinum, 2019.

Kukral, Michael. *Prague 1989: Theater of Revolution.* Boulder, CO: East European Monographs, 1997.

Luers, William H. "Czechoslovakia: Road to Revolution." *Foreign Affairs* 69, no. 2 (1990): 77–98. www.jstor.org/stable/20044305.

Mareš, Petr, Jana Kreuzigerová, and Jan Marian. *Zahraniční pomoc v Česku a Československu po roce 1989: Cíle, formy a výsledky.* Prague: Asociace pro mezinárodní otázky, 2006.

McMaster, Irene. "Privatisation in Central and Eastern Europe: What Made the Czech Republic So Distinctive?" *University of Strathclyde in Glasgow: European Policies Research Centre Regional and Industrial Research Papers,* no. 49 (November 2001). https://pureportal.strath.ac.uk/en/publications/privatisation-in-central-and-eastern-europe-what-made-the-czech-r.

McRae, Rob. *Resistance and Revolution: Vaclav Havel's Czechoslovakia.* Canada: Carleton University Press, 1997.

Mertlík, Pavel. "Czech Privatization: From Public Ownership to Public Ownership in Five Years?" *Eastern European Economics* 35, no. 2 (1997): 64–83. www.jstor.org/stable/4380082.

Milo, Daniel, and Katarína Klingová. "Vulnerability Index: Subversive Russian Influence in Central Europe." Bratislava: GLOBSEC, 2017. www.globsec.org/wp-content/uploads/2017/08/globsec-vulnerability-index.pdf.

Mlčoch, Lubomír. *Úvahy o české ekonomické tranformaci.* Prague: Vyšehrad, 2000.

Myant, Martin. "Podoby kapitalismu v České republice." In *Kapitoly z dějin české demokracie po roce 1989,* edited by Adéla Gjuričová and Michal Kopeček, 265–87. Prague: Paseka, 2008.

National Democratic Institute for International Affairs. "Statement by the International Observer Delegation to the Czech and Slovak Federative Republic Elections" (June 10, 1990). www.ndi.org/sites/default/files/1369_sk_elec_5.pdf.

Naval, Concepción, Murray Print, and Ruud Veldhuis. "Education for Democratic Citizenship in the New Europe: Context and Reform." *European Journal of Education* 37, no. 2 (2002): 107–28. www.jstor.org/stable/1503793.

Nellis, John. *The World Bank, Privatization, and Enterprise Reform in Transition Economies: A Retrospective Analysis.* Washington, DC: World Bank, 2002. http://documents.worldbank.org/curated/en/761441468758967175/The-World -Bank-privatization-and-enterprise-reform-in-transition-economies-a-retro- spective-analysis.

Newberg, Paula R., and Thomas Carothers. "Aiding—and Defining—Democracy." *World Policy Journal* 13, no. 1 (1996): 97–108. www.jstor.org/stable/40209465.

Nič, Milan, Marek Slobodník, and Michal Šimečka. *Slovakia in the EU: An Un- expected Success Story?* Berlin: Deutsche Gesellschaft für Auswärtige Politik, 2014. https://dgap.org/en/think-tank/publications/dgapanalysis/slovakia-eu.

North Atlantic Treaty Organization. "The North Atlantic Treaty" (April 4, 1949). www.nato.int/cps/en/natolive/official_texts_17120.htm.

Organisation for Economic Cooperation and Development. *Czech Republic.* Paris: OECD, 1998. www.oecd-ilibrary.org/docserver/eco_surveys-cze-1998-en.pdf? expires=1571753287&id=id&accname=ocid44008324&checksum=766BF978 EDEFD82A2C7D7910C9306AC2.

Peace Corps. "Peace Corps Holds Discussion on the Slovak Republic" (May 23, 2011). www.peacecorps.gov/news/library/peace-corps-hosts-discussion-on-the -slovak-republic.

Pehe, Jiri. "Czech Democracy Under Pressure." *Journal of Democracy* 29, no. 3 (2018): 65–77. https://muse.jhu.edu/article/698918/pdf.

Pithart, Petr. "Svobodné volby 1990: Jaké režimy od sebe oddělují?" In *Svobodné volby v Československu 1990. Referendum o dalším směřování státu a společno- sti*, edited by Pavel Krákora, 18–32. Prague: Epocha, 2010.

Polyakova, Alina, Torrey Taussig, Ted Reinert, Kemal Kirişci, Amanda Sloat, James Kirchick, Melissa Hooper, Norman Eisen, and Andrew Kenealy. *The Anatomy of Illiberal States: Assessing and Responding to Democratic Decline in Turkey and Central Europe.* Washington, DC: Brookings Institution, 2019. www.brookings.edu/research/the-anatomy-of-illiberal-states.

Prečan, Vilém, and Derek Paton, eds. *The Democratic Revolution in Czechoslova- kia: Its Precondition, Course, and Immediate Repercussions 1987–89: A Chronol- ogy of Events and a Compendium of Declassified Documents.* Prague: National Security Archive, Czechoslovak Documentation Centre, and Institute of Con- temporary History, 1999.

Prečan, Vilém, ed. *Prague–Washington–Prague: Reports from the United States Embassy in Czechoslovakia, November–December 1989.* Prague: Václav Havel Library, 2004.

Pullman, Michal. "The Demise of the Communist Regime in Czechoslovakia, 1987–89: A Socio-economic Perspective." In *The 1989 Revolutions in Central and Eastern Europe*, edited by Kevin McDermott and Matthew Stibbe, 154–71. Manchester University Press, 2015.

Quigley, Charles N., and Jack N. Hoar. "Civitas: An International Civic Education Exchange Program." In *Principles and Practices of Education for Democratic Cit- izenship*, edited by Charles F. Bahmueller and John J. Patrick, 123–46. Bloom- ington, IN: ERIC/ChESS 1999. http://files.eric.ed.gov/fulltext/ED434866.pdf.

Rieffer, Barbara Ann J., with Kristan Mercer. "US Democracy Promotion: The Bush and Clinton Administrations." *Global Society* 19, no. 4 (2005): 385–408. http://doi.org/10.1080/13600820500242654.

Risse, Thomas, and Kathryn Sikkink. "The Socialization of International Human Rights Norms into Domestic Practices: Introduction." In *The Power of Human Rights: International Norms and Domestic Change*, edited by Thomas Risse, Stephen Ropp, and Kathryn Sikkink, 1–38. Cambridge University Press, 1999.

Robinson, William H. "Parliamentary Development in Central and Eastern Europe." *Bulletin of the American Society for Information Science* 19, no. 4 (1993): 8–9.

Sajo, Andras. "Corruption, Clientelism, and the Future of the Constitutional State in Eastern Europe." *East European Constitutional Review* 7, no. 2 (spring 1998): 37–46.

Sampor, Željko. "Media Pluralism Monitor 2016: Monitoring Risks for Media Pluralism in the EU and Beyond Country Report: Slovakia." *Centre for Media Pluralism and Media Freedom*, 2016. https://cadmus.eui.eu/bitstream/handle/1814/46810/Slovachia_EN.pdf.

Savranskaya, Svetlana, Thomas Blanton, and Vladislav Zubok, eds. *Masterpieces of History: The Peaceful End of the Cold War in Europe, 1989.* Budapest: Central European University Press, 2010.

Schmidt, Jessica. *Rethinking Democracy Promotion in International Relations: The Rise of the Social.* New York: Routledge, 2016.

Sebestyen, Victor. *Revolution 1989: The Fall of the Soviet Empire.* New York: Pantheon Books, 2009.

Shafik, Nemat. "Making a Market: Mass Privatization in the Czech and Slovak Republics." *World Development* 23, no. 7 (1995): 1143–56. https://doi.org/10.1016/0305-750X(95)00037-D.

Šikulová, Ivana, and Karol Frank. "The Slovak Experience with Transition to Market Economy." Working Paper, *Welfare, Wealth, and Work for Europe Project.* Bratislava: Ekonomický ústav SAV, 2013. http://ekonom.sav.sk/uploads/journals/229_wp_49_sikulova_frank_experience_with_transition.pdf.

Školkay, Andrej, and Alena Ištoková. "Media Coverage of Corruption: The Role of Inter-Media Agenda Setting in the Context of Media Reporting on Scandals." *Środkowoeuropejskie Studia Polityczne*, no. 2 (2016): 125–40.

"Slovakia Corruption Index." Trading Economics. www.tradingeconomics.com/slovakia/corruption-index.

Snyder, Sarah. "The Foundation for Vienna: A Reassessment of the CSCE in the Mid-1980s." *Cold War History* 10, no. 4 (2010): 493–512.

———. *Human Rights Activism and the End of the Cold War: A Transnational History of the Helsinki Network.* Cambridge University Press, 2011.

Søndergaard, Rasmus Sinding. "Bill Clinton's 'Democratic Enlargement' and the Securitisation of Democracy Promotion." *Diplomacy & Statecraft* 26, no. 3 (2015): 534–51. https://doi.org/10.1080/09592296.2015.1067529.

The Foundation for a Civil Society. "Czech Republic Democracy Network Program: Quarterly Report for the Period of April 1 through June 30, 1995" (1995). https://pdf.usaid.gov/pdf_docs/PDABM061.pdf.

———. "Democracy Network Program Czech Republic: Final Program Report" (1997). https://pdf.usaid.gov/pdf_docs/PDABQ053.pdf.

The White House. *National Security Strategy 1995: A National Security Strategy of Engagement and Enlargement* (February 1995). http://nssarchive.us/national-security-strategy-1995.

The White House. *National Security Strategy of the United States* (January 1993). http://nssarchive.us/national-security-strategy-1993.

Ther, Philipp. *Europe Since 1989: A History.* Princeton University Press, 2016.

Thomas, Daniel. "Human Rights Ideas, the Demise of Communism, and the End of the Cold War." *Journal of Cold War Studies* 7, no. 2 (2005): 110–41.

———. "The Helsinki Accords and Political Change in Eastern Europe." In *The Power of Human Rights: International Norms and Domestic Change*, edited by Thomas Risse, Stephen Ropp, and Kathryn Sikkink, 205–33. Cambridge University Press, 1999.

———. *The Helsinki Effect: International Norms, Human Rights, and the Demise of Communism.* Princeton University Press, 2001.

Tomek, Prokop. "Akce Zásah: Československá lidová armáda v listopadu 1989." *Historie a vojenství* 4 (2015): 77–91.

Ulrich, Marybeth Peterson. "U.S. Assistance and Democratic Militarization in the Czech Republic." *Problems of Post-Communism* 45, no. 2 (1998). https://doi.org/10.1080/10758216.1998.11655778.

USAID. "20 Years of USAID Economic Growth Assistance in Europe and Eurasia" (July 2013). www.usaid.gov/where-we-work/europe-and-eurasia/20-years-economic-growth-assistance.

———. "2017 CSO Sustainability Index for Central and Eastern Europe and Eurasia" (September 2018). www.usaid.gov/sites/default/files/documents/1866/2017_CSO_Sustainability_Index_for_Central_and_Eastern_Europe_and_Eurasia.pdf.

———. "Monitoring Country Progress in Central and Eastern Europe and the Newly Independent States" (July 1999). https://pdf.usaid.gov/pdf_docs/PNADG905.pdf.

U.S. Congress. House. *Central Enterprise Development Commission: Hearing Before the Committee on Small Business.* 102nd Cong., 1st sess. (July 24, 1991).

———. *Democracy Building in the Former Soviet Union: Hearing Before the Subcommittee on International Operations of the Committee on Foreign Affairs.* 102nd Cong., 2nd sess. (March 18, 1992).

———. *Economic and Political Change in Eastern Europe: Report of Staff Study Mission to Poland, Hungary, Czechoslovakia, and the Former German Democratic Republic, August 1–12, 1990, to the Committee on Foreign Affairs.* 101st Cong., 2nd sess. (November 1990).

———. *Foreign Operations, Export Financing, and Related Programs Appropriations for 2001: Hearings Before a Subcommittee of the Committee on Appropriations.* 106th Cong., 2nd sess. (February 2000).

———. *Peace Corps: Meeting the Challenges of the 1990's* [sic]: *Hearing Before the Legislation and National Security Subcommittee of the Committee on Government Operations.* 101st Cong., 2nd sess. (May 22, 1990).

———. *United States Public Diplomacy in Eastern Europe and the Soviet Union: Hearing Before the Subcommittee on International Relations of the Committee on Foreign Affairs.* 102nd Cong., 1st sess. (July 30, 1991).

———. *U.S. Assistance Programs in Europe: An Assessment: Hearing Before the Subcommittee on Europe of the Committee on International Relations.* 108th Cong., 1st sess. (March 27, 2003).

———. *U.S. Assistance to Central and Eastern Europe: Hearing Before the Subcommittee on Europe and the Middle East of the Committee on Foreign Affairs.* 102nd Cong., 2nd sess. (June 3, 1992).

U.S. Department of State. "FY 2003 SEED Act Implementation Report: U.S. Government Assistance to Eastern Europe under the Support for East European Democracy (SEED) Act" (January 2004). https://pdf.usaid.gov/pdf_docs/PCAAB336.pdf.

———. "SEED Act Implementation Report: Fiscal Year 1992" (January 1993). https://pdf.usaid.gov/pdf_docs/PNABN454.pdf.

———. "SEED Act Implementation Report: Fiscal Year 1994" (January 1995). https://pdf.usaid.gov/pdf_docs/PCAAA701.pdf.

———. "SEED Act Implementation Report: Fiscal Year 1995" (February 1996). https://pdf.usaid.gov/pdf_docs/PCAAA735.pdf.

———. "SEED Act Implementation Report: Fiscal Year 1996" (February 1997). https://pdf.usaid.gov/pdf_docs/PCAAA736.pdf.

———. "SEED Act Implementation Report: Fiscal Year 1998" (March 1999). https://pdf.usaid.gov/pdf_docs/PCAAB179.pdf.

———. "Slovakia 2017 Human Rights Report" (2017). www.state.gov/wp-content/uploads/2019/01/Slovakia.pdf.

U.S. Embassy in Slovakia. "Joint Anti-Corruption Day Statement" (December 7, 2018). https://sk.usembassy.gov/joint-anti-corruption-day-statement-4.

———. "Notice of Funding Opportunity." https://sk.usembassy.gov/wp-content/uploads/sites/193/Annual-Program-Statement-FY-2019.pdf.

———. "U.S. Embassy Bratislava PAS Annual Program Statement." https://sk.usembassy.gov/wp-content/uploads/sites/193/Annual-Program-Statement-FY-2019.pdf.

U.S. Embassy in the Czech Republic. "Small Grants Program." https://cz.usembassy.gov/education-culture/small-grants-program.

———. "U.S.-Czech Anti-Corruption Efforts" (August 14, 2014). https://cz.usembassy.gov/wp-content/uploads/sites/22/2015/11/Anti-Corruption-One-Pager.pdf.

U.S. Embassy Warsaw. "United States SEED Act Assistance Strategy Update for the Czech Republic" (July 19, 1994). https://pdf.usaid.gov/pdf_docs/PNABU147.pdf.

U.S. Government Accountability Office. *Enterprise Funds: Evolving Models for Private Sector Development in Central and Eastern Europe.* NSIAD-94-77 (September 3, 1994). www.govinfo.gov/content/pkg/GAOREPORTS-NSIAD-94-77/html/GAOREPORTS-NSIAD-94-77.htm.

Veillette, Connie, and Susan B. Epstein. *State, Foreign Operations, and Related*

Programs: FY2008 Appropriations. Washington, DC: Congressional Research Service, 2007. https://fas.org/sgp/crs/row/RL34023.pdf.

Virkovic, Marian. "Quasi-Effective Governance: Slovak Mass Privatisation 1991–1996." *Journal of Economic Studies* 30, no. 3 (2003): 294–350. https://www.econstor.eu/bitstream/10419/125672/1/WWWforEurope_WPS_no017_MS23_Backgroundpaper1.pdf.

Waisová, Šárka. "Between Atlanticism, Anti-Americanism and Europeanization: Dilemmas in Czech Foreign Policy and the War on Terrorism." In *Czechoslovakia and Czech Republic in the World Politics*, edited by Ladislav Cabada and Šárka Waisová, 111–25. Plzeň: Aleš Čeněk, 2006.

Williamson, John. "Did the Washington Consensus Fail?" Peterson Institute for International Economics (November 6, 2002). www.piie.com/commentary/speeches-papers/did-washington-consensus-fail.

World Bank. *World Development Report 1996: From Plan to Market.* Oxford University Press, 1996. http://hdl.handle.net/10986/5979.

APPENDIX
Mandatory Declassification Review Request

To: Alden Fahy
From: Norman L. Eisen
Date: July 17, 2017
Subject: Request for MDR re: Embassy Prague from Aug. 1989 to Jan. 1990

Dear Alden:

As we discussed on Friday, here is a proposed request under EO 12958 and 22 CFR Part 171, Subpart C for mandatory declassification review regarding Embassy Prague. I have attempted to be precise in identifying the records, which are listed in chronological order between August 1989 and January 1990. I am of course ready to receive on a rolling basis or to trim back this list if that will expedite matters. To that end I have marked the most urgent items with asterisks. If there is a file list or other index that it might be possible to review to speed things up, that would be fine as well. I am of course open to any suggestions you have for how to edit or revise the list.

You will note, by the way, that some Embassy Prague cables for November–December 1989 were previously produced to researchers for a Havel Library publication in 2004. I am also sending the table of contents of that volume listing those cables to avoid duplication. There is no need to produce them a second time, and as you will see I have targeted materials not previously requested. I am sending this item under separate cover, lest the size of the pdf cause this email to get trapped in a filter.

I would of course still like to proceed on the other track we have been discussing for some time now, and I ask that we keep trying on that front. But given the uncertainties there I appreciate your considering this option as I am nearing my deadline to turn in my book manuscript (it is due September 30 of this year). All of the records herein are more than 25 years old and so would be subject to automatic declassification under FAM 485.

Once you have had a chance to look the enclosed over, please let me know your thoughts, including whether I also need submit a formal request by mail or fax.

Many thanks,

Norm Eisen

*   *   *

1. **Records regarding a meeting between Czechoslovak dissidents and U.S. Ambassador Shirley Temple Black on or around August 17, 1989. (NOTE: asterisks indicate priority records.)

2. Records related to an "oral warning" presented to Embassy Prague by the Czechoslovak Foreign Ministry prior to August 21, 1989, that the Ministry could not ensure the security of those within range of demonstrations. (Ref'd in: Prague 08087, November 20, 1989.)

3. **Any other records pertaining to the Prague protests of August 21, 1989, including the lead-up to the protest and its aftermath (other than the records listed herein and in the attachment).

4. Records regarding Ambassador Black's introductory meeting with Czechoslovak Foreign Minister Jaromir Johanes on or around August 22, 1989.

5. **Records regarding Ambassador Black's presentation of her credentials to Czechoslovak President Husak on or around August 23, 1989, and the conversation that followed.

6. Records regarding a meeting between Czechoslovak dissidents and four visiting U.S. Senators on or around August 24, 1989.

7. Records regarding Ambassador Black's Slovak trip of August 24–25, 1989, to attend the celebration of the Slovak National Uprising, including her confrontation with Vasil Bilak at the celebration on or about August 25.

8. Records regarding the meeting between U.S. Secretary of State Baker and Czechoslovak Foreign Minister Johanes at the United Nations General Assembly on September 27, 1989 (including the planning and follow-up).

9. **Records regarding a meeting between Vaclav Havel and Ambassador Black at the ambassador's residence on or around October 4, 1989, also attended by other USG personnel, film director Milos Forman and costume designer Doda Pistek.

10. Any other records pertaining to contacts or communications between Ambassador Black and Vaclav Havel between October 1, 1989, and the end

of January, 1990 aftermath (other than the records listed herein and in the attachment).

11. **Prague 7592, sent between October 28, 1989 and November 4, 1989, referencing the formal protest of Embassy Prague to the Czechoslovak government concerning the harassment of American journalists during the protests of October 28, 1989. (Referenced in: Prague 07736, November 4, 1989.)

12. Czechoslovak Foreign Ministry diplomatic note no. 317.572/89, sent in response to Embassy Prague's formal protest (contained in Prague 7592) and stating that Czechoslovakia would not ensure the safety of those present near unofficial demonstrations. (Referenced in: Prague 08087, November 20, 1989.)

13. Prague 7612, sent between October 28, 1989 and November 4, 1989, noting that 148 Czechoslovak citizens were held and charged with misdemeanors at a demonstration on October 28, 1989. (Referenced in: Prague 07736, November 4, 1989.)

14. Prague 7564, sent between October 28, 1989 and November 4, 1989, noting that eighteen foreigners detained on October 28, 1989 by Czechoslovak police were released. (Referenced in: Prague 07736, November 4, 1989.)

15. Prague 7534, sent between November 2, 1989 and November 4, 1989, noting that Czechoslovak press spokesperson Miroslav Pavel at a Thursday, November 2 press conference defended Czechoslovak police action in breaking up an independent demonstration on October 28, 1989. (Referenced in: Prague 07736, November 4, 1989.)

16. **Any other Records pertaining to the Prague protests of October 28, 1989, both in the lead-up to the protest and its aftermath (other than the records listed herein and in the attachment).

17. Records regarding the inspection visit involving Perry Shankle to Prague in late October and/or November 1989.

18. **Prague 8011, sent on November 15, 1989 or November 16, 1989, containing information regarding Embassy Prague conversations with Czechoslovak activists in the lead up to the November 17, 1989 student protests. (Referenced in: Prague 08031, November 16, 1989.)

19. Records regarding the Canadian-American reception co-hosted by Ambassador Black and Canadian Charge d'Affaires Robert McRae on the evening of November 17, 1989.

20. **Records regarding Ambassador Black's phone calls and other communications with the U.S. Department of State Operations Center, from roughly 12PM to 12AM ET, November 17, 1989. (Witnesses recall Ambassador Black repeatedly phoning State Ops.)

21. All Records pertaining to the Prague protests of November 17, 1989, both in the lead-up to the protest and its aftermath (other than the records listed herein and in the attachment).

22. Records regarding Ambassador Black's meeting with Czechoslovak Foreign Minister Johanes on November 28, 1989 to protest Czechoslovak government conduct.

23. **Records regarding Ambassador Black's first meeting in early January 1990 with the newly elected Chairman of the Federal Assembly of Czechoslovakia, Alexander Dubcek. The meeting likely occurred during the week of January 9, and in any case no later than January 19, 1990.

24. Any other records regarding meetings between Czechoslovak dissidents and Embassy Prague between August 17, 1989 and November 24, 1989 (other than the records listed herein and in the attachment).

INDEX

Figures and notes are indicated by f *and* n *following the page number.*

August 21st demonstrations (*cont.*)
to, 20–24; human rights updates
following, 47–50, 59–61, 71–75;
Johanes on, 52; media coverage of,
39, 58; organizational support for
demonstrations, 22–23; overview of
events, 9–10; police confrontation
and violence against demonstrators,
25, 32–33, 39–42, 57–58; protest
activities planned for, 22–23, 31–34;
public mood leading up to, 8–9,
19–20, 26–29, 31–34; purpose of,
9; regime's warning about, 17–18;
retrospective view of, 56–58; two
minutes of silence protest, 31, 33,
38, 39–40; warning to U.S. embassy
regarding, 29–31, 34–35

Babiš, Andrej, 170–72, 192n167
Baker, James, 10, 79–81, 100, 133, 152
Barry, Robert L., 162
Belgium, cancellation of foreign minister visit from, 130
Benešová, Marie, 171, 172
Bernthal, Lou, 55, 55na
BFWG (Business Facilitation Working
Group), 81, 81nb
Black, Shirley Temple: on attitude of
public, 8; on August 21st demonstrations, 9; Bratislava U.S. film
exhibit and, 65; career of, 175n7;
on demonstrations and violence,
11–12; dissent in Czechoslovakia
supported by, 4; on Havel's election, 148; human rights advocacy
and, 7–8; meeting with Johanes on
human rights, 9–10, 43–46; meeting
with Johanes on normalization of
U.S. relations, 13; meeting with
Ziebart, 35–37; on October 28th
demonstrations, harassment of
senior inspector during, 114–15;
security for, 69
Bok, John, 112
Brands, Hal, 150–51

Bratinka, Pavel, 134
Bratislava: criminal charges for activists in, 48, 59, 61, 72; cultural center
and consulate at, 66–67; Czechoslovak Republic for Human Rights
and Humanitarian Cooperation
committee in, 125; embassy report
on readiness for change in, 105–11;
general impressions of embassy
officers, 110–11; Slovak activist
activities in, 33, 48; U.S. film exhibit
in, 65
Bratislava Five, 59, 61, 109, 109na
Breaches of public order charges, 74
Brezhnev doctrine, 53, 53na
Bribery, 164–65
Bush, George H. W., 8, 43–44, 132,
151–52
Business Facilitation Working Group
(BFWG), 81, 81nb

CAEF (Czech-American Enterprise
Fund), 152–53
Čalfa, Marián, 134nb
Capitalism, 151
Čaputová, Zuzana, 169
Čarnogurský, Ján: criminal charges
resulting from August 21st demonstrations, 48, 61, 71, 72; embassy
officers' visit with father of, 108;
petition for release of, 83; reduction of charges against, 83; Slovak
state official criticism of, 107; U.S.
support for, 79, 99, 108
Carothers, Thomas, 155, 158–59, 184n64
Carter, Jimmy, 4
Catholic Church: bishop consecrations,
49, 72, 74–75, 87, 110; Civic Forum
on, 137; consecration ceremonies
for new bishops, 49; as facilitator of
open dialog, 21, 23; Saint Agnes of
Bohemia canonization ceremony,
122, 125; Saint Wenceslas Day mass
and demonstrations, 84; Slovakia
and, 84, 110; support for democ-

racy, 137; warning on violence against demonstrators, 23

Center for International Private Enterprise (CIPE), 153–54

Cerny, Vaclav, 92

Chafee, John, 134

Charter 77: on canonization ceremony for Saint Agnes of Bohemia, 125; detention of members prior to October 28th demonstrations, 112; on October 28th demonstration plans, 84, 96, 104; publication of, 4–5; two minutes of silence protest and, 31, 33, 39–40

Chudomel, Jan, 119

Cibulka, Petr, 21, 21na, 23, 74, 96

CIPE (Center for International Private Enterprise), 153–54

Circle of Independent Intellectuals, 97–98

CivAir agreement, 56, 64

Civic Democratic Party, 166, 170

Civic Forum (OF): Adamec's meeting with, 132, 134; Čalfa, support for, 134nb; communications equipment for, 143; creation of, 12; on democratic political structures, 135–36; economic aid for, 156; economic view of, 136; elections (1990), 148; elections (1992), 148; general strike (November 27th), 12, 134; meeting with U.S. senators, 133–37; on new coalition government, 134–35; peaceful transfer of power to, 6–7; presidential election timing controversy, 140–42

Civil society aid, 158–60, 185n69

CIVITAS International, 160

Clientelism, 164

Clinton, Bill, 152, 163

Cloud, John, 82

CoCom controls, 45, 51, 63, 142–43

Colasuonno, Francesco, 49

Cold War strategy, 4

Committee for the Defense of the Un-

justly Persecuted (VONS), 118, 119

Communist-era elites, 164–65

Communist Party of Bohemia and Moravia, 171

Communist Party of Czeckoslovakia (CPCz): canonization ceremony for Saint Agnes of Bohemia and, 125; ceding control of government, 12–14; CSS challenge to leading role in National Front, 91; election results for (1990), 148; forum of independent groups demanding resignation of members, 128–29; Jakeš as transitional figure in, 86–89; opposition leaders, meetings with, 13; party unity in, 88; presidential election timing controversy and, 140–42; reform efforts of, 12–13; Soviet diplomat on opposition within, 75–78

Conference on Security and Cooperation in Europe (CSCE): August 21st demonstrations and, 25; background of, 25na; Helsinki Accords and, 4–5, 8; on recognition of opposition political parties, 123; U.S.-Czech relations and, 62–63

Corruption: Communist-era elites and, 164–65; in Czech Republic, 170–73; privatization and, 164–67; in Slovak Republic, 167–69; tunneling phenomenon and, 165

Corruption Perception Index, 167

Counter-intelligence capabilities of U.S. embassy, 66

CPCz. See Communist Party of Czeckoslovakia

Cranston, Alan, 19, 25, 50–53

Credit market, 157–58

Crha, Miroslav, 73

Crime, 139, 144–45

Cultural exchange program, 63–65, 71

Cultural expression, 87

Czech-American Enterprise Fund (CAEF), 152–53

Czech and Slovak-American Enterprise Fund (CSAEF), 152–53
Czech Children, 22, 33, 96
Czech Municipal Finance Company, 158
Czechoslovak Academy of Science, 64
Czechoslovak Federal Assembly, 157
Czechoslovak Helsinki Committee, 74, 95, 98–99, 112
Czechoslovakia: August 21st demonstrations and, 29–31, 34–35, 43; exports to Soviet Union, 87–88; force reduction of, 51; gold claims, settlement from WWII, 80, 80*na*; Helsinki Accords, signing of, 4–5; Hungarian relations, 54–55, 57, 107; incentives to increase human rights, 8, 24–25, 177*n*34; liberalization of political and economic policies, 36, 45–46, 45*n*b; Nagymaros-Gabcikovo dam dispute and, 54–55; Polish relations, 57; resistance to reform in, 86–89; Slovak relations, 106, 108; U.S. relations, 6–7, 13, 43–45, 51–52, 58, 62–71, 80, 131; Velvet Revolution (1989), 1–2, 6–7, 14; war memorials and, 80. *See also* Czech Republic; Economic reforms; *specific political parties*
Czechoslovak People's Party (Obrodny Proud), 97, 148
Czechoslovak Socialist Party (CSS), 89–92, 97, 122, 124
Czechoslovak TV, on sentence for Hungarian airline hijackers, 61
Czech Republic: Czechoslovak Great Lustration Act (1991), 164; EU membership, 163; NATO membership, 161; privatization and corruption in, 163–66, 170–73; Velvet Divorce (1993), 147. *See also* U.S. support for democracy

Democracy. *See* U.S. support for democracy

Democracy Network (DemNet) Program, 159
Democratic Initiative (DI), 33, 95, 122, 123, 123*na*
Demonstrations and protests: diplomats and journalists attending, 7, 11, 30, 34, 44*nb*, 113, 128, 131–32; environmental, 125–26; general strike (November 27th), 12, 134; government permits for, 84, 96, 122–23; Palach self-immolation commemoration (January 19th), 18; in response to police violence (November 20-26, 1989), 12; Velvet Revolution (1989) resulting from, 1–2, 6–7, 14. *See also* Foreign participation in demonstrations; Police confrontation and violence against demonstrators; *specific demonstrations and protests*
Deník N (media outlet), 172
Detentions and arrests: August 21st demonstrations and, 39, 42, 47–49, 60, 112; of Charter 77 members, 112; of Havel, 6, 111–12; of Helsinki Committee members, 72, 74, 98–99, 112; of Hungarian activists, 49, 52, 54–55; of Independent Peace Association activists, 22; of *Lidove noviny* editors, 93–95, 99–100, 122, 124; of Movement for Civil Liberties activists, 95, 96, 122, 124; of Několik vět supporters, 84–85; of Obroda members, 21, 93; of Obrodny Proud members, 97; October 28th demonstrations and, 111–14, 118–19; of RFE correspondent, 133; of Wehrwolf activists, 23–24. *See also specific people*
Deutsch, Tamas, 49
Devátý, Stanislav: background of, 47*na*; conviction for incitement, 59–60; house search resulting from support of Několik vět, 18; hunger strikes of, 47, 60; legal appeal of, 59, 83–84; pe-

tition of support for, 72–73; release and trial set for, 47; U.S. support for, 72, 79, 99

DI (Democratic Initiative), 33, 95, 122, 123, 123*n*a

Diamond, Larry, 158, 161

Dienstbier, Jiří: background of, 20*n*b; as editor of *Lidove noviny,* 95; harassment of, 20, 22, 37; meeting with Gershman, 117; telephone disconnection of, 22, 37, 47, 50; on violence against fellow citizens, 32

Dillon, Kenneth, 56, 56*n*a

Dillon, Zuzana, 56, 56*n*a

Disrupting public order, criminal charges, 49

Ditsworth, James, 127

Dubček, Alexander: background of, 41*n*a; on charges against Carnogursky and Kusy, 71, 72, 83; demonstrations and, 41; Havel presidential candidacy and, 140, 141; Slovak state official criticism of, 107

Dubska, Irena, 24

Dubsky, Ivan, 24

Dubsky, Jakub, 24

Eagleburger, Lawrence, 137–38

Economic aid: Civic Forum on, 136; civil society and independent media, 158–60; for democracy support, 155–61; from European Union, 163; to fight corruption, 164; for free market support, 150–55, 150–51*f,* 183*n*46; graduation from USAID transition, 161–63; institutions of democratic contestation, 156; lessons from, 173–74; public governance institutions, 156–58

Economic reforms: Civic Forum on, 136; free market transition and, 149; human rights improvements and, 10; Johanes on, 52; labor unrest resulting from, 101–04; market liberalization, 149; resistance to,

87–88; Slovakia and, 106, 110; U.S. relations and, 63

Edwards, William Donlon "Don," 142

Eisen, Norman, 1–3, 147, 187*n*99

Elections: Civic Forum on, 135; civil society aid and, 160; corruption and, 168; Havel victory in presidential election (1989), 14, 148; political party participation in (1992), 148; timing of, 135, 140–42; U.S. economic aid for, 156

Enterprise with Foreign Property Participation Act (1989), 45, 45*n*a

Environmental issues, 45, 55, 87, 98, 125–26

European house concept, 46, 46*n*a

European Union (EU), 163, 166

Evangelical Church of Czech Brethren, 85

Exchanges Agreement (1986), 63–64, 65

EXIM Bank credits, 45, 51, 63

Exit visas, 38

Expert advice, 154

Fagan, Adam, 185*n*69

Fico, Robert, 167–69

Filippov, Vasiliy, 75–78

Fishman, David, 1

FOIA (Freedom of Information Act) requests, 2–3

Fojtík, Jan, 82, 116, 120, 137–38

For a Decent Slovakia, 169

Ford, Gerald, 4

Foreign aid. *See* Economic aid

Foreign participation in demonstrations: August 21st demonstrations, 40, 42, 49, 52, 54, 57; detention of journalists, 113; Johanes on, 52; October 28th demonstrations, 113

Foreign Service Nationals (FSNs), 67

Foundation for a Civil Society, 159

Freedom of Information Act (FOIA) requests, 2–3

Freedom of press, 53

Free markets, 14, 149, 150–55, 150–51*f,*
165–66
Fukuyama, Francis, 158

Gabal, Ivan, 117, 134, 134*n*a, 135
Gabalova, Zdenka, 117
Galbraith, Shelley, 143
Galston, William, 180*n*1
Gawronski, Mary, 38
Gelb, Bruce, 80, 116
General strike (November 27th), 12,
134
Generational changes, 57
Germany: East German refugees, 37,
127; Honecker regime, pressure to
reform, 86; peaceful demonstra-
tions in, 105
Gershman, Carl, 117–18
Gilchrist, Narrelle, 1
Gold claims, settlement of, 80, 80*n*a
Goldman, Michael, 56
Gorbachev, Mikhail: advocacy for uni-
fied Europe, 46*n*a; end of Commu-
nism in Soviet Bloc, 3–4; political
liberalization of Czechoslovak and,
6; reforms of, 36, 36*n*a, 43, 43*n*a, 53;
on use of force during demonstrations, 58
Governance institutions, 156–57
Graham, Bob, 51, 53

Hajek, Jiri, 74, 78, 117
Havel, Václav: arrest of, 6, 111–12;
Atlantis publishing house, support
for, 97; Civic Forum and, 7, 12;
as editor of *Lidove noviny,* 95; on
forum of independent groups, 128;
German booksellers peace award to,
97; hospitalization prior to October
28th demonstrations, 111–12, 114,
118–19; Mazowiecki's message to
regarding charges against Carnogursky and Kusy, 83; Několik vět
petition launched by, 8; Olof Palme
Prize awarded to, 126; petition to

release, 21, 79; on potential violence
against demonstrators, 38, 57; "The
Power of the Powerless," 158–59;
presidential candidacy of, 140, 141,
156; presidential election of (1989),
14, 148; on transition period in
Czechoslovakia, 8, 126; Union of
Young Democrats (Fidesz) demonstrators in support of, 40
HAWG (Humanitarian Affairs Working Group), 81, 81*n*a, 120–21, 127*n*b,
131–33
HDM (Human Dimension Mecha-
nism), 6, 72, 72*n*a, 177*n*34
Hegenbart, Rudolf, 88, 142
Helsinki Accords (1975): Czechoslovak
Helsinki Committee, 74; on free
movement of diplomats, 30; on
free trade, 51; Human Dimension
Mechanism, 6, 72, 72*n*a, 177*n*34;
human rights protections and, 4–6,
8; public opinion on, 27
Helsinki Commission, 5
Helsinki Committee, Czechoslovak,
74, 95, 98–99, 112
Helsinki Final Act (1975), 177*n*30
Helsinki Watch, 98, 108, 121
Honecker, Erich, 86
Hornblow, Michael, 120–21
Houštecký, Miroslav, 25, 25*n*b, 44
Houžvička, Josef, 46, 46*n*b
Hradilek, Tomas, 33, 119
Human Dimension Mechanism
(HDM), 6, 72, 72*n*a, 177*n*34
Humanitarian Affairs Working Group
(HAWG), 81, 81*n*a, 120–21, 127*n*b,
131–33
Human rights issues: August 21st
demonstrations and, 20–24, 47–50,
59–61, 71–75; Czechoslovakia and
U.S. relations and, 62; Czech rebut-
tal by pointing out U.S. violations,
52; demonstrations and, 9–11; em-
bassy request for department state-
ment on, 99–100; emigration and,

Tunneling phenomenon, 165

21st anniversary of Soviet invasion. *See* August 21st demonstrations

Two minutes of silence protest during August 21st demonstrations, 31, 33, 38, 39–40

Uhl, Petr, 24, 47–48, 50, 60, 119

Ulrich, Marybeth Peterson, 161

Unijazz, 117

Union of Socialist Youth (SSM), 11, 92, 92*n*a, 107, 122–23

Union of Towns and Communities (UTC), 157

Union of Young Democrats, 40

United Nations General Assembly, 79–81

United States: August 21st demonstrations, television coverage of, 39, 58; Civic Forum on need for support from, 136–37; Czechoslovak relations, 6–7, 13, 43–45, 51–52, 58, 62–71, 80, 131; detention of journalists in October 28th demonstration, 113; embassy request for statement on human rights, 99–100; free press in, 53; gold claims, settlement from WWII, 80, 80*n*a; Helsinki Commission, 5; human rights advocacy, 3–14, 43–44, 173, 177*n*30; human rights issues in, 52; National Science Foundation, 64; national security and democratization abroad, 151–52; Panama, intervention in, 145, 145*n*a; recommendations for reactions to violence in Prague, 24–25; Support for Eastern European Democracy Act (SEED Act, 1989), 152, 155, 157, 161, 162; violence against journalists in November 17th demonstration, 128, 128*n*a, 131–32. *See also* U.S. support for democracy

United States Agency for International Development (USAID): assistance in drafting SEC-type regulatory body, 154; assistance in transition to liberal democracy, 147; civil society aid, 159; Civil Society Organization Sustainability Index for Central and Eastern Europe and Eurasia, 172; graduation from assistance, 147, 161–63; local governance aid, 157–58; losses in Czech Republic, 153

United States Information Agency, 157

United States Information Service (USIS), 71

Universal Declaration of Human Rights, 177*n*30

Urban, Jan: economic reform and, 101–02; hospitalization of, 37, 49; house search resulting from support of Několik vět, 18; mandatory military duty of, 21, 37, 49; telephone disconnection of, 47, 50

Urbánek, Zdeněk, 38, 92–93, 132

Urban Institute, 157

Urban management training, 157, 184*n*54

U.S. embassy in Prague: access to Czech government officials, 80; administrative section of, 70–71; consular section of, 70; contractors for, 68; Czech harassment of staff, 114–15, 118, 144, 144*n*b; Defense Attaché Office, 71; financial support for initiatives in Czech Republic, 162, 187*n*99; housing for staff of, 65, 80; human rights advocacy, 4–5, 7–14, 173, 177*n*30; office space and equipment for, 68–71; OIG inspection of, 62–71, 138; personnel of, 65–68, 70; political/economic section of (POLEC), 64, 67–68, 70; security for, 66, 69–70; sit-ins at, 120; threat assessment of Prague, 139, 144–45; travel advisory issued by, 129; war memorials and, 80